CONTENTS

THE EAL TEACHING BOOK

WITHDRAWN

Sara Miller McCune founded SAGE Publishing in 1965 to support the dissemination of usable knowledge and educate a global community. SAGE publishes more than 1000 journals and over 800 new books each year, spanning a wide range of subject areas. Our growing selection of library products includes archives, data, case studies and video. SAGE remains majority owned by our founder and after her lifetime will become owned by a charitable trust that secures the company's continued independence.

Los Angeles | London | New Delhi | Singapore | Washington DC | Melbourne

THE EAL TEACHING BOOK

PROMOTING SUCCESS FOR MULTILINGUAL LEARNERS

JEAN CONTEH

3RD EDITION

Learning Matters
An imprint of SAGE Publications Ltd
1 Oliver's Yard
55 City Road
London EC1Y 1SP

SAGE Publications Inc.
2455 Teller Road
Thousand Oaks, California 91320

SAGE Publications India Pvt Ltd
B 1/I 1 Mohan Cooperative Industrial Area
Mathura Road
New Delhi 110 044

SAGE Asia-Pacific Pte Ltd
3 Church Street
#10-04 Samsung Hub
Singapore 049483

First published in 2012
Second edition published in 2015
Revised second edition published in September 2015
Third edition published in 2019

Editor: Amy Thornton
Senior project editor: Chris Marke
Project management: Deer Park Productions,
Tavistock
Marketing manager: Catherine Slinn
Cover design: Wendy Scott
Typeset by: C&M Digitals (P) Ltd, Chennai, India
Printed in the UK

Library of Congress Control Number: 2019931378

British Library Cataloguing in Publication Data

A catalogue record for this book is available
from the British Library

ISBN: 978-1-5264-7268-7
ISBN: 978-1-5264-7267-0 (pbk)

At SAGE we take sustainability seriously. Most of our products are printed in the UK using responsibly sourced papers and boards. When we print overseas we ensure sustainable papers are used as measured by the Egmont grading system. We undertake an annual audit to monitor our sustainability.

ABOUT THE AUTHOR

Jean Conteh was a senior lecturer in the School of Education at the University of Leeds where, among other things, she was in charge of the English component of the PGCE Primary and ran a Master's course for teachers on EAL and Education. She has worked in many countries and has published widely in the field of EAL in primary education, both for teachers and for academic audiences. Her research focuses on ways to promote success for those pupils who are often labelled 'disadvantaged' in our education system, and covers the role of language in teaching and learning in primary classrooms and the expertise and professional roles of bilingual teachers.

ACKNOWLEDGEMENTS

I wish to thank the following teachers and researchers who contributed case studies from their practice to the second edition of the book:

Oksana Afitska	Shila Begum	Anita Conradi
Zofia Donnelly	Dianne Excell	Ana Korzun
Ali O'Grady	Catherine Porritt	Pete Ruse
Linda Sandler	Georgina Vince	Charlotte Wood

Also Naomi Cooper, Dianne Excell and Ilona Szolc, who contributed additional case studies to this third edition.

Thanks are also due to my former students Shannele Cowban and Anna Grant who have contributed to this book by providing examples of children's work and classroom activities. I also wish to acknowledge Louise Wood and Jane Andrews for their helpful and insightful comments on my final draft of the new Chapter 4 on multilingual learners in the Early Years. These helped me to make a few final changes which greatly improved the quality of the chapter.

I wish to thank Tracey Burns of the OECD for the use of the cartoon on p. 53.

The extract from *The Iron Man* by Ted Hughes is reproduced by kind permission of Faber.

INTRODUCTION

This book is a new edition of *The EAL Teaching Book: Promoting Success for Multilingual Learners* (2015), itself the second edition of *Teaching Bilingual and EAL Learners in Primary Schools*, which was published in 2012. This new edition contains all the content of the previous editions. Facts and figures related to policies and social trends have been updated, some sections have been rewritten in the light of new research and policy, and there are two brand new chapters, one focusing on EAL in the early years (Chapter 4) and one on EAL and literacy (Chapter 5). Another new feature in this edition is the inclusion of Master's level study sections at the end of each chapter.

The overarching aim of this book is to show the ways in which 'EAL' needs to be a central aspect of the professional knowledge of all teachers. The term 'EAL' has been in common use for many years in England to describe pupils who are learning English as an Additional Language in mainstream schools. It has become a shorthand for a huge variety of issues across the whole range of schools and ages of pupils. The professional standards for teachers, introduced by the government in 2011, make it very clear that all teachers need to have training and professional development in order to meet the diverse needs of all the pupils they are expected to teach. This is part of Standard 5, which says that all teachers must:

> . . . *have a clear understanding of the needs of all pupils, including those with special educational needs; those of high ability; those with English as an additional language; those with disabilities; and be able to use and evaluate distinctive teaching approaches to engage and support them.*

The professional standards show how theory and practice always need to be closely connected in teaching. This book shows the ways in which the two can be linked in a pedagogy that plays to the strengths and helps to raise the attainments of EAL learners. Indeed, such a pedagogy will contribute to enhancing the learning of all pupils in mainstream schools, not just those who may have been placed in the category of 'EAL'. The use of case studies to show the integration of theory and practice proved very popular in the second edition and so has been extended in this new edition. These case studies have all been written by practising teachers, from mainstream schools, complementary schools and universities.

Soon after the first edition of the book was published in 2012, we had the introduction of the new national school curriculum which has two short statements that lay down some requirements for teachers in their work with multilingual and EAL learners. These are:

> *Teachers must also take account of the needs of pupils whose first language is not English. Monitoring of progress should take account of the pupil's age, length of time in this country, previous educational experience and ability in other languages.*

> *The ability of pupils for whom English is an additional language to take part in the national curriculum may be in advance of their communication skills in English. Teachers should plan teaching opportunities to help pupils develop their English and should aim to provide the support pupils need to take part in all subjects.*

(DfE, 2013: 8)

Though brief, these statements are important and they align with the key aims and messages of this book in articulating clear principles for EAL. They recognise the need to understand what pupils bring to their learning in mainstream schools, as this is the basis on which they will build their new learning and their identities as speakers and writers of English – a key element of the sociocultural theories of learning that are explained in Chapter 2. Secondly, they emphasise two crucial points. First, for many EAL pupils, learning English needs to go on simultaneously with learning all the subjects of the curriculum. Second, that many will have greater knowledge of some subjects than they can express in English. These have implications for the whole cycle of planning, teaching and assessing EAL learners and so underpin the ideas presented in all the chapters in Part 2 of the book.

The DfE introduced another change in 2016, related to the assessment of EAL learners. This is the DfE Proficiency Scales, which are covered in this new edition, mainly in Chapter 8 on assessment. Though introduced as part of the national schools' census rather than the curriculum and now – sadly – not an official requirement on schools, the scales offer a useful tool for teachers to understand the needs of their EAL learners and can be used effectively as part of formative assessment processes.

This book raises issues and challenges misconceptions about language teaching and learning generally and about EAL learners in particular. Such misconceptions have, in the past, contributed to what could be termed a 'deficit' model of EAL. EAL learners are sometimes perceived as being on the margins of mainstream education, with problems that need to be sorted out before they can be included fully. This book argues strongly for a positive perspective on diversity and in particular a view of language diversity as a resource and an opportunity for learning, for all pupils. This is why the term 'multilingual' features in the title of the book, reminding us that EAL learners are members of our contemporary multilingual world where using different languages in daily life is normal and natural. It is my hope that the book will instil in our next generation of teachers enthusiasm and passion for an aspect of their work which offers in return a great deal of professional reward and satisfaction.

The prime audience for this book is people who have chosen to become teachers, no matter what route they are taking, from the well-established, university and college-based degree-level and PGCE courses to the vast array of school-based training programmes that are being developed round the country. It is also relevant for other audiences, such as tutors in initial teacher education, NQTs and their mentors, teachers and other professionals working with multilingual and EAL learners in schools, and those engaged in continuing professional development (CPD) and working towards higher qualifications. A new feature in this third edition is the addition of sections at the end of each chapter that provide extra reading and critical questions for Masters' students and tutors. Each one focuses on a different reading, which is easily available online or from a university or college library. Together, these readings constitute a sound basis for Master's level study. Here they are:

	Chapter	Reading
1	Introducing multilingual and EAL learners	K. Safford and R. Drury (2013) 'The "problem" of bilingual children in educational settings: policy and research in England', *Language and Education*, 27 (1), pp. 70–81.
2	All about language and learning	Chapter 2: 'A sociocultural view of language and learning', in P. Gibbons (2006) *Bridging Discourses in the ESL Classroom*. London: Continuum.

	Chapter	Reading
3	What does it mean to be multilingual?	J. Cummins (2008) 'Teaching for transfer: challenging the two solitudes assumption in bilingual education', in J. Cummins and N. H. Hornberger (eds), *Encyclopedia of Language and Education, Volume 5: Bilingual Education.* Boston, MA: Springer, pp. 65-75. Available at https://link.springer.com/referenceworkentry/10.1007/978-0-387-30424-3_116
4	EAL in the Early Years: beginning schooling in a new language and culture	Chapter 3: 'The idea of intercultural competence', in P. Baldock (2010) *Understanding Cultural Diversity in the Early Years.* London: Sage.
5	EAL and literacy: learning to read independently in a new language	Chapter 4: 'The context of the mind', in E. Gregory (2008) *Learning to Read in a New Language: Making Sense of Words and Worlds.* London: Sage.
6	Planning for learning across the curriculum for multilingual and EAL learners	P. Sandoval-Taylor (2005) 'Home is where the heart is: planning a funds of knowledge-based curriculum module', in N. Gonzalez, L. Moll and C. Amanti (eds), *Funds of Knowledge: Theorizing Practices in Households, Communities and Classrooms.* New York: Routledge, pp. 153-65.
7	Assessing multilingual and EAL learners across the curriculum	S. Hopewell and K. Escamilla (2014) 'Struggling reader or emerging biliterate student? Reevaluating the criteria for labeling emerging bilingual students as low achieving', *Journal of Literacy Research,* 46 (1), pp. 68-89.
8	Promoting independence: using home languages and cultures in learning	J. Conteh and A. Brock (2010) '"Safe spaces"? Sites of bilingualism for young learners in home, school and community', *International Journal of Bilingual Education and Bilingualism,* 14 (3), pp. 347-60.

This book provides a theory-informed, accessible, comprehensive source of practical guidance for meeting the needs of children categorised as EAL learners in the early years, primary and secondary schools. As such, it is perhaps still the only book of its kind.

STRUCTURE AND ORGANISATION OF THE BOOK

The book is in two parts. The first part comprises Chapters 1–3 and the second Chapters 4–9. In between the two parts there is a set of principles which are intended to show how theory and practice always need to be integrated in considering the best provision for bilingual and EAL learners – indeed any learners.

PART 1: UNDERSTANDING MULTILINGUAL AND EAL LEARNERS – THEORIES OF LEARNING AND LANGUAGE

The chapters in the first part of the book provide theoretical and contextual information to frame the more practical ideas that form the second part of the book. Essentially, this part aims to provide:

- a contextualisation of the issues surrounding multilingualism both globally and in England, including a discussion of the development of the idea of EAL and illuminative vignettes of children who would come under its umbrella;

- an overview of key theoretical models and principles and their practical implications, which explain the role of language in learning generally and the development and learning of pupils who can be defined as 'EAL' and 'multilingual'.

Chapter 1: Introducing multilingual and EAL learners begins by providing some facts and figures which explain how our present 'superdiverse' society in England has come about and is constantly changing. Following this, it aims to answer the question 'who are EAL learners?' by offering vignettes of individual pupils, using terminology from policy documentation over the years. This section covers pupils in five categories, showing the need to be aware of the complexities and uncertainties in understanding their strengths and needs. It ends with a case study about Gypsy Roma pupils in a secondary school. The final section raises some common myths and misconceptions about language diversity and learning which are addressed at different points in the book and returned to at the end of Chapter 9.

Chapter 2: All about language and learning provides a theoretical overview of language, culture and identity in the field of EAL and multilingualism. It explains what is involved in the **functional approach** to understanding grammar and texts, showing the value of this for teaching and learning. The second section provides an introduction to sociocultural theories of learning, in which talk is a central element, and it argues for the importance of talk in working with **multilingual** and EAL learners in particular. Finally, the **funds of knowledge** concept is introduced, which is an important one for understanding the role of home and community in learning.

Chapter 3: What does it mean to be multilingual? addresses relevant theories about multilingualism and their practical implications in making the best provision for multilingual and EAL learners. Beginning with an overview of global contexts, it moves on to consider research related to multilingualism and education, in particular the work and ideas of Jim Cummins. A case study illustrates what it is like to be a multilingual learner in a mainstream school in England. The chapter ends by emphasising the importance for pupils' success in school of understanding the nature of home and community learning experiences that multilingual and EAL learners bring to school.

Part 1 closes by articulating some 'key principles' for promoting success for EAL learners, which are illuminated with practical examples in Chapters 4–9.

PART 2: PROMOTING LEARNING – PRACTICAL APPROACHES FOR MULTILINGUAL AND EAL LEARNERS

Based on the key principles identified in the first part of the book, the second part (Chapters 4–9) focuses on practical classroom issues. It covers the important themes of planning, classroom strategies, resources, assessment, language across the curriculum and making links with home and community contexts.

Chapter 4: EAL in the Early Years: beginning schooling in a new language and culture provides overall guidance and examples of practical strategies for working with multilingual and EAL learners in the early years. The funds of knowledge philosophy underpins the whole chapter, along with its practical implications. It illustrates the ways in which different settings can support children's active learning in the early years and the importance of learning through play. There is an extended section on literacy, which introduces the notion of **emergent literacy** and its importance for multilingual and EAL learners in the early years.

Chapter 5: EAL and literacy: learning to read independently in a new language provides a brief account of what independent readers need to do and the place of phonics within the whole picture of reading. It argues that phonics have been given too dominant a role in the teaching of reading in recent years. The chapter provides examples of ways of using multilingual and EAL learners' full language repertoires to open out learning to read. Finally, it addresses two key issues for multilingual and EAL learners – understanding **academic language** in different subjects across the curriculum and the importance of developing reading for pleasure.

Chapter 6: Planning for learning across the curriculum for multilingual and EAL learners provides guidance for planning language-focused activities across the curriculum using a framework (the Cummins' quadrant) which makes clear the ways that planning can support the progression of learning from simple, context-embedded tasks to more complex, more academic levels. There is a wealth of ideas and suggestions for developing activities that link language learning and content learning. Case studies illustrate the role of talk in primary science, the ways subject and 'EAL' teachers can work together, planning for collaborative talk and including new arrivals in your lessons.

Chapter 7: Assessing multilingual and EAL learners across the curriculum begins by raising issues for EAL learners related to the national, standardised models of assessment in place in England and suggesting some principles for assessing EAL and multilingual learners. It stresses the importance of assessment for learning (AFL) and introduces activities which can be used with pupils to enhance their future learning. The new 'Proficiency in English' Scales for EAL learners are introduced and discussed. Case studies are included on assessing learners across the curriculum in a secondary school, teachers' and pupils' views on science in primary schools and newly arrived pupils' views on their experiences in their first year of schooling in England. The possible confusions between language needs and special needs are addressed and the chapter ends with some practical advice on AFL, observing pupils and consulting with parents.

Chapter 8: Promoting independence: using home languages and cultures in learning discusses the importance of promoting independent learning and practical ways of doing it in multilingual classrooms. Following this, it discusses ways of involving families and communities in learning and briefly introduces the work of **complementary/supplementary schools**. Then there are sections on bringing home languages and cultures into school, and the use of dual language books in promoting independent learning. The final section, on using personal funds of knowledge, includes two case studies: the first on using Spanish as a means of including one newly arrived multilingual learner in science lessons and the second on learning place value through a counting song in Bangla.

Chapter 9: Conclusions: synthesising learning and moving on revisits the myths identified in Chapter 1 and the principles at the end of Part 1. It invites readers to reflect on their developing professional knowledge and suggests ways of moving on in order to extend and strengthen their professional expertise related to multilingual and EAL learners. It ends with an annotated list of further reading.

The new case studies in this revised edition provide a rich resource of classroom practice over a range of topics and learners.

REFERENCE

Department for Education (DfE) (2013) *The National Curriculum in England: Key Stages 1 and 2 Framework Document.* London: DfE.

PART 1

UNDERSTANDING MULTILINGUAL AND EAL LEARNERS – THEORIES OF LEARNING AND LANGUAGE

1
INTRODUCING MULTILINGUAL AND EAL LEARNERS

— LEARNING OUTCOMES —

This chapter will help you to achieve the following learning outcomes:

- develop understanding of the importance of your own experiences of language diversity and ethnicity for your professional knowledge as a teacher;

- gain awareness of the history of language and cultural diversity in England;

- develop awareness of the diverse range of experiences and knowledge that multilingual and EAL learners bring to their classrooms.

INTRODUCTION

This chapter introduces you to the pupils you will be teaching who come under the umbrella term of 'EAL', i.e. those learning English as an Additional Language. The term 'EAL' has been defined in policy and practice in many different ways and there is still no agreed definition. The chapter raises questions about how we define and label our pupils, and challenges you to consider your own perceptions of these issues. One of the main aims is to help you, as a beginning teacher or a more experienced one, to understand the importance of recognising and valuing all the knowledge and experience that your multilingual and EAL learners bring with them to school.

The chapter begins by providing some background information about the cultural and language diversity of British society today. Then it provides a set of vignettes of individual pupils, through which you will gain a sense of the rich diversity of the social and cultural experiences that many multilingual and EAL learners bring to their mainstream classrooms. Following this, there is an extended case study by Georgina Vince, who works in a secondary school attended by growing numbers of Roma and Gypsy pupils. Georgina describes the positive ways in which her school works with the pupils and their families. What she says has relevance for both primary and secondary settings. Finally, there is a set of common 'myths and misconceptions' about teaching EAL learners which – after reading the chapter – you may have questions about. We will come back to these at the end of the book in Chapter 9.

Interspersed through the chapter there are questions and activities to help you to think further about the ideas that you will read about, as well as their practical implications for your own practice in different classrooms. There are some suggestions for further reading at the end of the chapter, along with some critical questions for those working at Master's level.

These are the main sections and subsections of the chapter:

1 Defining difference

    1.1 Behind the facts and figures

    1.2 'Superdiversity' in England

2 Who are 'EAL learners'?

    2.1 Advanced bilingual learners – Safina (Secondary)

    2.2 New to English pupils – Stefan and Jan (Primary)

    2.3 Asylum-seekers and refugees – Joseph (Secondary)

    2.4 Isolated learners – Radia (Primary)

    2.5 Sojourners – Hamida (Early Years)

       Roma and Gypsy pupils – case study by Georgina Vince

3 Language diversity and learning – some myths and misconceptions

1 DEFINING DIFFERENCE

1.1 BEHIND THE FACTS AND FIGURES

┏━ RESEARCH FOCUS ━━━━━

Since 2009, as part of the annual schools' census data, the Department for Education has collected information about the languages spoken by pupils who attend mainstream schools. In 2018 (DfE, 2018), the figures showed that about 21.2 per cent of pupils in mainstream primary and 16.6 per cent in secondary schools in England were identified as 'EAL' (English as an Additional Language) learners. Figures for academies were only slightly lower. It is not easy to find a figure for the total number of languages currently spoken by pupils in schools in England, but it is thought to be about 350 (BBC, 2007). The proportion of ethnic minority pupils is different from those defined as 'EAL'; currently this is around 33 per cent for primary schools and 30 per cent for secondary schools (DfE, 2018). The data on ethnicity come from the National Census, which is carried out every ten years. The most recent census was undertaken in 2011 and the categories for ethnicity used are shown in Figure 1.1 below.

The percentages for ethnic minority pupils are much higher than those for language diversity, so it is clear that there are many ethnic minority pupils in schools in England for whom English is *not* an additional language. But it is also clear that many pupils can be defined as *both* EAL *and* ethnic minority, because they belong to an ethnic minority group and also speak another language besides English. It is important to understand, especially for pupils such as those in this second group, that language knowledge and cultural knowledge are interlinked. This idea is discussed further in Chapter 2, along with the implications for teaching. There are also pupils who would ethnically be part of the 'white' majority but who could actually be defined as 'EAL', because they do not have English as their first language and their families are from countries where English is not the official language.

A. White
British
English/Welsh/Scottish/Northern Irish/British Irish
Gypsy or Irish traveller
Any other White background

B. Mixed/multiple ethnic groups
White and Black Caribbean
White and Black African
White and Asian
Any other Mixed

C. Asian/Asian British
Indian
Pakistani
Bangladeshi
Chinese
Any other Asian background

D. Black/African/Caribbean/Black British
African
Caribbean
Any other Black/African/Caribbean background

Other ethnic group
Arab
Any other ethnic group

Figure 1.1 Categories of ethnicity in the 2011 National Census

ACTIVITY 1.1

Who are you?

In Figure 1.1, you can see the categories of ethnicity used in the 2011 national census. The categories change with every census, as the ethnic makeup of British society changes. Look at the categories and think about the following questions.

1. Did you complete the most recent census? If so, which category did you place yourself in? If not, which category would you place yourself in?

2. Could you place yourself into more than one category?

3. Do you find it difficult to place yourself, and if so, why?

4. Would it be difficult to place anyone you know?

5. Would it be difficult to place any pupils you teach or have worked with?

6. How do you think these categories were arrived at?

Despite the ever-increasing numbers of pupils from different ethnic and language backgrounds in our schools, the vast majority of teachers in England are still from 'white British' or 'English' backgrounds and do not speak other languages besides English. This means that most teachers who have pupils in their classes who speak other languages do not share those languages. This can sometimes feel like quite a challenge on top of everything else you need to know about and be able to do as a teacher. Vivian

Gussin Paley (2000, pp. 131–2) in her book *White Teacher* describes her experiences as a 'white majority' teacher in a school with increasing numbers of pupils from diverse backgrounds. She soon realised that, in order to understand their needs and make the best provision for them, she had to understand more about her own identity and how it influenced her attitudes to her pupils. She concludes:

> *Those of us who have been outsiders understand the need to be seen exactly as we are and to be accepted and valued. Our safety lies in schools and societies in which faces with many shapes can feel an equal sense of belonging. Our pupils must grow up knowing and liking those who look and speak in different ways, or they will live as strangers in a hostile land.*

Ethnicity is a very hard concept to define, and because we talk about 'ethnic minorities' we may sometimes think of it as a term only relevant for people who can be thought of as belonging to a 'minority' group. Of course, the reality is that we all have ethnicity. We all belong to different ethnic, cultural and social groups. But ethnicity in terms of language, ancestry and nationality is only one part of what makes us who we are. In your role as a teacher, thinking about your pupils, the notion of **identity** is a more useful one than ethnicity. It helps you think about all the factors that contribute to your individuality, and the personal and social issues that are so important in teaching and learning. As I suggest in Chapter 2, it is vital that you understand how your personal identity is an important aspect of your professional identity as a teacher, especially when you are teaching pupils from different language and cultural backgrounds from yourself. You need to understand how important (or not) your own ethnicity, language knowledge and other aspects of your personal makeup are to you, and how you might feel if any of them were threatened or undermined. This will help you understand the needs of the pupils you will be teaching. As Gussin Paley argues, this is an essential step to developing positive, trustful relationships with the pupils you teach and with their families.

The following activity will help you to think about your 'ethnicity' as part of your identity, in other words who you are.

ACTIVITY 1.2

How does it feel to be different?

You can do this activity on your own but it would be better if you could do it as a group discussion task, with some of your fellow trainees or colleagues in a school setting.

- First, look at the census categories and think about how you would define your own identity. Is it enough just to think about your 'ethnic background' as defined in the categories of the census? What other aspects of your identity are important to you? Where your family comes from might be an important part of your identity, but what else might count for you?

- Make a list of 6-8 attributes that you would say were important aspects of your identity. Compare your list with those of your colleagues.

- Can you think of a time when you were made to feel different and that you did not belong? This could have been when you were a child or as an adult in a work situation or in a social context. What did you feel was different about you? How would the quote from Vivian Gussin Paley reflect your feelings? Write a few sentences about how it felt to feel different and perhaps excluded.

1.2 'SUPERDIVERSITY' IN ENGLAND

In about 120 AD, soldiers from the Roman Empire built a fort at the mouth of the river Tyne and named it Arbeia (Tyne and Wear Archives and Museums, 2018). You can still see the remains today in South Shields near Newcastle upon Tyne. Some historians think the Romans who lived in the fort named it after their original homelands in what are now Syria, Libya and Spain. Britain has always been multicultural and multilingual – a small island which has experienced successive waves of immigration and emigration from and to all over the world. The English language reflects this, as it contains words from all the languages of the people that have come to this island and enriched its vocabulary over the centuries.

Over recent years, the population of England has changed greatly. The addition to the EU of the A8 'accession countries' in 2004 meant that people travelled within Europe much more than they used to. It has become quite normal for people from Poland, the Czech Republic, Slovakia and other eastern European countries to come to England to work, and then return to their countries of origin or move on elsewhere. This has been described as 'circular migration' and is a worldwide phenomenon. Migration has also been influenced by other global events. Many British cities now are what have been called **superdiverse** communities. People with vastly different languages, histories, cultural and social backgrounds and religions live side by side. Sometimes, new migrants arrive and join with communities from their countries of origin that have lived in the city for generations.

VIGNETTE

A superdiverse corner shop

The photo of a corner shop in a Yorkshire city shows clearly the effects of 'superdiversity' on everyday life in a typical community.

Figure 1.2 Shop front in a 'superdiverse' city

A Lithuanian heritage family owned the shop from the 1950s until they sold it to a Pakistani heritage family in the 1980s. A few years ago, this family sold the shop to a Polish man. He put up a new sign, covering up the old Lithuanian name. He kept the small '**halal** meat' logos from the Pakistani heritage owners at the edges of the sign to show that he still provides meat for the local Muslim

(Continued)

(Continued)

community. He also sells phone cards to customers from all over the world. He placed a bright yellow banner in the shop window (at the bottom right of the picture, but difficult to see) to show how he catered for the changing community around the shop: 'Everyone welcome English, Arabic, Kurdish, Polish, Slovakia', it says. There are now many multilingual communities like this in cities all over England, where many of our multilingual and EAL pupils live.

It is important also to remember, as we see below in section 2, that an increasing number of multilingual and EAL now also live in towns or villages where they may previously have been very few other such pupils.

ACTIVITY 1.3

Language and cultural diversity in school

If you have a placement in a school where there are pupils learning English as an additional language, or in the school where you work, try to find out the following information.

- How many pupils in school are defined as 'EAL learners'?

- How many different languages are spoken by pupils in the school?

- How does the school find out about and record the languages?

- Does the school have a policy for EAL or language diversity?

- How are EAL issues managed in the school?

If you cannot undertake this activity in your placement school, see if you could arrange a visit to a school where it would be possible to do it.

2 WHO ARE 'EAL LEARNERS'?

Sometimes the term 'EAL' is applied only to pupils who are new arrivals in school and who are better thought of as being 'new to English'. 'EAL' is an umbrella term, used for many different groups of pupils who bring a vast range of experience and knowledge of languages, literacies, cultures and schooling to their mainstream classrooms. The title of this book refers to 'multilingual' and EAL learners to make the point that we cannot think of the pupils whose learning we are considering as one, uniform group. Different terms have been used over the years in policies and strategy documents to describe the EAL learners you may meet in your classrooms – some of them may not be very relevant any more. You need to remember that some pupils you teach may belong to more than one group, such as a child who is new to English and whose family are spending a short time in England. Here is a list of the terms:

- ***Advanced bilingual learners*** – learners who are second- and third-generation members of settled ethnic minority communities.

- **Pupils new to English** – learners who are recent arrivals and new to English, some of whom have little or no experience of schooling. Others may already be literate in their first languages.

- **Asylum-seekers and refugees** – learners whose education has been disrupted because of war and other traumatic experiences.

- **Isolated learners** – learners who are in school settings with little prior experience of bilingual pupils.

- **Sojourners** – learners whose parents are working and studying and are in England for short periods of time.

ACTIVITY 1.4

Thinking about multilingual and EAL learners

Before you read the vignettes that follow, think about the pupils in your current class or one you have recently taught. Do you think any of them would fit into any of the groups listed above?

Write a list of the names of the pupils, and identify which group (or groups) you think each would belong to.

What follow are five vignettes and then one case study by Georgina Vince, who works in a large secondary school in Leeds. They will help you to understand something about the complexity of the term 'EAL'.

2.1 ADVANCED BILINGUAL LEARNERS – SAFINA (SECONDARY)

Safina is 13 years old and in a **Year 9** class in a large, multilingual secondary school in a former industrial city in the north of England. Most of her classmates are from similar backgrounds to herself. She represents the largest group in our list of different categories of EAL learners – advanced bilingual learners. She was born in England, the granddaughter of a man who arrived from the Kashmir area of Pakistan 40 or 50 years ago to work in the woollen mills in the city. Safina is multilingual. English is her dominant language, so 'EAL' is not really a helpful way to describe her. As well as English, she speaks Punjabi and Urdu. She is also **multiliterate** (Datta, 2007). With her sisters and female cousins, she is learning the Koran in Arabic from a Muslim teacher who visits her home. Her brothers go to the local mosque, which is in a converted cinema close to their house. Her mum is teaching her to read and write Urdu, their national heritage language. All these languages have important, but different, roles to play in her life. While English may be the most important, there is no sign that the other languages are fading away. Indeed, the signs are that they will continue to be important for Safina and her community (see Chapter 3). Punjabi has an important, though unofficial, role in British society; over half a million British people speak it, making it the most commonly spoken language after English. Pupils whose families originate from Bangladesh have very similar histories to Safina, with Bengali and Sylheti as their community languages. Bengali is the second most commonly spoken foreign language by British people (Wikipedia, 2018). Safina is doing well in school so far. She is very talkative and keen to answer questions, but is finding things increasingly difficult as she progresses through secondary school. She struggles to understand the range of subjects she is expected to study and to meet the demands of written assessments.

When Safina reached the end of Year 2, she completed the KS1 **Standard Attainment Tests (SATs)**, which were compulsory at the time. The expected level was level 2, and Safina attained this in English and level 3 in mathematics. In the KS2 SATs, which she completed at the end of Year 6, she attained level 4 in English and level 5 in maths, which is above the expected standard. But the data over the years show that she may struggle to attain such a high level in her GCSEs when they come around. Her family are very supportive of her education. Her father helps her a lot in mathematics at home, in Punjabi. Her mother and aunts do a lot of sewing and Safina is very good at this and other practical activities. When she was younger, her grandma told her and her siblings lots of stories from Pakistan, in Punjabi. She loved this and knew many of the stories by heart. In her primary school, where most of the pupils were multilingual, teachers encouraged the pupils to tell the stories in school. This benefited Safina's literacy by helping her to understand story structures and the kinds of language found in stories, which is different from spoken language. Pupils like Safina are exactly those whom Deryn Hall describes as 'living in two languages' (Hall et al., 2001), and who are discussed further in Chapter 3.

2.2 NEW TO ENGLISH PUPILS – STEFAN AND JAN (PRIMARY)

Stefan and Jan are both ten years old and in the same **Year 5** class in a small Roman Catholic primary school in a big, multilingual city in the north of England. They have both been attending the school for a couple of years, having arrived from Poland at almost the same time with their families. About 40 per cent of the pupils in the school are from Pakistani-heritage backgrounds and the numbers of pupils from Poland, the Czech Republic and Slovakia grew steadily over a few years to reach about 10 per cent, that is two to three pupils per class. Stefan and Jan's class teacher is a bit puzzled by the two boys. When they entered her class from Year 4, she checked the school records and noticed that, since coming to the school, both new to English, their progress had been very different though they seemed to start off from a relatively similar position in relation to their knowledge of English. Both have become fairly confident and fluent in spoken English over the two years they have been in the school. They can answer questions in class, hold conversations with their teachers and their peers and take part in social activities in school. But, while Stefan has made good progress with reading and writing and is beginning to perform in assessments at similar levels to his peers, Jan is struggling. He has taken part in various intervention activities but never seems to be able to catch up with Stefan or his other classmates.

The class teacher is considering what can be done to support Jan to help him catch up before he encounters the KS2 SATs in Year 6. She wonders whether yet another intervention activity is the answer. In studying part-time for her MA she comes across the work of Cummins (see Chapter 3) and other writers on bilingualism and multilingualism. She finds their ideas about the links between languages in pupils' learning very intriguing and decides to find out a little about Stefan and Jan's knowledge of other languages, especially their home language, Polish. To her surprise and interest, she finds out that Stefan is an accomplished reader and writer of Polish, and that he regularly attends the Polish Saturday school in the city where pupils study Polish to GCSE and 'A' level (see Chapter 8, section 2.1). Jan, on the other hand, can only read and write a little Polish – his early schooling in Poland was disrupted because of his family situation. He went to the Saturday class for a short while but then dropped out.

As an experiment, the teacher asks Stefan if he can bring some of his Polish books into school and tell the class about some of the things he does in the Saturday school. Stefan's dad comes along too, and tells the class a story in Polish, which Stefan translates into English. The visit is a huge success. Afterwards, to her surprise, the teacher notices how Jan seems much more enthusiastic and motivated. So she decides to give the pupils in her class opportunities from time to time to work together in same-language groups where they can discuss things with each other, using their home languages and then report back or write in English (see section 3 of Chapter 6 for more information about planning and organising groupwork and Chapter 8 for discussions of using home languages in school). As time goes on, Jan's reading and writing slowly begin to improve while his confidence steadily grows.

2.3 ASYLUM-SEEKERS AND REFUGEES – JOSEPH (SECONDARY)

Joseph is 15 years old and is moving into **Year 11**. He came to England as a baby with his mother, Jenneh, who had had to escape from her home town in Sierra Leone when it was overrun by fighting during the civil war that ended about 15 years ago. His father was a solicitor and his mother an administrator in a large secondary school in the town. At first, Joseph and his mother lived temporarily in bed and breakfast accommodation in London, and after 18 months they moved to a small town in the north-west of England where Jenneh had a Sierra Leonean friend. Other friends helped with accommodation and Jenneh found a job in a supermarket. They settled fairly well, although they were the target of racial abuse for a while. But because of the unsettled situation in Sierra Leone, they had lost touch with Joseph's father. Jenneh applied for political asylum and, after a long struggle, she gained it.

Though they had been in their new home for two years by the time Joseph began school, their future was still uncertain. Events in Sierra Leone had calmed and Jenneh had made contact with her family. She found out that her husband had died. All the problems she faced were a great strain on Jenneh and she became depressed. The school was a fairly small, Church of England primary school with very few non-white pupils. At first, Joseph was a well-behaved little boy and he made a good impression on his teachers. He was very polite and spoke good English, as English is the official language of Sierra Leone and Jenneh had taught him well. However, the teachers knew nothing about his home country apart from the awful events that they had sometimes seen on television. This made the teachers feel sorry for Joseph and they did not push him very hard in his work. There were other ethnic minority pupils in the school, but none from Africa. As time went on, Joseph's attendance at school was sometimes irregular as he had to stay at home to look after his mother when she was unable to go to work. His school work suffered and he did not make many friends.

Joseph did not do well in the KS1 SATs in Year 2, and was placed in a special needs (SEN) group, where he became very withdrawn. He got further and further behind in his work and his behaviour also began to suffer as his anxiety about his mother grew. No one at school knew of his home situation. When he reached Year 6, he attained level 3 in both maths and English, below the expected national standard. This was commendable in many ways, but not a reflection of his true ability. Most of his classmates in primary school moved on to the local secondary school which was very much part of the community. Joseph did not get a place there but was instead given a place in a large, inner-city secondary school where he knew nobody and the teachers knew nothing of his background. No one suggested to his mother that they could appeal against this decision. Joseph has had a tough time in secondary school so far. In Years 7 and 8, he was very isolated and withdrawn, and as he moved into Year 10, he got into a bad set of friends and began truanting from school. The school took a somewhat punitive line on this, which led to Joseph being excluded on a couple of occasions. Now, as he approaches his GCSEs, his school record is very patchy and the signs do not look very good for his success.

2.4 ISOLATED LEARNERS – RADIA (PRIMARY)

Radia is in **Year 4** in a primary school in a village near to a small city in the south-west of England. The family have been living in England for five years altogether. She has been attending the school for two years, after moving to the village with her family when her father began a job at the local university where he had recently completed his PhD. When the family first arrived in England from their home country, Algeria, they lived in the city, near the university. Radia attended a large, busy, multilingual primary school where she had some friends whose parents were also students. She did very well and was happy. When the job offer came, Radia's parents decided to move to the village in order to have a bigger house and garden and – they hoped – better schooling for their three children, of whom Radia is the eldest.

All is not going as well as they hoped. Radia's mother is finding it lonely living in the village with no Algerian friends nearby. Although her neighbours are very pleasant, none of them visit her as regularly as she would like and she often spends days alone with her young child. She takes the two older pupils to school every day and would like to be able to talk to their teachers more than she does. But she never seems to be able to engage them in conversation. Radia has not settled very well into school. She misses the friends she made in her old school and has not really made any new friends in the village school. She is the only 'EAL' pupil in her class and one of only eight or ten in the whole school, all of whom are from well-educated, middle-class backgrounds, some from Islamic countries in the Middle East and others from China. Their parents are either students or former students, like Radia's, or professionals working for companies in the city.

The school has taken steps to find out how to support their new pupils. One teacher has been given responsibility for their induction and went on a training course which was part of the *New Arrivals Excellence Programme* (DfE, 2011). But she did not find anything very relevant for the pupils coming to the village school. They all seem to be very fluent in English so language does not seem to be an issue for them. One of the strategies recommended on the course was to form good relationships with the pupils' parents, and she would like to be able to do this. But when she meets them as they bring their pupils to school and come to collect them, she finds it difficult to think of ways to generate conversations with them. She has not had much prior experience of people from different cultural backgrounds. She raises this in a staff meeting, and this leads to a long discussion. One of the outcomes is a decision to organise a social event to give parents an opportunity to meet their pupils' teachers and see something of the work they do in class. This proves a great success and greatly helps the processes of communication in the school.

2.5 SOJOURNERS – HAMIDA (EARLY YEARS)

Hamida is four years old and in **Reception** in a large, mainly white school in a prosperous city in the south of England. She arrived in the city with her family from Saudi Arabia at the start of the school year. Her father is doing a PhD at the university and her mother also has plans to study once childcare arrangements are made for Hamida and her two younger brothers. Hamida speaks Arabic and is learning to read and write it in a Saturday class run by the wife of another Saudi Arabian student. Her parents are very keen for her to maintain her skills in Arabic, as they will be returning home in three or four years' time. They are also very eager for her to learn to speak English – indeed, this was one of the main reasons why they decided to bring her to England with them rather than leaving her at home with relatives as other students have done with their children. They want her to learn 'proper' English so that she speaks as far as possible with a **Received Pronunciation (RP)** accent which will afford her high status in Saudi Arabia. They also, quite naturally, want her to retain her Muslim identity and hope that the school are aware of, and sensitive to, Islamic rules and practices.

The reception class that Hamida has joined comprises mostly 'white British' pupils, though there is one other multilingual child whose parents are students like Hamida's. He is from Indonesia and – like Hamida – his family is Muslim. Both children are new to the English education system and have not had experience in nursery. The class teacher is very positive and enthusiastic about having them as her pupils, but is having to work hard to find relevant background information and resources such as stories and information books from their home countries. She is a little wary of the anticipated requirements related to the pupils' Muslim identities but willing to find out and to be flexible in her teaching. She is very keen to establish good relationships with the pupils' families as she sees this as a support for her in meeting the needs of their pupils.

ACTIVITY 1.5

Understanding diversity

Each of the six pupils in the vignettes have particular experiences and knowledge that can be seen as strengths as they benefit their learning in mainstream school and particular gaps in their experience that may create issues for their progress and their **achievements**. Make a chart like the one below and, in discussion with other trainees or colleagues in your placement school, list what you think could be seen as each child's strengths and needs, from the vignettes. There are some suggested answers at the end of the chapter.

Child	Strengths	Needs
Safina		
Stefan		
Jan		
Joseph		
Radia		
Hamida		

ROMA AND GYPSY PUPILS – CASE STUDY BY GEORGINA VINCE

When I first started working in my current school 12 years ago, we had 12 Roma students in the school. Since then, the number has increased dramatically so that we now have more than ten times as many and they are one of the largest ethnic groups in school. We have learnt a lot about this group, their backgrounds, the issues they face and how best to work with them and support them. I hope to share some of this experience with you here although I cannot say that we have any magic solutions and I know that there is still much more that we need to do and learn to continue to close the achievement gap and enable students in this group to achieve their potential.

(Continued)

(Continued)

Our school is a secondary school serving a highly diverse multicultural, economically deprived inner-city catchment area. Approximately 65 per cent of our students are EAL learners and about 50 per cent were born overseas, with students from a huge variety of backgrounds. Large numbers of international new arrivals come each year. Initially, most of our Roma students were new arrivals, but this has changed over time as the community has become more established. So now we have many Roma students who transfer from primary school and even some who were born here. The majority of our Roma students are from the Czech Republic and Slovakia with smaller numbers from Poland and Romania.

Understanding and celebrating Roma history and culture

When we first started working with the Roma, we knew very little about them. 'Funds of knowledge' research (see Chapter 2, section 2.3) suggests the importance of recognising the culture of different ethnic groups. I think this is especially true for the Roma, who may well have had to hide their culture in the past in their countries of origin. We worked with organisations such as the local Gypsy Roma Traveller Achievement Service in Leeds (see website details at the end of the chapter) and used different resources to learn more. This knowledge was further enhanced by visits to the Czech Republic which I describe below.

As you may know, it is believed that the Roma originated in India and gradually migrated across Europe over 500 years ago. There are now Roma living in most countries of Europe and further afield. We tend to use the word Roma to refer to Eastern European Roma but English Gypsies are believed to have the same origins. Most of our Roma students were completely unaware of this history until we did some assemblies about it with the students. What particularly brought it home to them was the language. Some of the resources we used showed the similarities between the Roma language and languages of India and Pakistan and it made their history seem more real when the Roma students realised how close numbers were in the Roma language to those in Urdu and Punjabi, familiar to our Pakistani-heritage students. This also helped to build bridges between the different groups of students in our school.

Following this initial assembly, we continued to have regular activities to teach students about Roma history, particularly during Gypsy Roma Traveller History Month in June (see website details at the end of the chapter). We have also brought issues around the treatment of the Roma in the Holocaust and discrimination into history and PSE curriculums. However, the most significant difference was made in recognising and celebrating Roma culture. We first found out about the musical abilities of some of our Roma students by chance as they turned up in the music rooms and started playing. Many of the boys especially were found to be highly skilled musicians, playing regularly at home and in the community - largely self-taught and playing by ear. We initially used music as a way to get them to feel happier at school and encourage attendance, before trying to encourage them to perform in public. As we got to know them, we also found out that many of them, especially the girls, did traditional Roma dance, so we set up a group at lunchtimes and bought some skirts. Initially they were reluctant to perform in front of the wider school and it took a lot of support and practice before they took part in a musical and dance performance for the school diversity day. This was a real breakthrough as, prior to this performance, the Roma students had been largely viewed negatively as students who didn't come to school and didn't speak English. Suddenly, people could see how skilled they were. Other students and staff came up and told them how great they had been, which was a huge boost to their confidence and made them feel like a real part of the school.

We followed this up by a Roma festival, organised by local schools and the council and held at our school. Roma students and parents from all over the city came and performed. This was so successful that we are now looking to organise a future festival ourselves. We have also tried to bring their culture into school in other ways, such as including Roma artists in art and music lessons and stories about Roma in English lessons.

One important point to remember is that not all Roma will want to celebrate their culture and may find it patronising to be told to, preferring for example hip-hop dancing, but it is important that their culture is there, as part of wider opportunities.

Understanding the situation of Roma in their home countries

As more and more Roma continued to come to our area, we started to wonder what it was that was causing them to leave their countries of origin. As we got to know our students, we gradually learnt more and this was reinforced by a project in which we took part, which linked schools in England with schools with large numbers of Roma in the Czech Republic. On visits to the Czech Republic, we found out more and saw how the Roma lived. This helped us understand some of the issues we faced with our Roma students.

Roma and Gypsies have faced huge amounts of discrimination throughout history; I believe that many were kept in slavery in Romania for a long time and this culminated in their treatment in the Holocaust in which nearly all Czech Roma were wiped out. This discrimination still continues to a lesser extent and is the main reason why so many Roma leave. Although some Roma in Eastern European countries now live a more integrated life with the non-Roma community, many continue to live separately, often in very deprived conditions. They suffer discrimination in areas such as employment and education. Prior to one of my visits to the Czech Republic, there had been large anti-Roma protests and attacks on Roma in a nearby town.

While there, I experienced Roma going to largely segregated schools despite this now being illegal. This is partly due to Roma living in such segregated communities and also due to Czech parents not wanting their children taught along with Roma. Some of these schools were quite negative towards their Roma students while others seemed more positive, but even in these schools there was never the expectation that Roma could achieve, such as going to university. Roma children also tend to be over-represented in special schools. This can be a sensitive subject - Czech people may deny it and obviously not all Czech people feel this way. Some Roma children may also be unaware of the true situation in their country. However, it is worth bearing this in mind, for example when looking for a Czech interpreter as Roma parents will quickly pick up on any prejudice.

Ascription

One issue that we regularly come up against is the reluctance of families to ascribe as Roma. This is understandable, given the situation they may face in their country if known as Roma and the advantages attached to hiding their identity. There may also be some misunderstanding as most feel that they are both Roma and Czech and therefore Eastern European. It could be argued that it is not important what it says on the official records as long as you know who your Roma pupils are and can monitor and support them. While this is true to a certain extent, I think it is important that students feel safe to acknowledge who they are and are proud of their identity. They should not feel they have to hide this. Imagine if you always had to keep such an important thing about yourself hidden; it cannot be good for a child growing up. In addition to having Roma culture visible around school, a strategy we have employed is to use a Roma student who is happy to identify as Roma in admissions meetings with new students. It is essential that all staff are aware of the issues around ascription and do not undermine work done by asking about it in an insensitive way.

(Continued)

(Continued)

Attendance

One particular problem schools often have with Roma students is attendance. Our Roma attendance has improved greatly over the years with strategies we have put in place and although Roma attendance is still below the school average, it is above Gypsy Roma attendance nationally. We have found that a mixture of 'carrot and stick' approaches works best. Firstly, it is important that the families understand the system in this country, which is very different to that in the Czech Republic and many other eastern European countries where attendance is not monitored and followed up in the rigorous way it is in this country.

This is an area where a Czech-speaking worker who can communicate with the families is invaluable. When we employed a Czech worker, it made a huge difference and led to an immediate improvement in attendance. She meets all new Czech and Slovak families and ensures they know the consequences of not coming to school and what to do if a child is absent. In addition, as families have been in the country longer and have got used to the system, attendance has improved anyway. Employment of a Czech worker has also helped greatly in following up absences and visiting families with attendance issues, whereas before this we had no real way of communicating with our Roma families.

However, I think that more important in improving Roma attendance has been the fact that they now feel part of the school community and happier at school. In addition, as their English has improved, they feel more confident to participate in lessons and see they are making progress. In addition to this, we have organised attendance groups where students who struggle with attendance meet our Czech worker each week and improvements in attendance are rewarded.

Working with families

Some of our feeder primaries have built up good relationships with families as parents bring their children to school each day, but we always struggled to get parents in to school. However, I think we started to have something of a breakthrough when the Czech worker tried to meet all families before they start at the school, either in admissions meetings for new arrivals or by visiting primary schools and organising meetings for the parents of Year 6 students who would be joining the school. She also ensures that there is good communication with parents through letters and phone calls in Czech telling them about important events in school. We have found that once parents understand what is happening at school they are in most cases keen to support their child and attendance at parents' evenings especially has improved greatly. It is also important to recognise that many of the Roma parents may have had very negative or little experience of school themselves – a number of our parents are not literate. We therefore tried to encourage them to come into school for fun events, such as music shows and the Roma festival, which proved successful. We have also offered them support through such things as ESOL classes and drop-in sessions with our Czech worker for help with benefits and job applications.

Raising aspirations and achievement

Once we had developed our understanding of our Roma students and their attendance had improved, we realised that this was not enough and that we needed to do more in order to raise their achievement. I had noticed the low expectations of Roma students at schools in the Czech Republic and this was reinforced when a number of our students who were predicted to have very good GCSEs said that what they wanted to be were hairdressers or mechanics. When we told their parents they had the potential to go to university, they were nearly in tears. We realised that we had to do more to raise students' aspirations, so we introduced a student mentoring programme with some of the older

Roma students mentoring some of the younger students and we are looking to develop this further. We also identify students with potential in the lower years and take them to visit universities. We are now looking to develop this further by getting university students to mentor some of our older students and getting some of our Roma students who have done well and gone on to higher study to come back and speak to the younger students. In addition, we noticed that some of the students who were joining us from primary school were struggling due to their lack of literacy in Czech or Slovak so we are introducing Czech lessons at school and also going into some of our feeder primaries to tackle these literacy issues at an earlier stage.

I hope that you have found our experiences useful and have learnt something. If you are interested in learning more, there are some sources of further information/support listed at the end of the chapter.

3 LANGUAGE DIVERSITY AND LEARNING – SOME MYTHS AND MISCONCEPTIONS

This brief, final section is intended to raise some questions about the best approaches to teaching EAL learners. You may already have experience of teaching English to pupils or adults in other countries, which is normally defined as **English as a Foreign Language (EFL)** teaching, and you may even have done a **Teaching English as a Foreign Language (TEFL)** course. There are parallels between EFL and EAL learners and some ideas from TEFL teaching can be very useful in EAL. But there are also important differences, as the vignettes and case studies in this chapter show. Some ideas from TEFL teaching may seem obviously appropriate, like common sense. But they can be seen as myths and misconceptions and may not seem to be so helpful when you understand something of the complexities of the experiences of many multilingual and EAL learners. You will read a lot about theories of language, learning and multilingualism in Chapters 2 and 3, which will develop your understanding of the needs of multilingual and EAL learners. They will also help you to see how these myths and misconceptions can sometimes be unhelpful. So, here are my 'myths and misconceptions' – we will return to them at the end of the book in Chapter 9.

- Languages should be kept separate in the classroom or learners will become confused (*this is sometimes called 'language interference'*).

- Pupils will 'pick English up' naturally in the classroom; they do not need to be explicitly taught (*this is sometimes called 'immersion'*).

- Language diversity is a 'problem', and it is better if pupils speak English all the time in classrooms.

- It is impossible, or very difficult, to learn a new language beyond a young age (*this is sometimes called 'the critical period'*).

CHAPTER SUMMARY

This introductory chapter has provided you with background information about the pupils who are categorised as multilingual and EAL learners, and their families and communities. This should have helped you gain awareness of the history of language and cultural diversity in England, and the

(Continued)

(Continued)

diverse range of experiences and knowledge that multilingual and EAL learners bring to their primary classrooms. One of the aims of this is to help you think about the importance of recognising and reflecting on your own views on language diversity and ethnicity for you as a primary teacher.

Self-assessment questions

1. In what ways do you think your own identity might influence your views and perceptions of the pupils you teach? Think about specific situations where this may have happened.

2. Why do you think it is important to understand something about the family backgrounds of the pupils you teach? (You will read more about this in Chapter 3.)

3. Think about the teachers mentioned in each of the vignettes in this chapter. Following what you have read in this chapter, if you had been the teacher for any of the pupils described, would you have responded in the same way or might you have done something different?

4. Think of a group of multilingual and EAL learners you know. Which of the categories introduced in section 1.2 would your learners fit into? Write a brief vignette of one of your learners, along the lines of those in the sections that follow.

5. What distinctive factors influence the learning and achievement of Gypsy and Roma pupils? How do you think stereotypes in the media may affect their success in school?

Suggested answers to activity 1.5 – understanding diversity

Child	Strengths	Needs
Safina	Strong speaking and listening skills Supportive home and community Diverse experiences of learning at home	Sustained support in developing writing skills in English
Stefan	Strong literacy in home language Opportunities to develop expertise and take exams in home language	Continued support in developing writing skills in English
Jan	Teacher who is interested in understanding the problems he is facing Positive attitude in class to recognising pupils' home languages	Personalised provision to develop his skills in English
Joseph	Good level of English language Loving relationship with mother	Understanding (on the part of his teachers) of the broader cultural background of Sierra Leone Personalised provision to help him catch up
Radia	Supportive home and family background Positive attitudes in school towards EAL pupils	Improved communication between home and school
Hamida	Supportive home and family background Positive attitudes in school towards EAL pupils	Greater awareness on the part of the school of cultural and religious factors underpinning Hamida's experiences

FURTHER READING

Gussin Paley, V. (2000) *White Teacher*, **3rd edn. Cambridge, MA: Harvard University Press.**

This is a personal account of teaching in a school which becomes increasingly diverse. Paley reflects on the way that even simple terminology can convey unintended meanings. She vividly describes what her pupils taught her over the years about herself as a 'white teacher'.

Hayes, D. (2011) 'Establishing your own teaching identity', in A. Hansen (ed.), *Primary Professional Studies***. Exeter: Learning Matters, pp. 118–33.**

This chapter encourages readers to think about their own values, motivation and self-identity, and the impact these have on becoming a teacher.

Sources of information about Gypsy Roma pupils:

http://www.natt.org.uk/ – National Association of Teachers of Travellers
http://www.grtleeds.co.uk/ – Leeds Gypsy Roma Traveller Achievement Service
http://www.everyculture.com/wc/Norway-to-Russia/Roma.html – information about Roma
http://qualirom.uni-graz.at/home.html – Roma language teaching resources
http://www.romaninet.com/?sec=home – Roma language and culture resources
http://romani.humanities.manchester.ac.uk/# – Manchester University's Roma resources, including excellent language DVD link

STUDYING AT MASTERS LEVEL

Critical reading:

Safford, K. and Drury, R. (2013) 'The "problem" of bilingual children in educational settings: policy and research in England', *Language and Education***, 27 (1), pp. 70-81.**

In this article, the authors address issues around why EAL is perceived as a 'problem' in mainstream schools in England. They review the history of policy and practice, and consider what kinds of research might open up the potential of multilingualism as a resource.

After reading, consider the following questions, ideally in discussion with colleagues:

1. What do Safford and Drury mean by 'colonisation in reverse' and how has this influenced perceptions of bilingual children in schools in England? In what ways have you experienced 'colonisation in reverse' in your personal or professional life?

2. On p. 7, Safford and Drury indicate several themes that Wallace and Mallows (2009) identify in their research into provision for EAL learners in mainstream classrooms. What are they? How many of these have you experienced in your own work in school?

3. What kinds of research do Safford and Drury advocate as offering the best means of understanding the experiences of bilingual children in school and identifying ways to support them and meet their needs? Try to track down some of the studies they mention, and read and discuss them with your colleagues.

REFERENCES

BBC (2007) *Multilingualism*, at http://www.bbc.co.uk/voices/yourvoice/multilingualism2.shtml (accessed 23 November 2018).

Datta, M. (2007) *Bilinguality and Biliteracy: Principles and Practice*, 2nd edn. London: Continuum.

Department for Education (DfE) (2011) *The National Strategies: New Arrivals Excellence Programme*, at https://www.naldic.org.uk/Resources/NALDIC/Teaching%20and%20Learning/nswsneapcpdmodule0004108.pdf (accessed 23 November 2018).

Department for Education (DfE) (2018) *Schools, Pupils and Their Characteristics: January 2018 – National Tables*, https://www.gov.uk/government/statistics/schools-pupils-and-their-characteristics-january-2018

Gussin Paley, V. (2000) *White Teacher*, 3rd edn. Cambridge, MA: Harvard University Press.

Hall, D., Griffiths, D., Haslam, L. and Wilkin, Y. (2001) *Assessing the Needs of Bilingual Pupils: Living in Two Languages*, 2nd edn. London: David Fulton.

Tyne and Wear Archives and Museums (2018) *Arbeia Fort*, at https://arbeiaromanfort.org.uk

Wikipedia (2018) *Bengali Language*, at https://en.wikipedia.org/wiki/Bengali_language#Geographical_distribution (accessed 23 November 2018).

2

ALL ABOUT LANGUAGE AND LEARNING

— LEARNING OUTCOMES

This chapter will help you to achieve the following learning outcomes:

• gain awareness and understanding of how language and learning are linked and can be understood theoretically;

• develop understanding of the functional approach to grammar and its importance for teaching and learning;

• understand the important role of talk for learning;

• understand what is meant by the 'funds of knowledge' concept and what it means for understanding the needs of EAL learners in mainstream schools.

INTRODUCTION

Together with Chapter 3, this chapter introduces you to the theories related to language, learning and multilingualism that underpin the book. Good teachers understand that theory is not something that is 'applied', but that it is actively constructed through all aspects of their professional experience. Teachers' theories come from their understanding of how language works and how children learn. This understanding is developed from practical experience as well as reading and study. Good teachers know how to use theory to inform practice in their planning and teaching. There is no one particular 'grand' theory that dictates all you should do in the classroom, but good teaching benefits from a range of theoretical perspectives that complement each other. An understanding of theory can also help you to critically evaluate official policy and use it in the most effective ways to support your pupils' learning and development.

The theories about language and learning outlined in this chapter are relevant for your work with all pupils in early years, primary and secondary settings, not just those who are defined as multilingual, EAL learners. They will help you to understand the experiences of the multilingual and EAL learners, such as those you read about in Chapter 1 and those you will meet in your own classrooms. They will help you also to understand more about the role of language in learning generally. The practical outcomes of these theories flow through the ideas presented in Part 2 of the book and will help you to make informed, strategic decisions about the best ways to help your pupils to succeed.

There are questions and brief activities interspersed throughout the chapter to help you think about how the theories relate to your own experiences as both a teacher and a learner.

These are the main sections and subsections of the chapter:

1   All about language

1.1 What is language?

1.2 Language, culture and identity

1.3 Thinking about teaching languages – the functional approach

2   Language and learning

2.1 Sociocultural theories of learning and the Zone of Proximal Development

2.2 The importance of talk for learning

2.3 The 'funds of knowledge' concept

1 ALL ABOUT LANGUAGE

1.1 WHAT IS LANGUAGE?

Language pervades everything we do, in our social lives at home with our families and in our communities, as well as at school and work. Indeed, according to the Vygotskyan, sociocultural model of language and learning that is discussed in section 2.1 below, language is the medium through which our private thoughts are given life and meaning. We experience language in an infinite range of ways, both within and outside school: orally through our everyday conversations with family, friends and all the other people we engage with, as well as in written modes through traditional forms of print such as books and newspapers and through all the growing range of social media. We use spoken language to engage in face-to-face conversations with the people near us and in **multi-modal** modes of 'conversing' to communicate virtually with others. For all of us, **language diversity** is a normal and natural part of our lived experiences, even if the only language we speak and write may be English. If we happen to live in families and communities where different languages are used for different purposes on an everyday basis, this means that language diversity is an even richer aspect of our lives. Many children in England, as in other parts of the world, live in families where English may be the most commonly used language between themselves and their parents and siblings, but other languages are used naturally in interactions with grandparents or other relatives who live nearby or in conversations by phone or social media with relatives in other countries.

Through language, we interact with others in the social groups we belong to, and in this way construct our understandings of the world. This makes the learning of languages in school, whether in literacy, English literature or foreign languages (FL), very different from learning other subjects, in two main ways. First, language is not only the medium of communication; it is also the substance of what is being learnt. Second, learning English in mainstream schools in England is always cross-curricular in that the language itself forms the basis of learning in all the other areas of the curriculum. For all pupils, language learning takes place in every subject across the curriculum. For many multilingual and EAL learners who need to develop fluency in English, this fact is even more crucial.

Language learning does not only take place in mainstream schools for many multilingual and EAL learners, but also in community-based schools (sometimes called **complementary or supplementary schools**), where they learn what is sometimes called their **heritage language**. Even though this language is not taught in their mainstream school, they may be taking a GCSE or 'A' level in it. Many complementary schools make arrangements with the mainstream schools that their pupils attend for them to take exams in languages they have been studying out of school hours. This is the reason why Polish is rapidly becoming one of the most popular languages at GCSE. There is much more about this aspect of being multilingual in Chapter 3, and about complementary schools, their roles in learning and ways that bridges between complementary and mainstream learning can be built in Chapter 8.

As British citizens and members of different social and cultural groups, we all live in a multilingual society. It is important to remember that all the pupils you teach, not just those who are categorised as EAL or multilingual, have knowledge and experiences of languages and of varieties of English outside school that are different from those they use and learn in school. One of the central arguments in Chapter 3 is that the world is becoming more and more multilingual, while at the same time English is spreading in its use and power. Besides all the different languages that we may hear and read around us, we are all continually exposed to different forms and varieties of the English language in our everyday lives. We may hear and use different **dialects** of English, which have grammar and vocabulary different from **standard English**. We may speak English in different **accents** from the ones most commonly used in school, those that are widely regarded as appropriate for educated people to use. All of us, whether we regard ourselves as multilingual, bilingual or monolingual, have our own **repertoires**, or personal resources, of language. This is one feature of what is meant by language diversity. It means that we have a wide range of ways of speaking and writing from which we can choose when we interact with others.

We use our language repertoires to speak and write in order to get done all the things that we need to do – in other words, to perform different functions with the languages we know. We make choices from our language repertoires according to a range of factors, which are often called the '5Ws':

- *who* we are speaking to or writing for (audiences);

- *when* and *where* (contexts);

- *what* we say or write (topics);

- *why* we say or write these things (reasons and purposes).

Here is an example of some of the things I can do with my language repertoire in an ordinary working day. I may wake up to Radio 4 on the radio alarm, mumble a few words to my husband while eating breakfast, then set off down the road to the station, greeting our neighbour as he walks past with his dog. When I get to work, I head up the stairs to my office, switch on the computer, read and reply to several e-mails and compose a few of my own. After that, perhaps, I have to give a lecture to rows of students in a lecture theatre. This involves a very different way of speaking from the ones I have used so far – an academic form which is more like writing in many ways. Later on, I may meet a smaller group of students in a classroom for a tutorial. Here, I need to use yet another way of speaking from the others I have used so far, one which is much more tentative and conversational than the lecture but still academic. As I take part in the discussion, I need to listen carefully to my students' viewpoints and adapt the ways I speak in order to respond to their questions. On the way home from work, I may make a couple of quick calls on my mobile phone – yet another form of speaking, different from all the others I have already mentioned. In all of these interactions and for all of these functions, I choose the ways I speak or write from my language repertoire, depending on the '5Ws' indicated above – who, when, where, what and why.

ACTIVITY 2.1

Your language repertoire

Make a chart like the one below and list some of the ways you speak and write during a typical day. Answer the '5Ws' questions for each, following the examples given.

Activity	What	Who	When	Where	Why
Speaking	greetings	neighbour	early morning	in the street	to be friendly
Writing	e-mail	student	lunchtime	in the office	to answer a question

The notion of language repertoires is a very useful one in helping us understand how language works and in thinking about how your teaching can be made more focused and effective. It switches our attention from the language itself to the users of the language and the things they want to do with it. One of its key aspects is the notion of appropriacy, which emphasises the idea that there is always a range of different ways of saying and writing things, and that what we need to do is to choose the one that is most appropriate. This calls into question the idea that there is only one correct way to say or write something, and thus all other ways are wrong. It underpins what is known as the functional approach to language and grammar, a model which focuses on the purposes for which we need to use language, rather than just the language itself. If we help pupils to understand the functions – the '5Ws' – of the language in any task they are expected to do, then their thinking will be more focused and their language learning, through the activity, will be more meaningful, purposeful and successful. The functional approach to language is further explained in section 1.3 below.

1.2 LANGUAGE, CULTURE AND IDENTITY

In addition to being an essential tool for learning, language is an inextricable part of our personal and social lives, of the cultures we live in and of who we are. It is one of the main ways in which we develop a sense of where we belong and how we fit in with the social worlds that surround us. In other words, it is part of our identities.

RESEARCH FOCUS

There is a great deal of evidence to show that, if pupils have a sense of belonging and of being valued in their classrooms, their attitudes to learning will be much more positive and this will help their achievements to improve. In Conteh (2003, pp. 41-57), I show the range of knowledge and experiences that many multilingual and EAL learners bring to their mainstream classrooms, and suggest how these can support their learning in positive ways if they are recognised and valued. On the other hand, pupils can very quickly gain the sense - even if it is unintended - that their languages are not welcome and must be kept hidden from the teacher. This can have a negative effect on their learning, as the following example shows:

Five-year-old Rukshana began school speaking no English. Punjabi was the language of her home. Twenty years later, when she was training to be a teacher, she wrote about the way she felt as a child when, as a new child in the class, the teacher did not allow her to use Punjabi when assessing her knowledge of colours. This is part of what she wrote: 'The teacher left me staring blankly at the other pupils. Every one of them was doing something: playing, reading, working or talking in English, I sat back and felt sorry for myself. The teacher was probably thinking 'just another incident with an Asian child who does not know colours', this was a day I felt so many emotions inside me. Feelings that I had never experienced before. I did not want to be myself.

Multilingual and EAL learners need to feel that their home languages are recognised and valued in the classroom in order to feel that they themselves belong. To do this is often not difficult and it does not involve complex changes to the curriculum. Actions that may seem very small, such as doing the register in different languages or choosing a story with a particular setting or theme can make pupils feel recognised and valued and that they belong in the classroom. This can open out their potential for learning, as the following vignette shows.

▬ VIGNETTE ▬

Valuing language diversity – making 'safe spaces'

A trainee teacher found out that there was a new child in her class who had recently arrived from Sierra Leone in West Africa. She went to the library and chose a story to read to the class which was set in the child's country of origin. It contained words in a language that neither the class teacher nor the trainee knew. She found out from the child's mother that the words were actually greetings in one of the languages that the family spoke (Mende). With the trainee's (and her mother's) encouragement and support, the child taught the class how to say the greetings. The rest of the class enjoyed this very much. When the story was over, a little girl came up to the class teacher and the trainee and said, 'Miss, I can speak Arabic, and my dad teaches me every day. Shall I show you how to say hello?' The teacher was surprised, but pleased, and asked her to teach the class, which she did with a beaming smile on her face. The teacher told the trainee afterwards that the child had never done anything like that before. They concluded that she might have felt able to do so because of the 'safe space' (Conteh and Brock, 2010) that had been opened up for her by the story that the trainee had chosen for the new pupil and the subsequent experience of learning greetings in a new language in the context of an enjoyable whole-class activity.

The links between identity, language and culture are strong. Languages are formed in the cultural settings in which they are situated, their meanings shaped through everyday use. The meanings of English words can change from country to country – light bulbs in Australia are called globes; roundabouts in West Africa are called turntables. Word meanings vary even in different parts of England. There is a story about some road signs put up about 30 years ago at level crossings in Lincolnshire and Norfolk, which read, 'Wait while lights are red.' Some drivers waited until the lights turned red, then tried to race across the track before the train thundered past! It quickly became clear that, in that part of the country, 'while' and 'until' had very similar meanings and the confusing signs were rapidly changed. As teachers, we may sometimes need to think carefully about what our pupils are trying to say and respond positively to their meanings, even though they may not always be expressed in terms that are familiar to us.

Many pupils from Pakistani-heritage backgrounds, even when they are fluent in English, sometimes talk about their extended family members as 'brother cousins' and 'sister cousins'. When I first heard this, it reminded me of how people in Sierra Leone, where I lived for several years, sometimes talked about their relatives. In a setting where a man might have more than one wife, they would describe the relationships very precisely: 'he's my brother, same mother, same father' and so on. When I asked the Pakistani-heritage pupils I was teaching why they talked about their cousins in this way, they told me that in Punjabi there were different words for 'cousin', so they could distinguish whether it was mum's sister's son, mum's brother's daughter and so on. I found this fascinating, and it led to several interesting discussions about families, comparing the different ways that we could think and talk about families in different cultures and the words we used to describe them – see Chapter 4, section 2 for further discussion of this. This is an important way of learning (it certainly was for me), with clear links to personal and social education. It is also an excellent language-learning activity.

It is very important for our self-confidence and identity as learners that we feel we belong and are valued in the communities in which we are learning. Multilingual pupils need to feel that their home languages are recognised and valued in school, even if their teachers do not speak them. These languages, along with English, are often a significant part of their social lives outside school. Also, if they are in the early stages of learning English, the languages will form a large part of their thought processes and the ways they make sense of the world, as we will see in the discussion on multilingualism in Chapter 3. If you do not share your pupils' languages, you can still do a lot to show that you value them through using multilingual labels in the classroom, choosing stories from their own cultures and dual language texts, of which there are now many available. Dual language texts can also be produced in the classroom, as shown in Chapter 8. Resources such as these help pupils to transfer their thinking from one language to another and support the development of **additive bilingualism** (Chapter 3, p. 52). Valuing pupils' out-of-school experiences and understandings in this way is part of a **'funds of knowledge'** (Gonzalez et al., 2005) approach to their learning, and is discussed more fully in section 2.3 below.

1.3 THINKING ABOUT TEACHING LANGUAGES – THE FUNCTIONAL APPROACH

Like any subject we are expected to teach, we need to understand it ourselves. We need a way of thinking and talking about the English language in order to understand how it works so that we can help pupils to learn it. In other words, we need a language to talk about language, and this is part of what **grammar** can offer. Grammars, essentially, are ways of describing languages; they are not prescriptions for how they should be used. We sometimes think of grammars as sets of rules to be followed rather than descriptions of language. We can get very worried about what is 'correct', and anxious about making mistakes. However, when thinking about language and how to teach it, the question of what is or isn't absolutely correct is not always a very helpful one.

There are many different kinds of grammar. Some are not very helpful in teaching as they have other purposes; they can quickly become abstract and complex, the terminology difficult to remember and use. The functional approach to grammar offers a more useful way to think about grammar for teaching. As I said above, a key element in this approach is the idea of repertoire. This helps to give a focus on the choices we make – often intuitively – in using language to do the things we need to do. We all make choices and we all have repertoires of language to choose from, whether we think of ourselves as multilingual or not. A functional approach to grammar encourages us to think about how we can make the best choices, how we can say and write what we want to in the best ways possible. Using the '5Ws' described above (p. 29) helps us to consider the choices available and make the most appropriate ones.

Within the functional approach, grammar can be thought of as a set of tools to help us to analyse our language choices and decide what to do next. Thinking differently about language and asking different questions, such as whether the messages in the text have been conveyed in the most appropriate ways possible for that particular text, is often more productive. And the answers to these questions about appropriacy will be different from text to text – what is appropriate for one text will be inappropriate for another.

ACTIVITY 2.2

Saying things in the most appropriate ways: Ted Hughes and *The Iron Man*

Look at the following text which is from the beginning of *The Iron Man*, one of the best children's stories ever written (in my view!). In the traditional way of thinking about grammar, there are many features that may be described as 'incorrect'. Try to identify them. Think about why Ted Hughes (who was poet laureate, so knew a thing or two about language) might have decided to open his story in this way. There are some suggestions to help you check your responses after this activity.

CRRRAAASSSSSSSH

Down the cliff the Iron Man came toppling, head over heels.

CRASH!

CRASH!

CRASH!

From rock to rock, snag to snag, tumbling slowly. And as he crashed and crashed and crashed

His iron legs fell off.

His iron arms broke off and the hands broke off the arms. His great iron ears fell off and his eyes fell out. His great iron head fell off.

All the separate pieces tumbled, scattered, crashing, bumping, clanging, down on to the

rocky beach far below.

A few rocks tumbled with him.

Then

Silence.

Ted Hughes

These are some of the text features you might have noticed:

1. There are words in capital letters and a mis-spelt word at the start – here they help you to imagine the Iron Man tumbling and crashing down the cliff.

2. There are lot of exclamation marks at one point – often they are thought to be 'bad' punctuation if over-used, but here they help with describing the crashing of the Iron Man.

3. The sentence beginning 'From rock to rock …' has no stated subject, so could be considered 'wrong'. But we all know that it is about the Iron Man, and it helps us, again, to imagine him rolling down the hill.

4. The next sentence begins with 'and'. But it is very effective in carrying on the idea of the Iron Man tumbling down the cliff. (And this sentence starts with 'but' – but I think it is the most appropriate way to express what I want to say!)

5. The section of the text beginning with 'His iron legs fell off …' is rather repetitive, with simple sentences, all with the same structure. But, again, it is effective as we imagine the pieces of the Iron Man falling off, one after the other.

6. There are no descriptive adjectives in the whole text, yet it is wonderfully descriptive without them. The words which do most of the job of describing things in interesting ways are the verbs.

Taking a functional approach means that we look at the ways in which language is used in the text to do the job it is trying to do. Language is used to construct whole **texts** in their **contexts of use**, so we need to consider this rather than just the language itself without any context. The main practical implication of this is that in their learning of language, whether it be of literacy in English, literature in a foreign language, the language of science or maths or English as an additional language, pupils need to experience listening, speaking, reading and writing as authentic activities through which they can make meanings and do things, not just as sets of decontextualised skills, such as lists of spellings to be learnt. In a functional approach to teaching, teachers explain and model and learners discuss and analyse the ways in which words are chosen and sentences are structured and brought together to construct whole texts such as stories, letters, reports and so on. All pupils – and particularly multilingual learners – need to encounter examples of **authentic language** in their learning, not just made-up examples of language in exercises, worksheets, tests or traditional grammar books. They need to hear and read, think about, discuss and argue about real texts which writers have written for real purposes and audiences. Grammar can be a useful tool in doing all this. But the grammar will only make sense to them when they can relate it to real texts in this way.

Pupils learn much more effectively about how different texts work and are constructed if they have authentic purposes and audiences for their tasks. Rather than teaching text types in an abstract, mechanical way in literacy lessons, it is far more effective to introduce them through real tasks in different subjects across the curriculum, where they are used to accomplish different functions, e.g. a report in science, a narrative in history and so on. You can see some examples of this in Chapter 6 in the discussion of planning. Understanding of the features of different texts can be reinforced and practised in literacy lessons with meaningful content that is about something that your pupils are learning about in other subjects. There are ideas to help you to do this in activities across the curriculum in Chapter 6 and in literacy lessons in Chapter 5.

ACTIVITY 2.3

Thinking about the functions of texts

All of the following are examples of authentic texts in particular contexts of use. They are the kinds of texts you will have come across in your everyday lives, not just as a teacher. Decide what kind of texts they are and what contexts they come from (you could use the 5Ws questions to help you to do this). Then, think about what language features (grammar, punctuation, choice of words, etc.) the speakers or writers have used to make their texts meaningful and purposeful. There are some possible answers to these questions below, but you may have other relevant ideas which you can discuss with your course mates or colleagues.

Texts

1. 'Cheap day return to Manchester Piccadilly, please.'

2. To make wholemeal rolls, divide the dough into 18 equal portions. Each should weigh about 50g. On an unfloured surface, roll each piece of dough into a ball inside your cupped hand.

3. Parvana was small for her 11 years. As a small girl, she could usually get away with being outside without being questioned. 'I need this girl to help me walk,' her father would tell any talib who asked, pointing to his leg. He had lost the lower part of his leg when the high school he was teaching in was bombed. His insides had been hurt, somehow, too. He was often tired.

4. The Cold War is always portrayed as a global struggle between Communism and capitalism but in the early 1960s the world's Communist superpowers, China and Russia, also fell out. After a few border skirmishes they decided to continue their struggle in the rest of the world. So the Russia-China Cold War spread to Africa where they competed for allies.

CONTEXTS OF USE AND LANGUAGE FEATURES

1. This is a spoken text with a very simple purpose: the speaker wants to buy a rail ticket. They do not know the ticket seller personally, so they make their request in a very simple, straightforward way with no greetings or personal language. In some cultural settings, it would be appropriate to preface the request with a simple greeting, but this is not usually necessary in 'British' culture. The speaker ends their request with 'please', which is the way to express politeness in 'British' culture. In other cultural settings politeness is expressed in different ways.

2. This is a written text, a recipe. In some ways it is similar to the first example in that it is dealing with precise instructions in an impersonal way. So, it needs to be very clear in order to make sure that the reader has all the information they need to carry out the task. It uses imperative verbs (sometimes called 'bossy' verbs in primary schools), and the writer has made sure that all the actions needed to follow the recipe successfully are placed in the correct order and all measurements are accurate. The writer also uses some 'technical' language, e.g. 'on an unfloured surface', from time to time and also illustrates what needs to be done by connecting the instructions with everyday examples that can be easily visualised, e.g. 'roll … into a ball inside your cupped hand'.

3. This is a written fiction text, in fact a short extract from Deborah Ellis's book *Parvana's Journey*, a fascinating children's novel about a young girl in Afghanistan during the rule of the Taliban, which Ellis wrote after she had visited refugee camps and found out about the lives of women and children there. This short extract from the beginning of the book quickly sets the scene and raises questions in the reader's mind – why might Parvana be questioned if she is found outside? Why was her father's school bombed? Who did it? Who (or what) is a talib? What has happened to the rest of their family? The language is very simple, but we quickly gain an impression of the problems that Parvana faces.

ritten non-fiction text, a short extract from Richard Dowden's book *Africa: Altered States,* *Miracles*. Richard Dowden is a journalist, so his style is straightforward, with the main ...s presented at the start of the piece and reasons and explanations coming later on. He uses a popular kind of personification in the way he presents the 'struggle' between China and Russia in globalism and communism. They are described as 'falling out', like two people who have had a quarrel. This is a very vivid way of helping his readers to understand the events he is describing. If he were writing a history textbook rather than a general book for a wider audience, he would probably have used a more formal style, perhaps with longer, more complex sentences.

2 LANGUAGE AND LEARNING

2.1 SOCIOCULTURAL THEORIES OF LEARNING AND THE ZONE OF PROXIMAL DEVELOPMENT

RESEARCH FOCUS

Learning is often theoretically described as 'sociocultural'. This suggests that learning is not simply the transmission of knowledge, but a process of negotiation and co-construction between teachers and learners. Vygotsky was one of the originators of the sociocultural theoretical framework, which he developed through his research with pupils with special needs. He argued that all learning is social in origin, and that young pupils develop and learn through 'externalised' social interactions with their teachers and their peers. As they progress, they develop the capacity to 'internalise' the interactions and to learn more independently. He developed the idea of the **Zone of Proximal Development (ZPD)** to describe in a theoretical way this social mediation between teachers and pupils, suggesting that pupils learn interactively 'through problem solving under adult guidance or in collaboration with more capable peers' (Vygotsky, 1978, p. 86).

The sociocultural theory of learning has very important implications for all pupils in school, and particularly for multilingual and EAL learners. Sonia Nieto (1999) uses Vygotsky's theories to develop a model to describe the kinds of learning that will best support multilingual learners. She makes the point that it will promote learning for all pupils. Here are the four main elements in her model:

- learning is actively constructed;

- learning grows from and builds on the learner's prior experiences;

- there are cultural differences in the ways that pupils learn;

- learning is socially mediated and develops in cultural contexts.

One important conclusion we can draw from this is that while learning is something that we all do and so is a common human experience, the specific ways in which pupils learn will vary from individual to individual, depending on the knowledge and experiences they bring to the classroom. This is part of what Nieto means in her use of the word 'context' in the fourth point above. In using that word, she is referring to more than just the learning environment in terms of the physical setting that surrounds the learners. Her concept of context includes all the social, cultural, emotional, affective and cognitive resources, including languages, that both learners and teachers bring to their classrooms. Other researchers besides Nieto argue that it also includes the political and historical influences reflected in the policies, resources and practices that make up the teaching and learning activities. As Nieto points out, this is a very empowering idea, as it means that every child is capable of learning. Most, if not all, pupils can learn successfully if their teachers understand how to help them mediate all of the factors that influence their learning.

Bruner used Vygotsky's theories of learning to develop the notion of **scaffolding** for planning and teaching. His ideas are sometimes called 'a theory of instruction'. They are a way of thinking about how to develop teaching strategies to construct the best kinds of contexts to promote learning for individual pupils. To scaffold learning is more than providing 'support' – it is not just about helping pupils to do things, but helping them to do them more and more independently. Beginning with context-embedded activities and gradually moving, with talk and action, towards less context-embedded work means that pupils are never left without support. At the same time, they are encouraged to move forward to the new knowledge which is the object of the activity. Scaffolding is thought of as being future-oriented rather than simply being about helping pupils to get through the task in hand. It can be developed through a variety of practical resources and multi-sensory experiences and there are many examples of these in Part 2, particularly in Chapters 4, 5, 6 and 8.

2.2 THE IMPORTANCE OF TALK FOR LEARNING

▬ RESEARCH FOCUS ▬

There is a great deal of research that shows how collaborative classroom dialogues and discussions support cognitive development in individual learners. In *Constructing Knowledge Together*, Wells and Chang-Wells (1992) provide examples of talk from multilingual classrooms where pupils engage in 'collaborative sense-making' with their peers. Using Vygotsky's key concept of 'internalisation', they reveal how shared talk develops thinking. This could be seen in the way the pupils could take part in discussions with each other, using much more complex language to consider and express their ideas than they would have been able to do on their own. The examples are similar to the discussions I reported in Conteh (2003: 81-7), where pupils in Year 4 are negotiating how to carry out a 'fair test' in science to see which ball will bounce the highest. In the following example, Rehana, Yasmin and Nahida engage in collaborative talk about how to do the test, using language they probably would not be have been able to use on their own and co-constructing their understanding of what a fair test entails.

JC (teacher): ... To answer the question, 'this is how I will make my test fair'.

Rehana: Fair, I know how to make it fair.

JC: Yes.

Rehana: With the ruler, if you hold it like that ...

JC: Yes.

Rehana: Move it with your hand you've got to ... and I'll tell you something else, you've got to bounce it from the same height.

(Continued)

(Continued)

Yasmin:	*Do it from the same height ...*
Nahida:	*Same height.*
JC:	*Why is it important to have a fair test?*
Nahida:	*Because like, if the other ball, and they bounce it in a different way, and then ... the other balls won't bounce like that, this way.*

As Wells and Chang-Wells argue, this kind of discussion is essential to help pupils to develop the ability to think in analytical ways that they need to become fully literate, and so become good readers and writers. Taking part in discussions, in any subject across the curriculum, is also one of the key means through which pupils become confident in using the academic language they need to develop the **cognitive academic language proficiency (CALP)** that is so essential for multilingual and EAL learners and which is discussed in Chapter 3. In the Expert Panel Review of the National Curriculum (DfE, 2011, pp. 52–4), the importance of oral language across the curriculum is very clearly stated:

Whilst it should find a particular place within the National Curriculum for English, it should also be promoted more widely as an integral feature of all subjects.

Unfortunately, this emphasis has not come through to the 2014 curriculum. Despite the fact that most learning is mediated and accomplished in different ways through talk, we need to remember that the evidence of learning that matters is usually in writing, and pupils are almost always formally assessed through writing. It remains true that literacy is, of course, the main route to academic success in our education system. But it is essential that, as pupils progress through school, talk remains a central element of their learning. Not only do they need to *learn to talk*, pupils also need to be able to *talk to learn* across the whole curriculum. This has many implications for your planning, which are discussed in Chapter 6.

ACTIVITY 2.4

Talk for learning across the curriculum in the classroom

Using the '5Ws' again, make a chart and record all the examples you can think of across one day in your classroom where you think pupils were using talk for learning in any lesson across the curriculum. This will show you the range of ways in which your pupils are developing their talk repertoires.

Here is an example from mathematics with a Year 1 class:

Activity	What	Who	When	Where	Why
Mathematics mental starter	Addition and subtraction up to 10	Whole-class question and answer	Start of lesson	On the carpet	To practise number bonds
Mathematics group work	Worksheet with addition and subtraction in word problems	Small peer group (4–5 pupils)	Towards the end of the lesson	At tables	To reinforce knowledge of number bonds in word problems

2.3 THE 'FUNDS OF KNOWLEDGE' CONCEPT

I have talked a lot in this chapter about funds of knowledge and in this final section I explain briefly where the ideas that underpin the concept came from and why it is such a powerful theory in understanding the best ways to help multilingual and EAL learners to succeed in school. I also provide some concrete examples showing how pupils used their funds of knowledge in different ways to construct their own learning. The funds of knowledge concept was developed in the USA by Luis Moll and his associates (Gonzalez et al., 2005) in their work with Mexican-American families. Their definition of 'funds of knowledge' is as follows:

> *Historically developed and accumulated strategies (skills, abilities, ideas, practices) or bodies of knowledge ... which are developed in homes and communities in ways that provide pupils with ... ample opportunities to participate in activities with people they trust. (pp. 91–2)*

Funds of knowledge are developed in activities at home and in communities, often through extended families and wider communities working together across geographical and political borders in such activities as farming and animal husbandry, building houses, trading goods and so on. Children's roles in these activities, though small, are often vital to the success of the whole enterprise. In their engagement with such activities, children learn a wide range of skills and knowledge. Just as importantly, they also develop a profound sense of belonging and of their own place in their communities. Such learning entails 'maximum identity investment' (Cummins and Early, 2011), an idea which links with the arguments I made in section 1.2 of this chapter to foreground the importance of identity and belonging for success in school. Another important factor that Gonzalez et al. discuss is that the children's mainstream teachers usually know very little about the ways that their pupils are learning outside school. But the positive side of this is that, once teachers become aware of them, they can go on to find ways to successfully integrate such knowledge into the mainstream curriculum. There are many examples of this and the positive outcomes in Gonzalez et al.'s book.

The funds of knowledge concept has clear links with the work of Cummins, discussed in the next chapter, and implications for **pedagogy**. The **common underlying proficiency (CUP)** concept, for example, which you can read about on p. 56, suggests that all the input from the different languages that an individual experiences feeds into one common resource for meaning making and expression. Both theoretical concepts of funds of knowledge and CUP surely lead us to see the need for a pedagogy that allows teachers to build on all 'the language and cultural experiences of students, their most important tools for thinking' (Moll, in Gonzalez et al., 2005: 276). All pupils, and particularly EAL and multilingual learners, need safe spaces to use all their language and cultural resources in their learning, and to feel that their identities are valued and respected in the classrooms they inhabit.

I recently wrote a 'key concepts' piece on funds of knowledge in the *EAL Journal*, published by NALDIC (Conteh, 2018, pp. 50–3), and in it I gave the example of Anupom, a boy I taught many years ago. Anupom found his own ways to mediate what was happening in the classroom where I was responsible for teaching him, and was able to learn to read and write in English very quickly in the spaces afforded him. He showed me the importance of valuing the funds of knowledge that our pupils bring to the classroom. Similarly, the pupils I wrote about in Conteh (2015, pp. 58–9) used their funds of knowledge in small but important ways to develop their own understandings of the English vocabulary they were learning. For example, one child, Hibah, linked the vocabulary of telling the time with the ways her mother talked about measurements when she was buying fabric. In this way, she was able to make a meaningful link between the two that helped her to understand better the ways we talk about telling the time in English. A key factor in both these examples was that it was the child who did the linking of ideas, not the teacher. The teacher's role was to provide the space, and to recognise and value the learning that ensued.

CHAPTER SUMMARY

There are four learning outcomes for this chapter. They each focus on a particular theoretical aspect of language and learning which is introduced in the chapter. The first is based on sociocultural theories and the notion of the ZPD; the second is based on functional grammar; the third is based on theories of learning and the role of talk in learning; and the fourth is based on funds of knowledge. Look back over these sections in the chapter, particularly the Research Focuses, and consider the following questions.

Self-assessment questions

1. What are some of the general implications of sociocultural theories of learning and the notion of the ZPD for organising and planning learning activities for primary pupils in general and for multilingual and EAL learners in particular?

2. What are some of the differences between functional grammars and more conventional grammars?

3. In what ways do sociocultural theories of learning help us to understand the importance of talk for learning in multilingual classrooms?

4. Why is it important to develop talk across the curriculum? Look at the National Curriculum Review (DfE, 2011) and follow up some of the references to talk across the curriculum.

5. What kinds of funds of knowledge do you think pupils that you work with might possess?

FURTHER READING

Cummins, J. (2001) *Negotiating Identities: Education for Empowerment in a Diverse Society,* **2nd edn. Ontario, CA: California Association for Multilingual Education.**

This is perhaps the most comprehensive of Cummins' books. It explains in detail in a very readable way his ideas about the theories discussed in this and the following chapter and much more.

Gregory, E., Long, S. and Volk, D. (eds) (2004) *Many Pathways to Literacy: Young Children Learning with Siblings, Grandparents, Peers and Communities.* **London: Routledge.**

This is a collection of papers from across the world, which illustrate the range of ways in which children learn to read and engage with literacy. The introduction provides a clear explanation of the sociocultural approach to learning and its implications for practice.

STUDYING AT MASTER'S LEVEL

Critical reading: Chapter 2, 'A sociocultural view of language and learning', in Pauline Gibbons' book:

Gibbons, P. (2006) *Bridging Discourses in the ESL Classroom.* **London: Continuum.**

Gibbons describes one of the key aims of her book as 'to explore the usefulness of bridging differ-ent fields of study to theorize pedagogy.' In Chapter 2, she expands on many of the ideas I have discussed in this chapter, showing how functional grammars are relevant to sociocultural theories of learning. She argues that, together, they offer ways forward in developing pedagogies that support and enhance the learning of multilingual pupils.

After reading Chapter 2, consider the following questions, ideally in discussion with colleagues:

1. In the first 5-6 pages of the chapter, Gibbons discusses the concepts of knowledge as a 'com-modity' and language as a 'conduit'. What implications does she suggest they have for learning, and specifically for the learning of so-called 'disadvantaged' students?

2. In her discussion of Vygotsky's ideas, Gibbons foregrounds the concepts of 'mediation' and the ZPD (Zone of Proximal Development). How does she conceptualise the role of language in these? Why and how did Mercer develop the concept of ZPD into the IDZ (Internal Development Zone)?

3. What does Gibbons suggest are the key features of Systemic Functional Grammars (SFGs)? What are the key distinctions she makes between functional grammars and the grammars in Chomskyan linguistics?

4. On p. 36, Gibbons talks about the need in teaching to move pupils to use 'spoken but more context-reduced language' in their learning. What does this mean and what do you think are the practical implications?

REFERENCES

Conteh, J. (2003) *Succeeding in Diversity: Culture, Language and Learning*. Stoke-on-Trent: Trentham Books.

Conteh, J. (2015) '"Funds of knowledge" for achievement and success: multilingual pedagogies for main-stream primary classrooms in England', in P. Seedhouse and C. Jenks (eds), *International Perspectives on ELT Classroom Interaction*. London: Palgrave Macmillan, pp. 49–63.

Conteh, J. (2018) 'Funds of knowledge', *EAL Journal*, Spring, pp. 50–3.

Conteh, J. and Brock, A. (2010) '"Safe spaces"? Sites of bilingualism for young learners in home, school and community', *International Journal of Bilingual Education and Bilingualism*, 14 (3), pp. 347–60.

Cummins, J. and Early, M. (eds) (2011) *Identity Texts: The Collaborative Creation of Power in Multilingual Schools*. Stoke-on-Trent: Trentham Books.

Department for Education (DfE) (2011) *The Framework for the National Curriculum: A Report by the Expert Panel for the National Curriculum Review*. London: DfE.

Gonzalez, N., Moll, L. and Amanti, C. (eds) (2005) *Funds of Knowledge: Theorizing Practices in Households, Communities and Classrooms*. New York: Routledge.

Nieto, S. (1999) *The Light in Their Eyes: Creating Multicultural Learning Communities*. New York: Teachers College Press.

Vygotsky, L. (1978) *Mind in Society*. Cambridge, MA: Harvard University Press.

Wells, G. and Chang-Wells, G. L. (1992) *Constructing Knowledge Together*. Portsmouth, NH: Heinemann.

3

WHAT DOES IT MEAN TO BE MULTILINGUAL?

┌─ **LEARNING OUTCOMES** ───

This chapter will help you to achieve the following learning outcomes:

- develop understanding of what it means to be multilingual from the point of view of multilingual individuals and their families;

- develop awareness of current research and debates about multilingualism in education;

- understand the ways that multilingualism and EAL have been mediated in education policy in England, leading to the 2014 National Curriculum;

- understand why it is important to recognise and value the experiences of learning that children and young people have in their homes and communities.

INTRODUCTION

Together with Chapter 2, this chapter introduces you to the theories related to language, learning and multilingualism that underpin the book and which help you to understand the experiences of multilingual pupils in mainstream schools such as those you read about in Chapter 1. As I said at the start of Chapter 2, theory has a crucial role to play in teaching. The theories discussed in this chapter are based on extensive international research, mostly classroom based and much of it carried out by teachers. They will help you to understand more about the multilingual and EAL learners you teach and to make informed decisions about the best ways to help them, and all your pupils, to succeed. The theories flow through the practical ideas presented in Chapters 4 to 9. To illuminate many of the theoretical perspectives in this chapter, there is an extended case study by Zofia Donnelly of one multilingual learner's experiences in school and community. There are also questions and activities interspersed through the chapter to help you think about how the theories relate to your own experiences as well as their practical implications.

Following this chapter, which is the final one in Part 1, there is a set of 'key principles' for thinking about your planning and teaching, which will help you in planning and evaluating your own teaching strategies. These principles are illustrated by the practical examples in Part 2 of the book.

These are the main sections and subsections of the chapter:

1 WHAT DOES IT MEAN TO BE MULTILINGUAL?

1.1 THE GLOBAL CONTEXT

If the stereotypical image of the monolingual English speaker who believed that they could make themselves understood by speaking English wherever they went ever had any basis in reality, it is rapidly becoming outmoded. While it is true that English is still the most widely used language in the world, its dominance has reduced substantially in recent years. Ethnologue (Ethnologue, 2018), perhaps the best source of statistical information on the 7,000 languages of the world, informs us that in 2017 there were almost 400 million speakers of English as a first language in the world. And almost twice that number (almost 750 million) spoke English as a second or third language. But English is not the most common first language in the world; there are now over 900 million speakers of Mandarin and almost 450 million speakers of Spanish. And Urdu is not far behind English, with almost 330 million first language speakers. Around 80 per cent of people (and rising) in the world are multilingual. Being multilingual is thus the normal condition, and people who see themselves as monolingual are increasingly in the minority. So, for most people in the world, their normal everyday experiences are mediated in more than one language. Of course, this has many implications for education. Though people all over the world are interested in learning English, advancing their study and working in English-speaking countries, many more children around the world are educated in a second or additional language (most commonly English, Spanish or Mandarin) than in their mother tongue.

It is now generally accepted that being multilingual brings benefits in education. Dutcher et al. (1994), in an extensive review of global research into multilingualism, drew some strong conclusions about the role of multilingualism in learning, which include the following:

• Development of the mother tongue needs to be encouraged to promote cognitive development and as a basis for learning the second language.

• Individuals most easily develop cognitive skills and master content material when they are taught in a familiar language.

- Individuals most easily develop literacy skills in a familiar language.

- Cognitive/academic language skills, once developed, transfer readily from one language to another.

- Success in school depends upon the child's mastery of cognitive/academic language, which is very different from the social language used at home.

- Parental and community support and involvement are essential.

These ideas are illustrated and explored through the research presented in this chapter. They have important practical implications for thinking about working with multilingual and EAL learners.

1.2 BEING MULTILINGUAL IN MAINSTREAM EDUCATION IN ENGLAND

In Chapter 1, there is a full discussion about multilingual and EAL learners in England, with vignettes and case studies of pupils in mainstream schools who fit in that category. When I use the term 'multilingual' here, I include all those pupils who come under the 'EAL' umbrella, such as those that I described in Chapter 1, with their hugely diverse language experiences, knowledge, strengths and needs. I prefer the term 'multilingual' because I think it is broader and more inclusive than EAL. It is also more comprehensive than **bilingual**, and includes those pupils who speak two languages. As I illustrated in Chapter 1, 'EAL' is a rather problematic term; for example, for many multilingual pupils in England (those who would be categorised as 'advanced bilingual learners'), English is not an additional language at all, but often their first and most dominant language. Using the term 'multilingual' also represents more accurately the important idea that, for such children, all their languages contribute to their knowledge of the world and their language repertoires, which they can use in communication. Multilingual children and adults do not keep each of their languages separate – they naturally switch and mix between the languages they have at their disposal. If you listen to groups of multilingual people talking to each other, you will often hear words, phrases or even sentences from English mixed with the languages they are speaking. This has been known as **codeswitching** and is increasingly frequently being described as **translanguaging**. It is especially common in children whose families have been settled in the UK for two or three generations, and who still maintain strong links with their countries of origin.

━ RESEARCH FOCUS ━

A new term, **translanguaging**, is currently being introduced into the literature, which moves our understanding of multilingualism beyond the term codeswitching. The term links with the idea of repertoire that I introduced in Chapter 2 (p. 29) and helps us to consider the ways that multilingual people can use their language resources, fluidly moving across the languages they know to express what they wish to say in the most effective ways. Also, in Chapter 2, I argued that we need to appreciate the importance of identity for understanding language and learning; García (2009) suggests that the term translanguaging helps us think about a 'language identity' which is 'brighter and more intense' than a monolingual one, and is a reflection of the wider choices available to multilinguals to make meaning. She argues that children (and adults) move from one language to another in order to accomplish what they want to do and to reflect their language repertoires and identities. In their communication, they are often not consciously thinking about which language to choose but about what they want to communicate and to whom.

The following example shows this. It was collected in a small study I conducted of how children made links between their learning in **complementary** and in mainstream school settings. Sameena is an eight-year-old child, who is of third-generation Pakistani heritage. She was very proud of her ability in maths, reinforced by the fact that she gained level 3 in her KS1 SATs (level 2 is the expected standard). Here she describes how she uses her knowledge of Punjabi to answer her class teacher's 'hot mental' questions at the start of the daily maths lesson. The children were asked to count in fives from 20 to 40:

> We had to count in fives, so I did it in my head in Punjabi then I said it out in English. Eek, do, teen, cha ... twenty-five chey, saat, aat, nor... Thirty ... Eek, do, teen, cha ... thirty-five ...

Her voice varies as she demonstrates 'counting in her head' in Punjabi at the same time as saying the correct numbers in English out loud. She almost whispers when she says the numbers in Punjabi and then she says those in English out loud. She repeats the counting from 1 to 4 and then from 6 to 9 in Punjabi and says the relevant numbers in the 'counting to five' sequence in English in between. In this way, she accomplishes the task, in English, set by the teacher. Sameena is focused on answering her teacher's questions to show she is good at mathematics and to affirm her identity as 'level 3'. The language she needs comes naturally from her repertoire, which includes both English and Punjabi numbers. Evidence like this makes us question the commonsense myth, mentioned in Chapter 1, that in learning a new language, you should not use the ones you already know as they might interfere.

Multilingual children in England often speak different languages with different family members as a perfectly normal part of their lives. They may speak English with their siblings, friends and perhaps their parents, and their home languages with uncles, aunts and grandparents, who may be living with them or contacted regularly by phone or skype. They will also, often, be learning the language of the religious books of their community and their heritage languages in a complementary class, which I discuss further in section 3 and in Chapter 8. In a research project that was undertaken in 2003, Aitsiselmi (2004) studied the ways that people living in one area of the city of Bradford used languages. He revealed the complex ways in which members of different ethnic minority communities use all the languages and dialects in their repertoires. He notes the complications that some of his respondents faced when asked to name the languages they spoke. One simply said, 'we just call it apni zabaan (our language)'.

ACTIVITY 3.1

Languages interview

Arrange to carry out an informal interview with a multilingual child, or preferably a small group of children, in your class (or another class if there are no multilingual learners in your own class). The aim is to find out about the languages they speak at home, how they use them, who they speak them with, what other learning experiences they may have, etc. Here are some suggested questions. Do not turn it into a formal interview - try to have a conversation with your informants.

1. Tell me about the languages you know.

2. Do you speak other languages with members of your family? Which ones?

3. Can you remember how you learned the languages you know?

(Continued)

(Continued)

4.   Can you read any other language besides English?

5.   Do you go to a Saturday class or a class outside school to learn other languages?

6.   Do you go to any special clubs or places of worship where you speak other languages?

7.   Do you have relatives in other countries who you speak different languages with, or write letters, emails, etc.?

8.   Can you teach me a little bit of your language?

In talking about multilingualism in this way, we are not suggesting that EAL learners are fluent in all the languages they speak and write, but that – like the majority of people in the world – they have access to more than one language in normal and natural ways in their daily lives. The following is a useful working definition of this kind of multilingualism. It is helpful in understanding the experiences of many multilingual and EAL learners in schools in England. Hall et al. (2001: 5) say that multilingual pupils are those who

> ... *live in two languages, who have access to, or need to use, two or more languages at home and at school. It does not mean that they have fluency in both languages or that they are competent and literate in both languages.*

This way of thinking about multilingualism makes clear the links between language and identity that were discussed in Chapter 2. An understanding and appreciation of these links is very important for success in education. Research into multilingualism and multilingual education by Cummins (2001), García (2009) and many others resonates with the view of languages that Aitsiselmi discovered in his research in Bradford, that multilingual people translanguage as part of their everyday ways of communicating. It also challenges the myth, raised in Chapter 1, that when learning a second language, the learner's first language can 'interfere' and should be avoided.

As discussed in Chapter 1, in school, pupils can very quickly pick up negative messages about the languages they speak at home, even when these messages are unintended. They can feel that the languages have no place, and that being multilingual is of no value to their mainstream education and the ways they are assessed. This, after all, reflects in many ways the prevailing attitude in the wider society. I once had a long and interesting conversation with a group of Year 6 children about their languages, the ways they used Urdu, Punjabi, English, French and Arabic and how their 'monolingual' friends envied their knowledge. At the end, I asked them if they knew what the word 'bilingual' meant. One boy responded, 'Is it something to do with support?', suggesting that he linked it with those pupils in school who needed support for their learning.

It is essential that multilingual pupils recognise their own power and the potential for learning that being multilingual gives them – and if they don't begin to do this in the primary school, it will be too late. Underachievement at secondary school among minority ethnic pupils can be linked to the lack of support for their first languages as young learners, both in school and at home. This resonates with one of Nieto's key ideas about learning (see Chapter 2, p. 36), that it grows from the cultural contexts in which the learner is situated. Instead of focusing on the 'problems' of having children in mainstream classrooms who speak different languages in other contexts, it is much more positive to consider the possibilities that could open out if we see the children's languages as resources for their learning. As demonstrated in Chapter 8, research is beginning to show that multilingual learners are eager to use their home languages for learning, and that this can have positive benefits across the curriculum, not just for learning English and for literacy. Chapter 8 gives many examples of the ways that home languages can be used as a resource for learning in mainstream schools. The following case study demonstrates this.

ONE MULTILINGUAL LEARNER'S EXPERIENCE – CASE STUDY BY ZOFIA DONNELLY

At the time, Magda attended a primary school in rural North Yorkshire where just under 25 per cent of the pupils were multilingual. She arrived from Poland in July 2013 and joined Year 6 at the beginning of academic year 2013-14. She had learnt some English in Poland, but she felt this limited her initial interactions with her English peers as she found that they spoke too quickly for her to be able to pick up elements of a conversation. A translated version of Magda's school report from Poland is shown below (see original in Figure 3.1).

Annual Learning Outcomes

Behaviour: The student is able to monitor her own behaviour independently. She is very sensitive. She is able to behave in conflicting situations. She controls her own emotions. She can concentrate for longer periods of time. Her behaviour is passive during lesson time. She works at a moderate pace. She can complete a group task. She respects group rules. She does not disturb other pupils during lesson time. She cares about her own safety. She speaks politely to her peers. She joins into various child- and teacher-led activities.

Religion/Ethics: Very good.

Compulsory Education: The pupil answers questions in a full sentence, sometimes using just one word. She reads in full sentences. Sometimes she does not understand the text. Often she makes mistakes in aural tasks/exercises. Her written responses are short. She knows parts of speech. Her addition and subtraction is not always correct, she is able to add and subtract up to 100. She needs to develop her ability to form longer responses in written tasks relating to text. She is aware of her immediate environment. She can recall the names of animals and plants. She is aware of 'stranger danger'. She knows the monuments in her locality. She completes artistic tasks carefully according to examples (demonstrated by the teacher). She is not a keen singer. She can play percussion instruments. She has wonderfully mastered all forms of physical activity. She cares for her personal hygiene. She is able to use a computer, the internet and various multimedia. She can recite longer versed poetry and can sing songs in English, remembering correct pronunciation; she can name objects and describe them.

The report evidences her personality and attitude to work. There is clear information about her performance in numeracy and literacy in her own language, as well as historical, geographical and general knowledge. This is crucial information for her new class teacher as it gives a bilingual overview of achievement for both the teacher and the student. These 'funds of knowledge' can help Magda immediately begin to feel that she is in a 'safe space' (Conteh and Brock, 2010) on her road to integration.

(Continued)

(Continued)

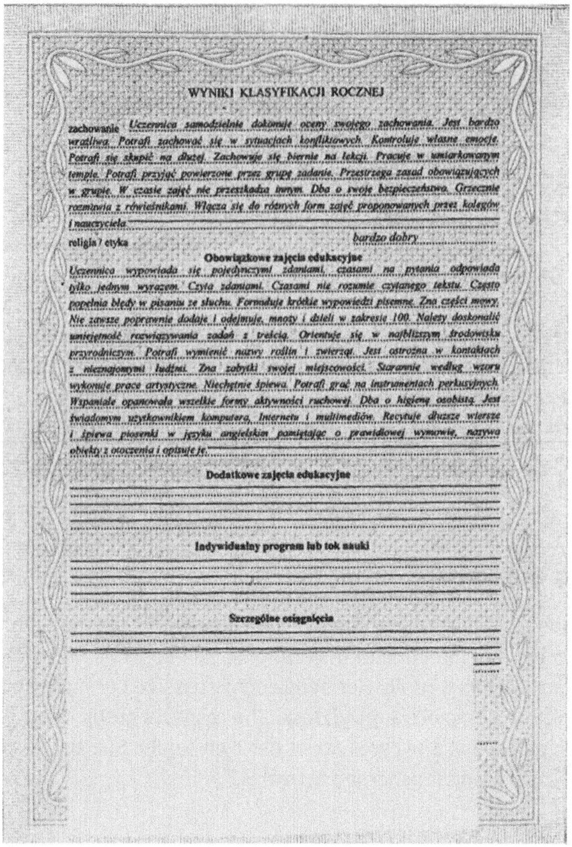

WYNIKI KLASYFIKACJI ROCZNEJ

zachowanie Uczennica samodzielnie dokonuje oceny swojego zachowania. Jest bardzo wrażliwa. Potrafi zachować się w sytuacjach konfliktowych. Kontroluje własne emocje. Potrafi się skupić na dłużej. Zachowuje się biernie na lekcji. Pracuje w umiarkowanym tempie. Potrafi przyjąć powierzone przez grupę zadanie. Przestrzega zasad obowiązujących w grupie. W czasie zajęć nie przeszkadza innym. Dba o swoje bezpieczeństwo. Grzecznie rozmawia z rówieśnikami. Włącza się do różnych form zajęć proponowanych przez kolegów i nauczyciela.

religia / etyka bardzo dobry

Obowiązkowe zajęcia edukacyjne

Uczennica wypowiada się pojedynczymi zdaniami, czasami na pytania odpowiada tylko jednym wyrazem. Czyta zdaniami. Czasami nie rozumie czytanego tekstu. Często popełnia błędy w pisaniu ze słuchu. Formułuje krótkie wypowiedzi pisemne. Zna części mowy. Nie zawsze poprawnie dodaje i odejmuje, mnoży i dzieli w zakresie 100. Należy doskonalić umiejętność rozwiązywania zadań z treścią. Orientuje się w najbliższym środowisku przyrodniczym. Potrafi wymienić nazwy roślin i zwierząt. Jest ostrożna w kontaktach z nieznajomymi ludźmi. Zna zabytki swojej miejscowości. Starannie według wzoru wykonuje prace artystyczne. Niechętnie śpiewa. Potrafi grać na instrumentach perkusyjnych. Wspaniale opanowała wszelkie formy aktywności ruchowej. Dba o higienę osobistą. Jest świadomym użytkownikiem komputera, Internetu i multimediów. Recytuje dłuższe wiersze i śpiewa piosenki w języku angielskim pamiętając o prawidłowej wymowie, nazywa obiekty z otoczenia i opisuje je.

Dodatkowe zajęcia edukacyjne

Indywidualny program lub tok nauki

Szczególne osiągnięcia

Figure 3.1 Magda's Polish report

Importance of the mother tongue

Magda's 'buddy' (see p. 137) speaks Polish, has a good command of English and is also her best friend, enabling her to integrate more easily into school life. The interaction between them involves all four elements of language: speaking, listening, reading and writing. She understands what is going on around her, feeling safe in a multilingual teaching and learning environment. Other children are keen to be friendly with Magda and her buddy. This learning environment influences Magda positively and develops a 'safe space' linguistically for her, which she can relate to. The class teacher's strategies emphasise the importance of first language maintenance. She feels that bilingual pupils benefit from being in a group in their own right. She acknowledges that language learning is gradual and therefore the first language is necessary for an extended period. She allows Magda to speak Polish as much as she needs to, which is a good example of translanguaging (García, 2009). Interestingly, the 'British' children are somewhat envious of Madga's and other EAL children's linguistic skills. This is positive for the EAL children as it raises their self-worth and sense of pride. The class teacher realises that different languages may share identical means of expression, for example personification in literacy, and that this can lead to effective teaching strategies in a particular subject. This provides a conceptual basis on which both the teacher and learner can linguistically and culturally build. Kenner et al. (2007) and Gonzalez et al. (2005) allude to this when they discuss the importance of 'funds of knowledge' (see p. 39).

García's (2009) theory of 'translanguaging' – counteracting the idea of a **monolingualising** society – was very much evidenced when the class teacher suggested that a bilingual member of staff would have sensitivity to the linguistic difficulties and obstacles experienced by Magda. She recognised that this would also contribute to building the 'safe space' for learning. The lesson observation transcribed below (from January 2014) illustrates how easy it is to misjudge a conversation with a multilingual child who is at the early stages of learning English, if the means of communication is solely English. Magda and her teacher are discussing the Christmas holidays.

T: *Good Christmas?*

M: *Yes*

T: *Stay here (pointing finger down) or Poland?*

M: *England*

T: *What presents did you get?*

M: *(Shrugs shoulders)*

T: *You get presents?*

M: *Ah, yes*

T: *What presents?*

M: *(Puzzled look)*

T: *You get book? Computer? Clothes (pointing to pictures in First Thousand Words)*

M: *Ah, yes, yes. Book, computer, trouser, big present. Christmas good (smile appears on face).*

Following this, I, as a visiting teacher, continued the conversation with Magda in Polish. The responses were now in full sentences. Adjectives and verbs were included and a fuller picture of Christmas was gained, without prompting, which included the Christmas Eve dinner and the members of the family present at the event.

T: *A jaka była pogoda podczas Boz˙ego Narodzenia?*

M: *Było bardzo zimno. Padał s´nieg. Sankowalis´my sie˛ (big smile).*

T: *Było Was duz˙o na Wigilii?*

M: *Cała rodzina zjechała sie˛. Wesoło nam było.*

T: *A co jedlis´cie na kolacje˛ wigilijna˛?*

M: *Jadłam barszcz, pierogi, karpia, uszka, róz˙ne sałatki, makowiec i sernik. Pyszne!*

T: *Gdzie poszłas´ o północy?*

M: *Cała rodzina poszła na Pasterke˛ gdzie s´piewalis´my kole˛dy.*

Translation:

T: *What was the weather like at Christmas?*

M: *It was very cold. It was snowing. We went sledging.*

T: *How many of you were present at the Christmas Eve dinner?*

(Continued)

(Continued)

M: *The whole family got together. We were happy.*

T: *What did you have to eat for the Christmas Eve dinner?*

M: *I had beetroot soup, dumplings, carp, ravioli, various salads, poppyseed cake and cheesecake. Delicious!*

T: *Where did you go at midnight?*

M: *The whole family went to the 'Shepherd's Mass' where we sang carols.*

The teaching assistant felt that while Magda needed to develop her competence in English, this had to happen alongside maintaining her appropriate, overall curriculum level. Staff agreed that the first language, where at all possible, should be accessed and maintained. Interestingly, although Magda is fluent in speaking her own language, there is evidence in her written work that she has some difficulties (see her report from Poland, above). It emerged that, for approximately 10 per cent of the time, she writes the words phonetically as she has heard them spoken. This then raises the issue of whether or not she is reading enough in Polish in order to internalise and memorise Polish phonics and spelling patterns to be able to maintain her written level parallel with her speaking and listening levels. This begs the question of whether Magda's native language is suffering and what impact this may have on her overall learning. Magda's lessons, where possible, are translated into Polish and tasks for written work are also set in Polish. Magda has taken part in lessons involving discussion as a member of a peer group where Polish is the main means of communication. With the help of the teaching assistant, the tasks were explained and completed in Polish and then the pupils' responses translated into English. Then the class teacher assessed the outcomes. She wrote positive and encouraging feedback in English, which was then translated into Polish. Assessment for learning was evident through peer-group marking, traffic lights, smiley faces and thumbs-up.

Learning across the curriculum

Magda accesses the full school timetable along with the rest of her class. She finds PE, games, music and drama similar to Poland and partakes fully in these activities, including performing in the school play about the Second World War. Magda felt it was easy to learn the songs for this because, as she said, 'the same thing was sung every time over and over, and it was easy to remember it' suggesting that repetition reinforced the meaning for her. The teacher is frustrated that there is insufficient time to devise tailor-made resources for a bilingual learner. She also feels that time constraints mean there is very little flexibility in shifting away from the National Curriculum in order to meet Magda's specific needs. There was a feeling that this was, to a degree, specialist work and the class teacher welcomed any support available from specialists.

As a visiting teacher, I was able to contribute to teaching in science and literacy. This paragraph gives brief examples of some of the outcomes. During a KS2 class-integrated science week, all the Polish-heritage children were grouped together and Magda worked with a Polish peer group, which gave a lot of opportunities for discussion. Tasks were explained and discussed in Polish and recording was done in English. Through this, Magda was able to understand deeply the notions of 'prediction' and 'result' relating to science experiments. This involved looking at which materials dissolve and do not dissolve, e.g. soil, sugar, salt, sand and taking part in the filtering of these materials. Answers were recorded in English. The literacy lessons related to the topic of the Second World War. The class had been reading *The Silver Sword* by Ian Serraillier (1956). Having learned about the Second World War in Poland, Magda was totally familiar with this area in literacy. She mentioned that she had spoken to her grandmother about the war, who was able to contribute historical information linked to the story's setting. This endorses Kenner et al.'s (2007) points about the important role that all members of a family play in teaching, learning and transcending knowledge through generations.

Learning outside school

The involvement of her grandmother in Magda's learning is a positive example of linking home and school, a key element of the funds of knowledge philosophy. Moreover, as the theories presented in Chapter 2 illustrate, learning the first language nurtures and influences consequent learning. Pedagogy and policy strategies relating to the multilingual child are found not only at the chalkface but very much in the school as a whole and in the wider community. Magda's profile illustrates this clearly and also demonstrates practical ways in which multilingual children can access the right to foster their linguistic and cultural heritage. To support this further, Magda was informed of the Polish school in the nearby large town and of its benefits, including Polish reading and writing and keeping in touch with Polish culture and traditions. Her involvement in this would work very much in her favour, not just in maintaining and developing her skills in Polish, but in developing her local knowledge, meeting more children from her background, learning and identifying with various groups and networks already in place. Magda's mum hopes to enable her family to uphold Polish values, celebrations and culture as she feels this is an important element of her children's identities. Being part of this complementary learning community supports a holistic approach to a child's well-being through family, school and community, echoing Bronfenbrenner's (1979) ecological theory relating to the role of the family and its links to community culture and language and identity. Magda has visited the complementary school and hopes to start attending in the new academic year.

2 MULTILINGUALISM IN EDUCATION

2.1 POLICY CONSTRUCTIONS: ASSESSMENT, ACHIEVEMENT AND THE 2014 CURRICULUM

No child should be expected to cast off the language and culture of the home as he [sic] crosses the school threshold, nor to live and act as though school and home represent two totally separate and different cultures which have to be firmly kept apart.

Zofia's case study of Magda illustrates this much-quoted advice from the Bullock Report (DES, 1975: 286). It is also supported by what we know from research about the best ways to promote children's learning. We need to know about how children learn in different contexts, both in and out of school, and to use this knowledge to develop official policies and classroom practices which are truly inclusive. But, of course, to achieve inclusion through recognition and acceptance of diversity in this way is not easy.

The National Curriculum, first introduced in 1988, recognised above all that every pupil has an entitlement to learn English, but did not consider the importance of their heritage and home languages. Its key aim was that, by the age of 16, all pupils would be able to use spoken and written standard English confidently and accurately. This is, of course, an important aspiration and through all the years since the introduction, of the National Curriculum it has not changed. But it has been described as a 'monolingualising' curriculum, as no specific references were made at the beginning to pupils who may have two or more languages in their repertoires. There was no sense that, for such pupils, their entitlement to English might need to be secured in different ways from 'monolingual' children.

The National Curriculum Council did produce some guidance about language diversity (NCC, 1991) but it epitomised what Safford (2003, p. 8) calls 'the contradiction at the heart of education policy in England' for multilingual pupils, i.e. that their the diversity of their home languages and cultures could be positively 'celebrated' in school, but that the means of assessment should be 'universal' and the same for everyone. It reflected the problem at the centre of aspirations for *equality* that treated children as if they were all the *same*. The circular welcomed language diversity as 'a rich resource', and went on to offer some guidance and support for teachers working with multilingual pupils. Essentially, it suggested that pupils could be encouraged to use their first languages for learning only until their proficiency in English was strong enough for them to move to the exclusive use of English. After this, other languages were not seen as relevant to learning.

This approach to accommodating pupils' home languages and cultures in their learning has come to be known as **transitional bilingualism** by many writers. It is based on the assumption that English and knowledge of English should replace rather than grow from knowledge of other languages. Research has shown that transitional bilingualism can lead to restricted concept learning and problems with attainment. Instead of this, the theoretical and practical ideas in this book all promote a model of **additive bilingualism**. I believe that the best way to help multilingual pupils learn and achieve to their fullest capacity is certainly to value their multilingualism from the start, but to go much further than this. The English language needs to be seen as part of their ever-growing language repertoires, not as a replacement for their other languages. There is a great deal of research that supports this idea, such as the work of Cummins (2001), which is described in the next section. The key practical implication of this is that we need to develop strategies that allow pupils to play to their strengths, using the languages they know best to take ownership of and manage their learning. This underpins the practical ideas discussed in the second part of this book, and particularly in Chapter 8.

When the National Literacy Strategy was first introduced in 1998, there was still no official recognition of the importance of different languages and multilingualism for learning. The first version of the Framework for Teaching (DfEE, 1998) – the famous 'blue file' and its accompanying 'lunchbox' of training materials – made no mention at all of multilingualism as a possible factor, either positive or negative, in learning to read and write. An additional section to the files was later distributed, which included provision for EAL learners, together with those with SEN and others. The simple link that was made between SEN and EAL was unfortunate. It masked the fact that many EAL learners actually have *language* needs rather than *learning* needs. It is no doubt true that they often need support, but this support can sometimes come from allowing them to use the languages they already know rather than ignoring this knowledge. The same link between EAL and SEN was made in subsequent versions of the National Curriculum, for example Curriculum 2000 had an introductory statement about 'inclusion' (DfE, 2012) that talks about the 'potential barriers to learning and assessment' for pupils 'with' SEN, disabilities and EAL. The 2014 curriculum (see below) has a more positive outlook in some ways, but still, I argue, retains the deficit ethos.

▬ RESEARCH FOCUS ▬▬▬▬▬▬▬▬▬▬▬▬▬▬▬▬▬▬▬▬▬▬▬▬▬▬▬▬▬▬▬

Assessment

Cummins (2001) argues, based on his research with French-English multilingual pupils in Canada, that the merging of multilingualism with SEN can have negative academic outcomes. It can lead to multilingual pupils being assessed as having learning needs and then being placed in SEN groups when in fact their needs are for specific language support in order to develop their competence in listening, speaking, reading and writing in order to cope with the demands of the curriculum. His theoretical models can help us to understand the ways in which multilingual learners' experiences of language and learning need to be seen differently from those of children who do not 'live in more than one language'. Some of his key ideas are explained in the next section.

Safford (2003, p. 8) suggests that we have 'two conflicting policy paradigms' in curriculum and assessment in England:

> ... the celebration of ethnic and linguistic diversity, and the universal model of language development and assessment.

For teachers working with multilingual children, assessment is a complex issue, as Safford (2003) shows in her teacher's account of trying to assess pupils from a wide range of language and cultural backgrounds following official requirements. Many writers (e.g. Baker, 1996) spell out the negative implications for children's learning when assessment policies demand that we treat children as if they are all the same and expect them to attain the same targets in the same ways. Ultimately, this denies multilingual learners the space to develop to their full potential and, in effect, closes the door to educational success for them. Providing 'equal access' does not mean that we should treat all children in the same way. Doing this means that we often ignore some of the things that some children can do and the skills they have. We need to recognise the ways that national testing procedures do not give us a 'fair test' of all our children's full capabilities.

Figure 3.2 A universal approach to assessment?

Imagine what the fish and the seal are thinking and feeling as they listen to what they have to do in the so-called 'fair' test in Figure 3.2! Can you also think about what skills and expertise they have, which they cannot use in climbing a tree? These skills are ignored in the 'universal' test. Allwright and Hanks (2009, p. 21) also point out the negative effects on teachers' views of their pupils, arguing that 'when teachers are constrained to operate standardised assessment procedures, they will find it difficult to resist the associated view of the learner'. In Chapter 7 you will find a full discussion of assessment across the curriculum in relation to multilingual learners.

THE 2014 CURRICULUM

Despite the recent, and continuing, rapid growth in numbers of multilingual pupils in our schools, there is very little reference to EAL learners in the new National Curriculum or guidance about how to meet their needs. In a document of 224 pages, there are 94 words that make direct reference to English as an additional language (DfE, 2012, p. 8). To repeat what I say in the introduction, here they are:

> *4.5 Teachers must also take account of the needs of pupils whose first language is not English. Monitoring of progress should take account of the pupil's age, length of time in this country, previous educational experience and ability in other languages.*

> *4.6 The ability of pupils for whom English is an additional language to take part in the national curriculum may be in advance of their communication skills in English. Teachers should plan teaching opportunities to help pupils develop their English and should aim to provide the support pupils need to take part in all subjects.*

The model of language that underpins the curriculum is very different from the one that I presented in Chapter 2, where I argued that we need to think about the ways that languages are used and who uses them, i.e. the functional model (see p. 29). Instead of this, the National Curriculum has what I call a 'naming the parts' model of language, where terminology and definitions take precedence over thinking about texts in their contexts of use. An example from the extensive glossary in the 2013 curriculum document illustrates what I mean (DfE, 2013, p. 9):

> *The surest way to identify nouns is by the ways they can be used after determiners such as 'the': for example, most nouns will fit into the frame 'The __ matters/matter.'*

> *Nouns are sometimes called 'naming words' because they name people, places and 'things'; this is often true, but it doesn't help to distinguish nouns from other word classes. For example, prepositions can name places and verbs can name 'things' such as actions.*

> *Nouns may be classified as common (e.g. boy, day) or proper (e.g. Ivan, Wednesday), and also as countable (e.g. thing, boy) or non-countable (e.g. stuff, money). These classes can be recognised by the determiners they combine with.*

Such an approach can drive teachers to think that they need to teach English through disconnected words, phrases and sentences to make sure that their pupils can reproduce the definitions and identify the **word classes** in formal tests. This is unhelpful, not just for EAL learners, but for most pupils. It is essential that we take a critical approach to the curriculum and recognise that, if we are genuinely committed to helping multilingual learners to succeed, a much more theoretically informed approach to pedagogy is needed.

This said, the guidance in the 2014 curriculum does begin to point the way forward, by indicating two key issues.

- First, it suggests the importance of knowing about where our EAL pupils come from, about the languages they speak and their educational backgrounds.

- Second, it makes the important point about how EAL pupils' subject and conceptual knowledge may be ahead of their knowledge of English.

The second is a key issue in planning and assessment, particularly at secondary le\ extensive coverage of this in Part 2.

Before we get too depressed, it is important to remember that, as teachers, we have knowledge and authority to make informed decisions about how we interpret official p....... are the experts, and the ones who know their pupils best. Zofia's case study above is just one illustration of the ways in which skilled and committed teachers can work together to develop learning opportunities for their EAL pupils that benefit their learning in positive and creative ways. The following section is a brief example of how teachers can use policy documents and the curriculum to develop effective learning for their EAL pupils in one curriculum area.

MAKING LINKS IN THE CURRICULUM – EAL AND MFL

It is very important to make links whenever possible across curriculum requirements in order to play to the strengths of multilingual learners. An example of where this can be done very fruitfully is in the teaching of other languages and in literacy. Pupils categorised as EAL learners bring positive resources into this area of the curriculum, if the approaches to teaching and learning are designed to help them make links between the languages they know and the new languages they are learning. Since 2002, the KS2 Framework for Languages (DfES, 2002) has offered new ways of thinking about language to primary teachers, and some of the ideas have been extended into secondary. This is the policy document underpinning the introduction of modern foreign languages into primary schools (PMFL), as part of the New Labour reforms. It is possible to find it easily online – see the references at the end of this chapter. The approach it advocates is very different from the way that 'foreign languages' are mediated in the 2014 KS2 curriculum, which is more akin to traditional secondary MFL teaching. Rather than seeking to develop proficiency in a specific language, PMFL is much more about building generic strategies for language learning and developing the positive values, attitudes and awareness that learning languages provides. The framework has two 'cross-cutting strands', Knowledge About Language (KAL) and Language Learning Strategies (LLS). These are intended to stimulate children's creativity and ensure an international dimension in learning across the curriculum. Different languages can even be used for different learning intentions across the strands.

The objectives in the two strands lend themselves to a wide range of activities that, besides promoting children's learning of different languages, can get them exploring their local communities and the wider society as they develop global awareness and understanding. They can be met in ways that include families and affirm their funds of knowledge as well as those of multilingual staff in the school. These kinds of activities promote the best kinds of learning for multilingual pupils and examples of these can be found throughout Chapters 4, 6 and 8.

KS2 FRAMEWORK FOR LANGUAGES: MAKING LINKS

Get hold of a copy of the KS2 Framework for Languages - see the reference below for links to the three parts, or you may find a hard copy in your school. Read the guidance on p. 11 about the structure of the framework, in particular the information about the Knowledge About Language (KAL) and the Language Learning Strategies (LLS). Then, look at the KAL and LLS objectives for one of the years (it doesn't matter which, but you could do this with colleagues and each focus on a particular year, then share your findings). Think about how they link with children's learning of literacy, and what activities you might do, to help your children achieve them.

CUMMINS' THEORIES: CUP, LANGUAGE INTERDEPENDENCE, BICS/CALP

RESEARCH FOCUS

Cummins' ideas are well known throughout the world and provide powerful explanations for many distinctive features of multilingualism. They show how the learning of first and additional languages is always linked and how proficiency in academic language needs time to develop. The key difference in Cummins' thinking and writing from many other writers about second language acquisition is that he includes learners' first languages in the processes of learning a new language. This is why his work is more relevant for understanding the needs of multilingual learners in England than models taken from other models of language learning such as **Second Language Acquisition (SLA)** and **English Language Teaching (ELT)**. I will discuss three of his main ideas that are very relevant to understanding the needs of multilingual and EAL learners; the first two, Common Underlying Proficiency (CUP) and **linguistic interdependence**, are helpful in understanding the ways that multilingual learners process and use their languages while the third, **BICS/CALP**, is a way of thinking about the kinds of language that successful learners need to know.

CUP AND LINGUISTIC INTERDEPENDENCE

It used to be believed that moving between different languages could be confusing for multilingual individuals. So, in teaching, one of the main 'myths' that developed (see Chapter 1, p. 23) was that the languages had to be kept separate in order to avoid the first language 'interfering' with the new language being taught. Cummins proved how wrong this was many years ago by observing the ways that multilingual children actually used their languages, both in oracy and literacy. He recognised that languages were not kept separate but that multilinguals switched between their languages in ways such as those described in section 1.2 above. So he concluded that, instead of a separate proficiency for each language that they could speak, read or write, all human beings have some kind of common underlying proficiency (CUP) for language. This could be imagined as a sort of reservoir of language understanding, knowledge and skills, which the individual can draw on to make the meanings that they need in the context in which they are situated. This clearly links with the ideas about language repertoires and choices that I discussed in Chapter 2 (p. 29).

Cummins' famous 'iceberg' diagram represents the CUP. My version is in Figure 3.3. The horizontal line is the boundary between the language user's inner capacity (the CUP) and the outside world. The tips of the iceberg represent the languages being used, whether it is LI, L2 or any further languages. These draw on the CUP, which is like an iceberg in that most of it is hidden but it supports all the language choices that the user makes.

The idea of the CUP clearly links with the notion of language repertoires. It also underpins the theory of linguistic interdependence, which Cummins describes as follows.

Knowledge and understanding of one language links to knowledge and understanding of new languages – this is especially significant in relation to literacy.

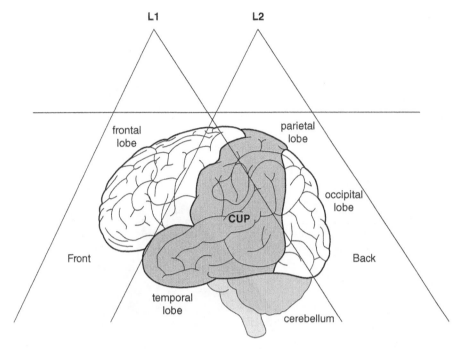

Figure 3.3 Cummins' iceberg diagram of the CUP

The reference to literacy is very important in education. It is not just about learning to read, but about developing the kinds of academic language that different subjects in school demand. The following vignette, of a nine-year-old 'new arrival', Mushtaq, provides compelling evidence of the ways that literacy in his first language opened up his learning of English.

VIGNETTE

Making links

Mushtaq was nine years old when he arrived in England from Bangladesh, unable to speak any English at all. On his first day in school, he was sent to join my 'language support' group where we were doing some story-based activities. He spent the whole lesson in silence while the rest of the group worked on an African story about the sun and the moon. The next day, Mushtaq gave me a piece of paper covered in neatly written script. I did not know what the script was, and was amazed when I discovered that on the paper was the sun and moon story, written out in Bengali. His classmate had re-told the story to him, and he had written it out for me. So it turned out that Mushtaq was already highly literate in Bengali. The following week, he contributed to a trilingual book that we made about the story. The writing in the top right-hand corner of the page is his (see Figure 3.4).

Over the next few weeks, Mushtaq contributed to several other trilingual books like this, and also made some story tapes where he read stories in Bengali for other children to listen to. Within six months, he was one of the best readers in his class – in English.

(Continued)

(Continued)

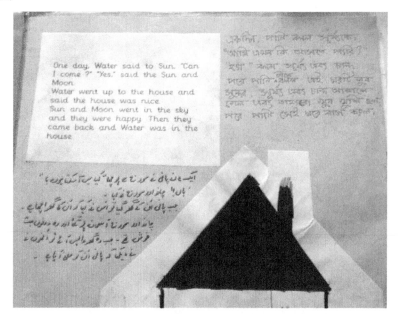

One day, Water said to Sun. 'Can I come ?' 'Yes.' said the Sun and Moon.
Water went up to the house and said the house was nice.
Sun and Moon went in the sky and they were happy. Then they came back and Water was in the house

Figure 3.4 Children's trilingual book

Once again, the key message here is that we must find out about the languages that our pupils can speak, read and write outside our classrooms. It does not matter if we cannot speak, read or write them ourselves – I cannot speak Bengali and did not even know what language it was when I first saw the script on Mushtaq's paper. We must value the knowledge that our pupils bring to the classroom and help them find spaces in which they can construct their own ways of learning, beginning from what they already know.

BICS/CALP

These well-known, but sometimes misunderstood, acronyms underpin an important idea that Cummins has developed over the years about the ways that languages are learnt and used. It has relevance for all pupils, but is of particular relevance for multilingual and EAL learners. Basic Interpersonal Communication 'Skills'/Cognitive Academic Language Proficiency (BICS/CALP) are sometimes described as 'skills' or even specific features of language to be taught and tested, but this does not reflect what they actually are. It is sometimes said that BICS is more to do with spoken language and CALP with written, but again this is not really what Cummins meant.

Basically, BICS refers to all the social, everyday things we do with language, embedded in face-to-face, familiar contexts, such as greetings, conversations, retelling, describing, recalling and so on. CALP, on the other hand, refers to all the things we need to do with language in order to achieve academic and cognitively demanding purposes, such as explaining, analysing, synthesising, arguing and so on. BICS relates to the kinds of language which develop first in learning a new language, usually in face-to-face, highly contextualised situations. CALP develops through engaging in more decontextualised situations and discussions, and so is often seen as more complex. CALP has two main dimensions: it is the **cognitive language** which we need in order to think and do academically demanding things, such as investigating, exploring ideas, analysing, hypothesising and solving problems. It is also the kind of **academic language** that we find in textbooks, lecture notes and so on, and which we need to learn to write in order to succeed as we progress through the education system. This often has features such as the passive voice, vocabulary with Greek and Latin roots, the use of metaphor and personification and the use of abstract nouns, such as 'information' from 'inform' and 'hunger' from 'hungry'.

Cummins has developed the notions of BICS and CALP over the years and he now writes of them as a continuum rather than as two separate aspects of language. Educated adults move back and forth along the continuum according to what they are trying to do with language, and we should be aiming to develop this capacity and confidence in the children we teach. The BICS/CALP model is relevant for all children – all children need opportunities to use a wide range of language and languages in different ways in their learning. The model also has implications which are specific to multilingual learners. Cummins found that children entering school with very little English would develop BICS (i.e. fluency in the kinds of language interactions suggested above) quite quickly, usually within 18 months to two years. But full capacity in CALP would take a lot longer, as it does with all pupils. Cummins concluded that this could take at least seven years. It is also clear that the progression from BICS to CALP is not automatic, and that children need to be supported as they move from learning through context-embedded activities to the more context-disembedded tasks they are expected to perform as they move through primary school and on to secondary. This is discussed in more detail in Chapter 6, on planning.

These ideas about BICS/CALP can help us to see through the confusion between language needs and learning needs that I talked about in section 2.1. Children may enter school unable to speak English and at first, they can seem to do very well. They learn to do all the social things they want to do in English and everything seems very promising. Then, things slow down as the long slog to develop CALP progresses. Sometimes, pupils do not seem to make any progress at all. This is because their thought processes are still largely in their first language and they are – literally – learning to think in a new language. Unfortunately, it is at this point, usually, that the assessment wheel starts turning and pupils can find themselves placed in SEN groups and even diagnosed with learning difficulties. Worse still, if they arrive at secondary age and begin in secondary school they can be placed in sets where they do not have the opportunity to attain high GCSE grades, no matter how hard they try. Often, all they need is time and the opportunity to continue using their first language to support their thinking in the new language.

3 THE IMPORTANCE OF LEARNING OUTSIDE SCHOOL

3.1 HOME, FAMILY AND COMMUNITY LEARNING CONTEXTS – 'FUNDS OF KNOWLEDGE'

As I explained in Chapter 1, it is important to remember that, for many multilingual learners, formal learning does not end when they go home from their mainstream school in the afternoon. Many attend community-based classes in mosques, synagogues, churches, temples and other settings where they learn to read and write their heritage languages and the languages of their religions. These are known as '**complementary**' or '**supplementary**' schools. Many students go on to take GCSE and 'A' level exams in Urdu, Gujerati, Bengali, Polish, Chinese and other languages. There is a growing body of research into the ways that children learn in their complementary classes, and the links that they can make between their complementary and mainstream learning, as with the example of

Sameena in section 1.2 of this chapter. In Chapter 8, you will find an extended discussion of learning in complementary schools and examples of activities of the kind that could easily be developed in mainstream classrooms.

Many multilingual pupils experience learning in different contexts, but often their teachers in one system know very little about what goes on in the other. There is no link between their different learning contexts, and children are left to make their own sense of the learning demands on them. One Year 6 boy, whom I interviewed as part of a small research project, talked about his learning in the mosque in a very insightful way, describing the different things his teachers did in his mosque school and his mainstream school. He ended with a very powerful and deeply felt comment:

> *I think the mosque and school should be together ... it's like the same thing ... you're teaching something, you're getting knowledge from people.*

As well as finding out about the languages that the pupils in your class speak, it is very worthwhile to find out about the different schools they attend, and what they are learning there. This will make them feel that you are interested in them and value them as individuals. It will also increase your knowledge of your pupils' home and community experiences.

ACTIVITY 3.2

Learning in home and community

In a school with EAL learners, find out what the policies are for working with parents and families to support their children's learning. Think about how they might help to access family 'funds of knowledge'.

Find out if the school has a home-school liaison officer (HSLO) and ask if you can talk to them about what they do and how they work to develop links between home and community and school. If you can, try to visit a community or complementary school.

We also need to be aware of the ways that children are learning in the home and how this contributes to the 'funds of knowledge' (see Chapter 2) that they bring to their learning in more formal, mainstream settings. Children are often involved in interpreting and translating for family members who may have very limited English; they take part in extended family activities such as weddings and celebrations for Eid and other religious events. They sometimes travel to their countries of origin or to visit relatives in other parts of the world. All of these experiences offer possibilities for learning, with the added benefit of affirming the children's identities as members of dynamic, diverse communities. Families mediate every child's first learning experiences and it is the responsibility of the school to build on this in whatever ways it can. Ideas for this, related to learning across the curriculum, are provided in Chapters 4, 6 and 8.

CHAPTER SUMMARY

The four learning outcomes for this chapter are all to do with understanding the language and cultural experiences of the multilingual and EAL learners you will be teaching. Here are some questions to consider in thinking about these outcomes.

Self-assessment questions

1. How have your views about multilingualism and multilingual learners been changed by the ideas you have read about in this chapter?

2. How do your personal experiences of language diversity and multilingualism in school and community compare with the ideas you have read about in this chapter?

3. In what ways could we assess multilingual and EAL learners' learning without depending on their capacities in English? Can you think about how you could do this with children that you teach?

FURTHER READING

Conteh, J. (2003) *Succeeding in Diversity: Culture, Language and Learning in Primary Classrooms.* **Stoke-on-Trent: Trentham Books.**

Based on research with successful multilingual KS2 learners and their families, this book develops many of the ideas discussed in this chapter and includes evidence from interviews with families and teachers and classroom observations to illustrate the arguments developed.

Hall, D., Griffiths, D., Haslam, L. and Wilkin, Y. (2001) *Assessing the Needs of Multilingual Pupils: Living in Two Languages*, **2nd edn. London: Fulton Books.**

A clear, practical and concise account of the tensions between 'EAL' and 'SEN', with useful guidance for planning. This will help you ensure that the language and cognitive demands of your activities provide support and progression for multilingual learners.

STUDYING AT MASTER'S LEVEL

Critical reading:

Cummins J. (2008) 'Teaching for transfer: challenging the two solitudes assumption in bilingual education', in J. Cummins and N. H. Hornberger (eds), *Encyclopedia of Language and Education, Volume 5: Bilingual Education.* **Boston, MA: Springer, pp. 65-75.**

You can also find this chapter online at:

https://link.springer.com/referenceworkentry/10.1007/978-0-387-30424-3_116

In this chapter, Cummins discusses 'the monolingual principle' which, he argues, underpins second language teaching but which has no basis in research. He traces its history and presents research evidence that questions its value, arguing that the notion of 'transfer' is a much stronger one from research and for pedagogy.

After reading the chapter, consider the following questions, ideally in discussion with colleagues:

1. What are Cook's four criteria for the use of L1 in language classrooms? How helpful do you think they are in planning and teaching?

(Continued)

(Continued)

2. How are Cummins' interdependence hypothesis and his notion of the common underlying proficiency (CUP) linked?

3. Cummins' proposes five possible types of transfer between and across languages. Which of them are illustrated in the account of the bilingual Urdu-English book written by three students?

4. How far do you think the bilingual strategies that Cummins' lists might be possible and helpful in classrooms familiar to you?

REFERENCES

Aitsiselmi, F. (2004) *Linguistic Diversity and the Use of English in the Home Environment: A Bradford Case Study*. University of Bradford, Department of Languages and European Studies, School of Social and International Studies.

Allwright, D. and Hanks, J. (2009) *The Developing Language Learner: An Introduction to Exploratory Practice*. London: Palgrave Macmillan.

Baker, C. (1996) *Foundations of Multilingual Education and Multilingualism*, 2nd edn. Clevedon: Multilingual Matters.

Bronfenbrenner, U. (1979) *The Ecology of Human Development*. Cambridge, MA: Harvard University Press.

Conteh, J. and Brock, A. (2010) '"Safe spaces"? Sites of bilingualism for young learners in home, school and community', *International Journal of Bilingual Education and Bilingualism*, *14* (3), pp. 347–60.

Cummins, J. (2001) *Negotiating Identities: Education for Empowerment in a Diverse Society*, 2nd edn. Ontario, CA: California Association for Multilingual Education.

Department for Education (DfE) (2012) *Including All Learners*. London: DfE. Available at https://webarchive.nationalarchives.gov.uk/20090815203352/http://curriculum.qcda.gov.uk/key-stages-1-and-2/inclusion/statutory-inclusion-statement/index.aspx (accessed 25 November 2018).

Department for Education (DfE) (2013) *The National Curriculum in England: Key Stages 1 and 2 Framework Document*. London: DfE. Available at https://assets.publishing.service.gov.uk/government/uploads/system/uploads/attachment_data/file/425601/PRIMARY_national_curriculum.pdf (accessed 25 November 2018).

Department for Education and Employment (DfEE) (1998) *The National Literacy Strategy: Framework for Teaching*. London: DfEE. Available at https://webarchive.nationalarchives.gov.uk/20100603153934tf_/http://nationalstrategies.standards.dcsf.gov.uk/primary/primaryframework/literacyframework (accessed 25 November 2018).

Department of Education and Science (DES) (1975) *A Language for Life* (Bullock Report). London: HMSO.

Department for Education and Science (DfES) (2002) *Key Stage 2 Framework for Languages*, Parts 1, 2 and 3. Available at https://webarchive.nationalarchives.gov.uk/20110511211850/http://nationalstrategies.standards.dcsf.gov.uk/node/85274http://webarchive.nationalarchives.gov.uk/20130401151715/http://education.gov.uk/publications/eorderingdownload/framework%20for%20languages%20-%20part%202.pdf (accessed 25 November 2018).

Dutcher, N. in collaboration with Tucker, G. R. (1994) *The Use of First and Second Languages in Education: A Review of Educational Experience*. Washington, DC: World Bank, East Asia and the Pacific Region, Country Department III.

Ethnologue (2018) *Languages of the World*, 21st edn. Available at https://www.ethnologue.com.

García, O. (2009) *Bilingual Education in the 21st Century: A Global Perspective*. Chichester: Wiley-Blackwell.

Gonzalez, N., Moll, L. and Amanti, C. (eds) (2005) *Funds of Knowledge: Theorizing Practices in Households, Communities and Classrooms*. New York: Routledge.

Hall, D., Griffiths, D., Haslam, L. and Wilkin, Y. (2001) *Assessing the Needs of Bilingual Pupils: Living in Two Languages*, 2nd edn. London: David Fulton.

Kenner, C., Ruby, M., Gregory, E. and Al-Azami, S. (2007) 'How research can link policy and practice: bilingualism as a learning resource for second and third generation children', *NALDIC Quarterly*, 5 (1), pp. 10–13.

National Curriculum Council (NCC) (1991) *Linguistic Diversity and the National Curriculum*, Circular No. 11. York: National Curriculum Council.

Safford, K. (2003) *Teachers and Pupils in the Big Picture: Seeing Real Children in Routinised Assessment*. Watford: NALDIC.

PART 2

PROMOTING LEARNING –
PRACTICAL APPROACHES
FOR MULTILINGUAL AND
EAL LEARNERS

The following six key principles for planning lessons and activities for multilingual learners have been developed from the ideas discussed in Chapters 1 to 3. In Chapters 4 to 9, I will use these principles to present practical examples of activities and strategies to promote multilingual children's learning in speaking and listening, reading and writing across the curriculum.

• Developing a positive ethos that reflects language and cultural diversity at whole-school level will support home–school links, and encourage families and schools to work in partnership.

• In the classroom, providing opportunities for multilingual pupils to use their first languages in everyday activities will open out potential for learning and affirm their identities.

• Pupils need every possible opportunity to explore ideas and concepts orally in all subjects across the curriculum.

• Before beginning extended writing activities, pupils need plenty of chances for collaborative discussion and practical experience.

• Promoting awareness of language systems and structures by allowing multilingual pupils to analyse and compare the different ways of saying things in the languages they know will help develop their CALP and also promote language awareness among their monolingual classmates.

• Providing extensive opportunities for hands-on experience will enhance language learning and learning more generally.

4

EAL IN THE EARLY YEARS: BEGINNING SCHOOLING IN A NEW LANGUAGE AND CULTURE

---- LEARNING OUTCOMES ----

This chapter will help you to achieve the following learning outcomes:

- develop understanding of key issues in working with multilingual and EAL learners in the early years;

- understand the importance of making links between home and school for children in the early years;

- understand the importance of speaking and listening and the links to literacy for children in the early years;

- gain some knowledge of practical activities to support multilingual and EAL learners in the early years.

INTRODUCTION

The terminology related to early years in the UK has sometimes been confusing, and has had different interpretations in both policy and practice. Palaiologou (2016) provides a comprehensive outline of the history and development of the current early years curriculum in the UK. In England, the Early Years Foundation Stage (EYFS) covers children from birth to five years, but provision is statutory only from the point that children enter a Reception class, usually at the age of four. Normally children begin nursery education at the age of three, and the ideas in this chapter are relevant for children from the age of three in nursery and reception settings until they begin formal schooling in Year 1.

Based on the theories about language and learning presented in Chapters 1–3, this chapter provides guidance and practical ideas for working with multilingual and EAL learners in the early years. Perhaps the most important theoretical perspective featured in the book for early years pupils is that of funds of knowledge. This underpins all the sections of the chapter, with the practical implications illustrated by many examples. The chapter illustrates the ways in which different settings can support children's active learning in the early years and of the importance of learning through play. In the section on literacy, a detailed case study by Ilona Szolc highlights many issues and draws together many themes introduced in the chapter. There are research focuses and tasks to help you think about how the theories relate to your own experiences, as well as their practical implications in the settings in which you work.

are the sections and subsections of this chapter:

1 OFFICIAL GUIDANCE FOR EYFS – SOME PRINCIPLES

The current guidance for early years practitioners in England (DfE, 2017) makes one substantial statement that refers directly to multilingual and EAL learners:

> *1.7 For children whose **home language** is not English, providers must take reasonable steps to provide opportunities for children to develop and use their home language in play and learning, supporting their language development at home. Providers must also ensure that children have sufficient opportunities to learn and reach a good standard in English Language during the EYFS: ensuring children are ready to benefit from the opportunities available to them when they begin Year 1. When assessing communication, language and literacy skills, practitioners must assess children's skills in English. If a child does not have a strong grasp of English language, practitioners must explore the children's skills in the home language with parents and/or carers, to establish whether there is cause for concern about language delay. (p. 9)*

Though the statement clearly recognises that young children may be exposed to different languages at home and in school, there is no recognition of multilingualism, including the need to work with interpreters, who may be willing to work with the school on a voluntary basis. The emphasis is on the development of English without reference to other languages. It suggests that other languages may have their place in the home but that they have no real place in school settings. English is the language of assessment, and the pressure is to learn it as quickly as possible in order to be ready to access the National Curriculum in Year 1. Indeed, there is even the worrying implication in the last sentence that if a child is not making satisfactory progress in English language, this may be a symptom of delay. As I argued in Chapter 2 (section 2.1, p. 51) this approach to assessment means that, for many learners in EYFS, we ignore the language skills and knowledge they have. In Chapter 7, I discuss this further and outline some approaches that do open out understanding of young learners' full language abilities.

The negative picture of multilingualism painted in the current guidance is different from that presented in 2007 by the Primary National Strategy, which is still available online (PNS, 2007). This lays out some key principles for supporting young multilingual and EAL learners in EYFS (PNS, 2007, p. 4), linking language and learning and stressing the importance of recognising that all the languages a child knows are part of their resources for learning. The guidance also, crucially, makes it clear that providing support should not lead to reduced cognitive challenge:

- Bilingualism is an asset, and the first language has a continuing and significant role in identity, learning and the acquisition of additional languages.

- Supporting continued development of first language and promoting the use of first language for learning enables children to access learning opportunities within the EYFS and beyond through their full language repertoires.

- Cognitive challenge can and should be kept appropriately high through the provision of linguistic and contextual support.

- Language acquisition goes hand in hand with cognitive and academic development, with an inclusive curriculum as the context.

- Secure and trusting relationships with a key person are vital to a child's development in all areas.

- Bilingual support is a highly desirable resource but it has to be accepted that appropriate first-language support may not be available for all children in all settings all the time.

Following this, the guidance follows the themes of the general EYFS requirements to spell out principles for effective practice. These offer a strongly positive view of all children as active learners, which is very appropriate for multilingual and EAL learners. The four themes are:

- **Theme 1: A Unique Child:** Every child is a competent learner from birth who can be resilient, capable, confident and self-assured (p. 7).

- **Theme 2: Positive Relationships:** Children learn to be strong and independent from a base of loving and secure relationships with parents and/or a key person (p. 10).

- **Theme 3: Enabling Environments**: The environment plays a key role in supporting and extending children's development and learning (p. 12).

- **Theme 4: Learning and Development:** Children develop and learn in different ways and at different rates and all areas of learning and development are equally important and interconnected (p. 14).

Together, these themes and principles provide a useful framework for developing appropriate pedagogy for multilingual and EAL learners in the early years.

2 LINKING HOME AND SCHOOL

2.1 UNDERSTANDING HOME AND COMMUNITY LEARNING

RESEARCH FOCUS

The funds of knowledge philosophy was developed through collaborative research done with academics, teachers and families of Mexican heritage in the USA. The teachers visited the homes of some of their pupils and carried out small-scale ethnographic studies, such as that described by Martha Floyd Tenery in Chapter 6 of Gonzalez et al. (2005: 119-30). As one of her conclusions, Tenery states, 'The characteristics of the families described in this chapter contradict many stereotypes of Mexican origin families' (p. 129). She continues, 'In all, an analysis of *la visita* portrays Mexican origin households as resourceful, connected, and full of life experiences.' The insights she gained from her research, she states, helped her to avoid 'jumping to erroneous conclusions' about her pupils and their responses to school.

In Conteh (2003: 51), I describe my first visit with Yasmin, one of the children in my PhD research, to her home. I walked with Yasmin and her younger sister from school to their home. When we arrived, I was ushered into a large kitchen with comfortable furniture on one side of the room while Yasmin and her sister went upstairs to change. This is an extract from my ethnographic description of the scene:

> *... I was left with Grandma and sleeping baby. We smiled at each other, then more people arrived ... the youngest woman made a cup of tea. The children sat in the corner of the room, Yasmin smiling proudly at me. Eventually, Mum arrived with two little girls, followed soon by Dad and another man ... So there we were, sitting on two settees; two grandmothers (who were sisters), mother, father, aunt, uncle and six children, including the baby, who woke up, totally calm, to be absorbed into the group.*

A lot of things interested me about this family scene, not least the baby, who sat up smiling and was then passed round from hand to hand, remaining calm and smiling throughout. I never worked out whose baby it was.

The home visits I made to Pakistani-heritage Muslim families as part of my research taught me about Pakistani extended family structures and the importance to the children of their grandparents, cousins, aunts and uncles. They helped me to understand why cousins formed such strong friendship groups in school and why, sometimes, adults who were not the parents of the child attended parents' consultations. They taught me the language of extended family relationships; for example, I learned from the children that there are at least six different words for 'cousin' in Punjabi – 'masayree' for mother's sister's daughter; 'masayr' mother's sister's son, and so on. In English, of course, there is only one. I finally understood why children from south Asian backgrounds often invent terms in English for family members, such as 'brother cousin' or 'sister aunty'. This does not reflect a flawed understanding of English, but a creative attempt to say what they want to say in a language that does not afford them the scope.

The practical message here is not about the need to go out and do ethnographic research, though it would be excellent if that were possible. Rather, it is about the need to get to know the children you teach and their families. It is about recognising the diversity of ways in which families can be constituted and not rushing to judge those that may be very different from ones that you are familiar with. Many early years settings have very good arrangements for involving families in their children's school experiences. Such arrangements need to recognise that this is a two-way process, that families are active and equal partners with knowledge and skills that are of value to the school, as well as the other way round. Chapter 8, section 2 (p. 172) contains many ideas for bringing home languages and cultures into school, which are also relevant for early years settings. A key difference, however, between EYFS and later phases is that children entering early years settings are leaving their homes and entering formal education settings for the first time. Clarke (2018) discusses the social nature of young children's learning and the need for young children to learn 'the rules and expectations of their new social world'.

It is important to remember that young children may be learning skills and knowledge in their homes and communities that are totally different from what you may expect. This astonishing picture in Figure 4.1 is taken from Rogoff (2003, p. 6).

Figure 4.1 Cutting a coconut with a machete

The picture shows an 11-month-old child from the Democratic Republic of Congo cutting a coconut with a sharp machete, watched over by his grandmother, who can just be seen in the background. I have known people to find the picture shocking and feel the child is being put at great risk, even being subject to abuse. But what he is doing is considered perfectly normal and safe in his own cultural context, though he would never be left alone to do it. Rogoff's book contains many similar examples of young children doing things that would be considered very unsafe in the kinds of western societies that most of us are used to, where we feel we need to protect children from dangers such a sharp instruments, fire, hot water and so on. Rogoff, and many others, take the sociocultural perspective that learning is essentially co-constructed 'guided participation' and so deeply grounded in the communities and cultures of the participants. They have argued that though there are commonalities across different cultures about what young children need to learn in order to become full members of their societies, there are huge differences in the ways that they learn.

71

Early years settings are certainly very child-friendly spaces, but they are organised in very particular ways that can seem very strange and even threatening to some children and their families. Children need opportunities to participate in activities and conversations with their peers in order to learn how to position themselves in the setting, and how they are expected to behave. Drury (2000) shows the processes of 'language socialisation' in an early years setting and also 'how children in the early stages of second language development create their own opportunities for rehearsing and practising class-room learning outside the school context.

Children who lack prior experience of the culture and language of the nursery or school may feel inhib-ited. Until a child has a shared language with their peers then it will be difficult to participate in the setting activities, which can lead to them becoming unwilling to take part in interactions with others. One of the aims of early years education is to develop children's self-motivation, so this could become a big problem. For example, as Clarke points out, children are often expected to choose an activity and participate in play. But some children may never have done this before, and even the equipment may be unfamiliar. Indeed, for some parents also, the expected behaviours in early years classrooms may feel somewhat strange and alien. It is important that such feelings are not allowed to persist and that families are quickly given a sense that they are welcome and that they belong in the setting.

Baldock (2010, p. xvi) introduces the useful notion of 'inter-cultural competence' and argues that it is 'necessary to develop skills in responding to cultural differences rather than just to acquire informa-tion about the cultures we expect to meet'. Suggesting that diversity is an 'intrinsic' aspect of social life, Baldock goes on (p. 33) to argue that the basis of inter-cultural competence is 'a readiness to learn from each other' and – linked to this – 'critical self-awareness' (p. 37). This resonates with the ideas I discussed in Chapter 1 (p. 12), about the importance of considering your own cultural identity in order to give you a perspective on the cultures of the children you work with. Understanding cultural diversity means more than acquiring a lot of facts about different cultures. We need to become more aware of the com-plexity and fluidity of the ways 'culture' is mediated in our superdiverse society (see Chapter 1, p. 13).

ACTIVITY 4.1

Home-school partnerships in the early years

Can you think of any kinds of activity in your own culture, such as those illustrated above, where young children are expected to do things that could appear very risky and dangerous? On the other hand, can you think of things that children are routinely expected to do in early years settings that could seem strange and risky to parents from different cultural backgrounds? Discuss this with col-leagues or fellow students if possible.

Get hold of some school policies for involving parents in their children's learning in the early years. Sometimes you find these online or you may be able to get access to some in a placement school or the school where you work. Read them and think about them in relation to the points raised in the section above about possible dissonances between school and home environments. Do you think the policies allow for a 'two-way conversation' between parents and school? If so, how do they do this? If not, how might they be adapted to allow such a conversation?

If possible, discuss the policies with colleagues or fellow students and identify the features in each which might offer positive or negative outcomes for home-school partnerships for children in the early years.

2.2 MULTILINGUAL DEVELOPMENT IN THE EARLY YEARS

— RESEARCH FOCUS ———————————————————

Although there are clearly individual and cultural differences in the ways children acquire an additional or second language, the evidence from most research is that there is a consistent developmental sequence. Clarke (2018) suggests that it is useful for teachers to have a framework against which they can make professional judgements about how each of their pupils is progressing and decide the best strategies for their learning. She summarises the overview provided by Tabors (1997, p. 39) of the ways young multilingual learners respond progressively to their first encounters with a new language:

1. There may be a period of time when children continue to use their home languages in the second-language situation.

2. When they discover that their home language does not always work in this situation, some children enter a non-verbal period as they collect information about the new language. They perhaps spend some time in trying out new sounds and language patterns privately.

3. Children begin to go public, using individual words and phrases they have picked up in the new language.

4. Children begin to develop productive use of the second language.

These stages are described in greater detail below and their practical implications are considered.

1. CONTINUED USE OF THE HOME LANGUAGE

Some young children, but not all, who enter early years settings may continue to use their home language and expect that everyone will understand them. If this is the case, it is essential that they are not made to feel as if their home language is wrong. Their introduction and gradual transition to the language of the classroom needs to be smooth. A classroom buddy who shares the same home language will be very helpful at this stage (see p. 137). This may be another child in the class, though this is unlikely in an early years setting. An older sibling or other relative or a member of staff who shares the same home language can take on the role.

The buddy may not be able to be present in the classroom all the time, but when they are present they can interpret for the child, ensuring that they are not left isolated and unsure about what is happening around them. They could perhaps make a list of helpful words and phrases in the home language for others in the setting. The child should be encouraged to use their home language to communicate while at the same time being given opportunities to hear and respond to the classroom language. The child's home language should be woven into the fabric of the setting as much as possible through displays, songs, rhymes, dual-language texts and so on. The child should be encouraged to play with other children who share the same home language, as well as any of the other children in the class.

2. THE SILENT PERIOD

All children who do not speak English as their first language need time to acclimatise to the new language of the early years setting. Many have been observed to respond to the new situation by not speaking or overtly responding to what is going on around them. This has been termed the 'silent period', a term which applies to a now familiar concept in language education, though it is still controversial. It does not mean that the child is inactive or passive as the word 'silent' may be thought to imply. Bligh and Drury (2015, p. 271) call it 'a crucial time for self-mediated learning' and present case studies of young learners in the silent period. Children may be doing lots of things, such as rehearsing the language silently to themselves and beginning to practise privately until they have the confidence to try out the language publicly. This is perfectly normal and children need reassurance at this time that they are accepted members of the group and encouragement to interact socially with those around them.

Clarke (2018) suggests ten useful strategies to support children's language development during this 'silent' stage:

- Continue talking to the child even though they do not respond.

- Keep including the child in small groups with other children.

- Use a range of different questions and don't worry if there is no response.

- Include other children as the focus in the conversation while the 'silent' child is in earshot.

- Maintain the use of the child's home language as much as possible.

- Accept any kind of response from the child, non-verbal as well as verbal.

- Praise any effort you notice, however minimal.

- Use English as well as the child's home language. Keep repeating the same language in English, e.g. greetings, instructions, simple conversations etc., counting, rhymes and songs.

- Provide as many opportunities as possible to encourage child-to-child interaction for the 'silent' child.

- Provide activities which reinforce language practice through role play and play more generally.

3. GOING PUBLIC

At the early stages of speaking publicly in English, many children begin to interact with others by using single words or formulaic phrases repetitively as ready-made responses to routine situations. These may include sequences from songs, rhymes and stories, routine language used at specific times in the setting, for example answering the register, asking to go to the toilet, eating lunch and so on. My own son, at the age of three, looked down at his newborn sister as she was waking up in her moses basket. 'She's got a gleaming hungry eye,' he declared, quoting his favourite story of the moment, Roald Dahl's *The Enormous Crocodile*.

At this stage, regular, repeated language is crucial for the young EAL learner. Listening to songs, rhymes and stories is even more vital than at other times. Provide opportunities for children to join in, without pressure, with familiar stories. Repeated oral readings of the same popular stories, allowing children to join in if they wish, will provide safe spaces for them to hear and reinforce their understanding of the same language. All kinds of props can support the story, providing different kinds of cues to the meanings of words as well as the elements of the story – plot, character, setting and so on. Although the child may be becoming more confident and comfortable in English, the home language should always be maintained. Some stories could be told bilingually with two adults collaborating, one of whom shares the children's home language. The use of dual language texts can also enhance the experience. Parents and older siblings can be invited in to the setting to share the text with the child. Section 2.4 in Chapter 8 (p. 180) provides some ideas for finding out about and using dual language texts.

In early years settings, the provision of resources for role play based on stories as well as on everyday situations such as going to the shops, visiting relatives, getting on the bus and so on generates language, both home languages and English. Children will take opportunities to try out their new knowledge and check that it works. At this stage, oracy and literacy are often not differentiated in the child's mind. Figure 4.2 shows a text that a young child once gave me in a nursery setting where I had gone in to visit a student teacher on her placement. She had set up a post office for role play with all kinds of artefacts, including some paper forms that she had picked up (with permission!) in a real post office, including a TV licence application. As I was standing watching what was going on, a child, who was almost four years old, came up to me and slipped the form into my hand. I looked at the marks she had made and noticed that they were almost in the correct places for completing the form. 'What does it say?' I asked. 'It says, "what's your name and where do you live?"', she replied quickly and confidently and dashed off to do something else.

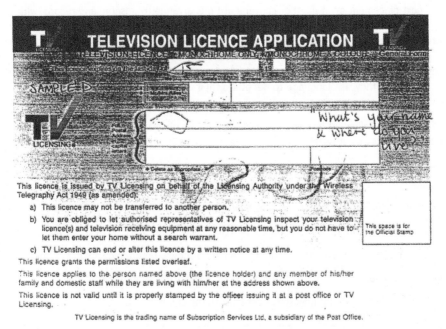

Figure 4.2 'What's your name and where do you live?'

4. DEVELOPING PRODUCTIVE USE OF THE NEW LANGUAGE

There is often not a clear distinction between this phase and the previous one. When children begin to develop productive use of the new language, you will observe that they often begin generating more creative language of their own by extending the use of the formulaic single words and phrases they have been using. They may combine some of these words and phrases in order to produce longer and more complex utterances to which they attach their own meanings, different from the original sources of the language. Careful observation is important to help track progress, as an individual child's language use may show a great deal of variety within the context of the setting. Section 3.2 in Chapter 7 (p. 154) gives you an overview of observing as a tool for formative assessment, which is equally relevant for children in the early years as well as those in primary and secondary settings. Remember, though, that in the early years it is important to observe actions as well as talk, especially for children who may be thought to be in the silent period of development.

As children explore the setting more extensively and freely, they need opportunities to try out their new language and to gain confidence in their identities as emergent speakers and writers. It is at this stage that translanguaging (see p. 44) may begin to be observed much more frequently, occurring naturally and showing how the child is using all the language resources at her disposal to achieve her own purposes. The need for careful observation on the part of the professionals grows.

ACTIVITY 4.2

Observing multilingual and EAL learners in the early years

On your next placement or at another convenient time, arrange to observe and record (with permission, of course) a group of multilingual and EAL learners in an early years setting during a time when they are choosing activities independently. Make sure that you have the consent of the children themselves, and that you follow the protocols of the school in relation to confidentiality. A period of 15-20 minutes will be enough to give you an insight into how the children respond to the environment and some of the ways they use language to negotiate their learning. Be prepared to be drawn in by the children to what is going on – there is nothing like non-participant observation in early years settings!

You could use the following questions as a guide to your observations and take notes of anything that interests, surprises or puzzles you.

1. What evidence can you see in the setting that the children's home languages are recognised and valued?

2. What evidence can you see of parental involvement?

3. Which activities seem to be most popular with the children and which do they pay less attention to?

4. Roughly how much time do the children spend at an activity before moving on to something else?

5. What do you notice about the ways that children make use of their home languages in their play?

6. What do you notice about how staff interact with the children?

2.3 WORKING WITH BILINGUAL PRACTITIONERS

All professionals in the early years have vital roles to play in ensuring that their young learners develop a positive attitude to learning and to themselves as learners. A central aspect of this, which has been emphasised at many points in the book, is the need to be recognised and valued for who and what you are. This includes acceptance and acknowledgement of identity in terms of ethnicity, religion, language and ability among other factors. Even very young children respond positively to having others around them who are like themselves or who are familiar with their home and community cultures.

This is perhaps the most important reason why it is very important to have practitioners in early years settings from the same or similar cultural backgrounds as the pupils. This does not, of course, negate the vital role of practitioners from all and any other backgrounds, but rather to make a plea for promoting diversity among professionals in all education settings.

In working closely with colleagues, it is important to develop collaborative ways of working, recognising and respecting the different kinds of knowledge, experience and power that each colleague brings to the setting. Chapter 8, section 3 (p. 181) contains strategies and activities for working with multilingual colleagues, with examples from primary and secondary contexts. The principles underlying these are equally appropriate in early years settings, but here there is the added need to interpret in home languages and to support young children in other ways who are at the very early stages of learning English in school. So, colleagues who share the same languages as the learners have a crucial role to play. Drury and Robertson (2008) and Drury (2007) illustrate the value of bilingual adults as mediators of culture and language for young multilingual and EAL learners. The following extract from Drury's work features a child, Nazma, and a bilingual teaching assistant, Mussarat, and demonstrates the way in which the adult can scaffold the learner's engagement with the processes of learning in the shared language. Nazma was finding the transition from home very difficult and, at the time the research was done, she spoke in nursery only in her home language and when Mussarat was present. This transcript, which is translated from Pahari, is from her first term in the nursery:

Mussarat:	What's this?
Nazma:	Apples
Mussarat:	What's this?
Nazma:	Pears
Mussarat:	What's this?
Nazma:	Lemon, yuk I don't like that [*making a face*]
Mussarat:	Don't you like it because it's sour?
Nazma:	Yes
Mussarat and Nazma:	1, 2, 3 green apples [*counting together*]
Mussarat and Nazma:	1, 2, 3, 4 pears [*counting together*]
Nazma:	We eat them, we like them, we get them, we go to a shop and we buy apples and pears … We went to the shops with mum and Hasnan. And we bought lollies. We had Hasnan's birthday.

We see here the vital importance of Nazma's home language for her learning. For her, Pahari had been the basis for almost all her cognitive and linguistic development to date. Her conversations with Mussarat were maintaining and extending her cognitive processing in ways that would not be possible if the two did not share the same home language while she settled into her new learning environment. Her interactions with Mussarat were helping her to learn about the early years environment as well as supporting her cognitive development. The teacher in charge of the setting, who most likely did not understand Pahari, could trust in the knowledge and skill of Mussarat to negotiate Nazma's experiences in the setting at this stage.

3 THE IMPORTANCE OF PLAY

The vast majority of children have a natural curiosity to explore and play offers them the medium to do so. The complex spaces of early years settings are set up to promote learning through play in as many ways as possible. Play is a very serious business, but it is different from work in that it is an activity self-chosen by the child, not something imposed by another. Through play children make sense of the world around them, develop social and cognitive skills, and gain the self-confidence required to engage in new experiences and environments. They learn a wide range of skills, knowledge, attitudes and ways of seeing themselves as well as others. Through this learning, they will develop confidence, creativity and independence both as learners and as individuals.

Play comes from the child's internal motivation, but it needs to be encouraged and supported by adult intervention. Play-based learning is grounded in the Vygotskian model of scaffolding, where the practitioner pays attention to the specific elements of the play activity that promote new learning and challenge for the child. The practitioner provides encouragement and feedback on the learning. The following three sections focus on creating a positive environment through play, the links between play and language learning and the importance of listening.

3.1 CREATING A POSITIVE ENVIRONMENT

It is not possible to plan children's play, but early years practitioners can plan *for* play. This involves making decisions and choices for the physical environment of the early years setting. Clarke (2004) provides a checklist of how a positive, play-friendly early years environment should be constructed, beginning with considering how young learners need to be able to access the setting. The setting needs to provide:

- flexible and open-ended periods of time for children;

- easy transitions from routine times to play;

- easy negotiation of the environment by children.

Children in the early years are expected to engage in a range of social groupings in order to learn to play and work alone and with others. The next part of Clarke's checklist provides a framework for the kinds of learning the physical space should provide, focusing on social interaction. It speaks to the need for flexibility in participation in the setting, where there should be:

- opportunities for two children to play together;

- spaces for small groups or single children to play;

- quiet retreats and privacy for children;

- active participation by adults where appropriate;

- freedom to play without adult intervention.

Finally, Clarke's checklist focuses attention on the range of activities that the early years setting should provide. There should be:

- space for physical activity – indoors and outdoors;

- spaces for music and movement;

- spaces for self-expression and creativity;

- spaces to facilitate:

  o cooperative play and communication

  o imagination

  o language development

  o development of positive self-esteem and respect for others

  o opportunities for open-ended play

  o development of concentration.

We could add to this list: the need for spaces for rest and relaxation and for 'time out' for those children who may need it.

As well as considering the physical space of the early years setting, it is important to think about the kinds of attributes and attitudes the setting should nurture – in other words, what kind of culture of learning the setting should promote. In this light, Clarke (2004) provides another useful checklist to help early years practitioners assess how far their setting is succeeding in establishing a positive learning environment. She suggests that early years settings should be set up in such a way as to:

- provide children with a sense of belonging and security;

- enable children to work at their own pace;

- foster pride in the children's cultural and linguistic heritage;

- encourage children to express their feelings in a safe and secure setting;

- provide a structure that encourages children to explore, experiment and make decisions as they play together;

- encourage children to achieve success;

- allow children to experiment within safe boundaries;

- allow children to work at their own pace;

- offer children consistent limits.

Of course, the ways in which all this can be achieved are many – each early years setting is unique and needs to reflect the languages, cultures and identities of all its participants and the context in which it is situated, as well as offering windows into new and different worlds.

3.2 PROMOTING LANGUAGE LEARNING THROUGH PLAY

During free play, children often engage in pretend talk, which is very much linked with the quality of the environment of the setting. The growth of language and cognitive skills during the pre-school years leads to more complex imaginary play. Curiosity about the environment results in greater interest in understanding how things are the same or different. Children at this age may enjoy sorting objects into meaningful groups or creating simple crafts. As they develop in the early years, children will often move from parallel play to cooperative play with their peers. An understanding of turn-taking and increased attention span allows children at this stage to also begin to play simple board games.

Adults can support all this development by engaging children in conversation, in much the same way as Mussarat does above, using questioning and feedback to help extend the child's thinking and develop the ideas they are expressing. There will also be opportunities to help the child develop important language skills in fun and supportive situations. The following strategies can be very useful:

- **Follow the child's lead**. Become observers of children's play and engage them in play activities that they find interesting. The more the child engages in play, the greater the opportunities for language acquisition and learning.

- **Practise turn-taking**. Establishing successful turn-taking routines will facilitate social and communicative skill development in young children. Techniques to facilitate turn-taking include using facial expressions, making eye contact and waiting, and asking questions.

- **Be an expander and a model**. This provides exposure to new vocabulary and correct grammar. Providing accurate language input can include adding a word or phrase to the child's short phrases, introducing synonyms or modelling the correct sentence structure. This needs to be tailored closely to what the child already knows. Here is an example:

Child: Car

Adult: Yes, it's a big car

Child: He goed fast.

Adult: Yes, it went fast.

Child: Big lorry!

Adult: Yes, you're right. It's an enormous lorry!

3.3 THE IMPORTANCE OF LISTENING

Language learning is not just about the production of language. Developing listening skills is also very important at this stage. Listening is a collaborative process, requiring the active participation of both adults and children. Adults need to take time to listen to children and children need to develop skills in listening to staff and to other children. Here are some suggestions (adapted from Clarke, 2004) for developing a positive listening environment in an early years setting:

- Model good listening habits by getting down to the child's eye level.

- Concentrate on what the child is saying, knowing when to listen and when to talk.

- Create a positive environment where background sounds or music is eliminated so that children can focus on listening.

- Ensure that all children can be heard – explain that everyone needs to have a turn.

- Make directions and instructions explicit and check that the learner has understood what you said.

- Plan listening activities and games based on the children's level of development, interests and experiences and supported with real objects and pictures.

- Use language strategies to increase active listening, such as:

  o *restating*: 'Who can tell me what we need to do before we do a painting?'

  o *summarising*: 'What did we do when we went on … ?'

  o *reflecting*: 'If you could … ?'

  o *self-assessment*: 'Tell us …'

- Provide a variety of games and activities where the focus is on listening (singing games, action rhymes and stories, sound and picture recognition games).

- Read and tell a wide variety of stories and involve the children as much as possible in patterned responses. Support stories with props and visual materials.

4 LITERACY IN THE EARLY YEARS

4.1 LINKS BETWEEN ORACY AND LITERACY – THE CONCEPT OF EMERGENT LITERACY

As I noted above, for many young children, at first there are no real boundaries between oracy and literacy. These develop as they learn the specific skills of literacy along with perceptions of what it is to be a writer and reader and their sense of themselves as readers and writers. Children need time and space to develop confidence in themselves as language users and communicators – this is especially important when they are bridging the languages of the home and the school. With the heavy pressure to begin formal instruction in phonics and other separate elements of reading from an earlier and earlier age, sometimes the time is lost in early years settings when children can experiment with their growing knowledge of how languages work, both in spoken and written forms. The following demonstrates what happens when a child has the space to develop their own understandings of written language and to create texts that are meaningful to them. It was produced spontaneously by a young child almost four years old in a nursery as part of the long-ago National Writing Project, a government-funded in-service programme at the time of the introduction of the National Curriculum in 1988. The child was able to bring her language resources together to produce a text that communicated something of vital importance to her and to every child – her own family and her place in it (see Figure 4.3).

Ng's home language is Chinese. At the point when she produced this text, she had been attending an English-medium nursery for about a year and a Saturday school where she was learning to read and write Chinese for a few months. Her text is remarkable in many ways, not least for the way it highlights her closeness to her family and its importance to her. It also shows how much she has learnt about literacy, both in English and Chinese, including the correct orientations for the two scripts. She has written her name in English script at the top left corner, and down the right side she has written the Chinese characters for 'mummy', 'daddy' and 'family' (though, as I have been told by several Chinese speakers, she has confused the strokes slightly and actually written 'horse'). She has also drawn pictures of herself and her parents and altogether – in her words – she has made a story of her family.

Figure 4.3 Ng's story about her family

Such creativity in young children's approaches to literacy is not unusual. Hall (1987) developed the concept of emergent literacy, based on the ideas of Marie Clay, to explain the ways in which young children make their own sense of written texts and can begin the process of becoming literate from the earliest age. Here are the main features of emergent literacy that can be observed in young children:

- **Print motivation**: showing interest and enjoyment in books.

- **Word knowledge**: knowing the names of things.

- **Print awareness**: knowing how to handle a book and knowing how to follow printed words on a page.

- **Narrative skills**: being able to describe things and events and tell stories.

- **Letter knowledge**: understanding that letters are different from each other, knowing their names and sounds, and recognising letters all around them.

- **Phonological awareness**: being able to hear and play with sounds, including sounds in words.

The idea of emergent literacy is a very important one for multilingual and EAL learners, and a key one for understanding that children learn important skills in the home before they begin school, and so for understanding the links between home and school. It is also helpful in understanding the links that young children make between listening, speaking, reading and writing, showing that maintaining a strict sequential progression through the four modes of language is not always helpful.

4.2 DEVELOPING LITERACY IN ONE EARLY YEARS SETTING

The following extended case study describes the practices of literacy in one multilingual early years setting. It shows the official requirements for literacy are met while providing plenty of opportunities for children to follow their own interests and motivations.

DEVELOPING BILINGUAL READING AND WRITING AS PART OF CHILDREN'S LITERACY IN EYFS – CASE STUDY BY ILONA SZOLC

Sharing books

Each morning starts with the same routine in both reception classes at St B's: once the children have changed their outdoor shoes to plimsolls, they are encouraged to choose a book from one of the reading boxes available in the classrooms and share it with a friend or an adult until registration time. The word 'share' is chosen deliberately because each child has the freedom to establish their own relationship with the reading process (at whatever stage of development it has reached). Some children choose to scan the pictures throughout a book and move on to the next one, others will thoroughly look through each page, attempt to read the headings or familiar words and with the help of illustrations will try to make sense of the text. Another group of children are fluent readers who may read to their less confident friends and discuss what they've just read about. There is one group of children who will ask an adult to read to them regardless of their own level of fluency.

All of the children mentioned above are engaging with the reading process in the way they have chosen themselves. So, where do we find the majority of EAL learners? You've probably guessed it correctly – they are usually the ones who ask the teacher to read to them, not because they cannot read themselves but because reading for multilingual learners at this stage is primarily associated with phonic decoding. This tends to limit fluent interaction with the text, removing the pleasure from the reading process and turning it into a 'mechanical' skill. However, when an adult reads with a child, this facilitates engagement with the text without rigid expectations on the child. The whole book-sharing process becomes more relaxed and enjoyable, without too much emphasis on being correct. It is also a great opportunity for the adult to find out what the multilingual learners already know. Sometimes it can come as a surprise, as in the following example where a group of 5–6 children (one of them was Z) was sharing a book with their teacher. Each page finished with '…', so the teacher asked if anyone knew what it was. None of the children in that group could answer the question, so the teacher told them that it was an 'ellipsis' – another type of punctuation. Then the teacher continued with the question if anyone knew why it was used to end each page. Suddenly, Z turned to the bilingual member of staff and whispered to her in Polish: 'Because the story is to be continued, it is not finished yet. It makes us want to carry on reading to find out more.' When asked how she knew all that, Z explained that in a fairy tale read to her by her mum, they'd come across ellipsis too and her mum mentioned to Z how it was used. Obviously, Z did not know the English term for this type of punctuation but she showed clear understanding of its use which was important for her future development of literacy in both languages.

Phonics

There is a separate time set aside on a timetable for teaching phonics. All the pupils in the reception class have been divided into two sets according to the amount of knowledge they already have in this area. EAL pupils have been distributed evenly within both groups right from the beginning of the school year. The teaching sessions usually last about 20 minutes each day and usually take place just before lunch or just after children return to class in the afternoon. While in one group EAL learners prosper, in the other group some really struggle to come to terms with blending, 'chopping' words into sounds and identifying the initial sound in words that name given pictures – never mind phase three digraphs and remembering the spelling of tricky words! Even the supporting Jolly Phonics strategies, where each phoneme is associated with an action, took a while to internalise for some bilingual learners at the start. The reason for this struggle may be the lack of context for learning separate sounds through a systematic synthetic phonics approach. In a way, it has detached this mechanical process of memorising phonemes from the main purpose for knowing them – reading for meaning and pleasure.

(Continued)

(Continued)

Writing

Despite the struggle with phonics, many of the pupils in this Early Years/Reception setting are particularly keen on writing as their free choice activity. They usually accompany their sentences or captions with supporting pictures. Those who are not confident about writing in sentences yet choose to produce story maps such as the one shown in Figure 4.4, which they successfully use to recount their ideas to the teacher or peers.

Figure 4.4 A story map of The Enormous Turnip

Some children enjoy retelling the stories they know in writing, particularly when repetitive story language is used. They frequently show incredible perseverance and concentration. For example, S copied the Enormous Turnip story map and then used it to help her retell the story. Her work is shown in Figure 4.5.

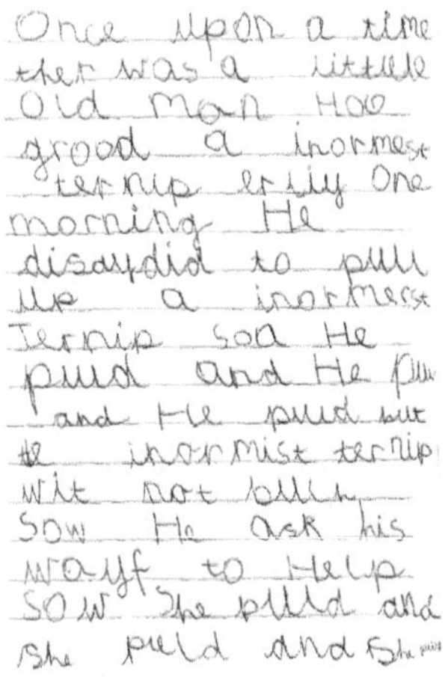

[Once upon a time there was a little old man who grew an enormous turnip. Early one morning he decided to pull up the enormous turnip. The lady pull the son, the son pull the daughter, the daughter pull the dog, the dog pull the cat, the cat pull the mouse. Is pull and pull and pull. Finally the enormous turnip is out of the ground with a bang. They is happily ever after. The end.]

Figure 4.5 Child's written telling of The Enormous Turnip story

When a story is chosen to introduce to the children, it is usually analysed for accessibility of the content in terms of culture and for the demands of the language. If available, the specialist EMA teacher introduces it in Polish to the whole class alongside the class teacher, who reads it in English. This not only makes it easier to understand for Polish-speaking EAL learners, but also increases the cultural and linguistic awareness of all the pupils.

M, who attends the local Polish community school on Saturdays, was the first to introduce differences in Polish script and phonics to her teacher, Miss F. He explains:

> 'In Polish, letter "ł" makes the same sound as letter "w" in English. If you want to write "beautiful" in Polish, you have to write "ładna" not "wadna". [Writes the correct Polish spelling on the whiteboard]

Miss F comments, 'This is really clever M. I like how you found a way to explain it to me. You can be our teacher of Polish.' More positive feedback from her teacher serves as encouragement for M to go to the 'writing' area; however, Miss F refrains from giving any further instructions. M announces, 'Now I am going to write a story in Polish like we did in English.' She spends about 15 minutes creating a picture story with sentences written under each of the five pictures in Polish. When it is ready, she takes it to Miss F and reads it out in Polish. The Polish-speaking EAL teacher discreetly comments to Miss F that M has used the same vocabulary structures as they did earlier in English. The teacher asks M, 'Can you help me understand it better, please? You could use gestures to help me with it.' M starts by re-reading her story in Polish but this time she accompanies 'Jednego dnia ...' ('One day ...'), 'Wtedy...' ('Then ...'), etc., with actions learnt from the work of Pie Corbett and used for storytelling sequences. When she finishes, Miss F retells in English what she has just heard in Polish. M beams with pride because the teacher has got it right. The EMA specialist teacher had attended Talk for Writing training which focused on Pie Corbett's storytelling techniques, and had then made the principles applicable to the early years by employing numerous EAL strategies and resources from the Talk for Writing website http://www.talk4writing.co.uk.

What we are witnessing in this positive interaction is, first of all, how a bilingual pupil shows an impressive metalinguistic awareness at such a young age in the way she can compare both languages. Then she proves that linguistic abilities are transferable by the way she uses the same story and vocabulary structures that were learnt previously in English in her Polish story. The teacher has acknowledged the equal value of Polish and English languages by emphasising them both as an effective medium for communication and understanding. Both the teacher and the pupil have gained something invaluable in this example: M displayed the use of naturally interconnected languages which supported her learning. At the same time, she incidentally introduced a piece of theory about the second-language acquisition to her teacher.

CHAPTER SUMMARY

The four learning outcomes for this chapter are about developing your understanding of the distinctive features and factors involved in working with multilingual and EAL learners in early years settings.

Self-assessment questions

1. It could be argued that intercultural competence is more important in the early years than at later stages in children's education. Do you agree? If so, why do you think this is the case? If not, why not?

(Continued)

(Continued)

2. What are some of the key differences between working with multilingual and EAL learners in early years settings and in primary classrooms?

3. How would you characterise the main differences between 'planning play' and 'planning *for* play' in early years settings?

4. How would you characterise the development of literacy in young multilingual and EAL learners who are exposed to writing in more than one language at the early stages?

FURTHER READING

Baldock, P. (2010) *Understanding Cultural Diversity in the Early Years.* **London: Sage.**

This thought-provoking book approaches the questions around cultural diversity in the early years from the position that diversity is normal and brings many advantages to teaching and learning. It establishes strong theoretical bases for this position, followed by a wealth of practical examples for working with young learners and their families.

Kenner, C. (2004) *Becoming Biliterate: Young Children Learning Different Writing Systems.* **Stoke-on-Trent: Trentham Books.**

This book presents case studies of six-year-olds growing up bilingually which reveal the processes involved in becoming biliterate. They show how children's learning is supported in home and community contexts and offer approaches to supporting literacy development and achievement in early years settings.

STUDYING AT MASTER'S LEVEL

Critical reading:

Chapter 3 'The idea of intercultural competence', in **P. Baldock (2010)** *Understanding Cultural Diversity in the Early Years.* **London: Sage.**

In this chapter, through introducing ideas and terminology from different countries in Europe, Baldock explores the notions of intercultural competence and cultural shock, and their relevance for early years practitioners in England.

After reading the chapter, consider the following questions, ideally in discussion with colleagues:

1. On p. 33, Baldock discusses the importance of 'intercultural interaction' and of learning from each other. How does he see this as different from multiculturalism and why does he consider it important?

2. On pp. 37-8, Baldock stresses the need for teachers working with multilingual and EAL learners in the early years to have 'the skills to respond to new situations'. What does he suggest that these skills involve? Are there any other attributes you think should be included?

3. As an issue related to 'cultural shock' Baldock discusses on pp. 40-1 the example of wearing the hijab. What arguments does he raise and where do you stand on this particular debate?

4. What cultural issues does Baldock raise around the practices of giving and receiving things and offering help? What implications do you think this might have for practitioners in the early years?

At the end of the chapter (pp. 45-7), Baldock provides a group exercise in the form of a simulation to illustrate the issues around intercultural interaction that he raises in the chapter. If possible, have a go at the activity with your course mates or colleagues.

REFERENCES

Baldock, P. (2010) *Understanding Cultural Diversity in the Early Years*. London: Sage.

Bligh, C. and Drury, R. (2015) 'Perspectives on the "Silent Period" for emergent bilinguals in England', *Journal of Research in Childhood Education*, 29 (2), pp. 259–74. Available at https://doi.org/10.1080/02568543.2015.1009589.

Clarke, P. (2004) *Creating Positive Environments that Promote Listening and Speaking*. Available at http://www.naldic.org.uk/Resources/NALDIC/Professional%20Development/Documents/Creatingpositiveenvironments.pdf.

Clarke, P. (2018) *The Social Basis for Learning: Considerations for the Bilingual Child*. Available at https://naldic.org.uk/teaching-learning/eyfs/eyfs-curriculum/.

Conteh, J. (2003) *Succeeding in Diversity: Culture, Language and Learning in Primary Classrooms*. Stoke-on-Trent: Trentham Books.

Conteh, J. and Kawashima, Y. (2008) 'Diversity in family involvement in children's learning in English primary schools', *English Teaching Practice and Critique*, 7 (2), pp. 113–25. Available at https://edlinked.soe.waikato.ac.nz/research/journal/view.php?article=true&id=526&p=1.

Department for Education (DfE) (2017) *Statutory Framework for the Early Years Foundation Stage*. Available at https://www.gov.uk/government/publications/early-years-foundation-stage-framework--2.

Drury, R. (2000) 'Bilingual children in the nursery: a case study of Samia at home and at school', *European Early Childhood Education Research Journal*, 8 (1), pp. 43–59.

Drury, R. (2007) *Young Bilingual Learners at Home and School*. Stoke-on-Trent: Trentham Books.

Drury, R. and Robertson, L. (2008) *Strategies for Early Years Practitioners*. Available at https://www.naldic.org.uk/Resources/NALDIC/Teaching%20and%20Learning/Documents/EYFSStrategies.pdf.

Gonzalez, N., Moll, L. and Amanti, C. (eds) (2005) *Funds of Knowledge: Theorizing Practices in Households, Communities and Classrooms*. New York: Routledge.

Hall, N. (1987) *The Emergence of Literacy*. London: Hodder & Stoughton.

National Association for Language Development in the Curriculum (NALDIC) (2011) *Response to the Revised Statutory Framework for the Early Years Foundation Stage*. Available at https://www.naldic.org.uk/Resources/NALDIC/Advocacy/Documents/NALDIC-Response-EYFS-revised-framework.pdf

Palaiologou, I. (2016) *Child Observation: A Guide for Students on Early Childhood*. London: Sage.

Primary National Strategy (PNS) (2007) *Supporting Children Learning English as an Additional Language: Guidance for Practitioners in the Early Years Foundation Stage*, https://www.naldic.org.uk/Resources/NALDIC/Teaching%20and%20Learning/ealeyfsguidance.pdf.

Rogoff, B. (2003) *The Cultural Nature of Human Development*. New York: Oxford University Press.

Tabors, P. (1997) *One Child, Two Languages: A Guide for Preschool Educators of Children Learning English as a Second Language*. Baltimore, MD: Paul Brookes.

5
EAL AND LITERACY: LEARNING TO READ INDEPENDENTLY IN A NEW LANGUAGE

LEARNING OUTCOMES

This chapter will help you to achieve the following learning outcomes:

* develop understanding of all the attributes involved in independent reading;

* gain awareness of the debates around the role of phonics in reading and the implications for multilingual and EAL learners;

* understand the importance of 'identity texts' in reading with multilingual and EAL learners and consider some practical examples;

* gain understanding of some of the wider issues around reading for multilingual and EAL learners, including academic literacy and reading for pleasure.

INTRODUCTION

Undoubtedly, the most important thing that all learners need to do in school is to learn to read independently. It not only gives access to the whole curriculum, but also opens doors to the world outside school. Being able to read means that we can function as full members of our communities and as citizens in the wider society. It also means that we have the keys to enter the multifaceted worlds of literature, the arts, science, humanities and culture that will enrich us throughout our lives. It is crucial that all pupils become independent readers by the time they leave primary school. Those who are still struggling at this stage will often find their opportunities for success in school become more and more limited. Despite (or perhaps because of) the importance of reading, there is still little real agreement about the best ways to teach it – to all pupils, not just those categorised as EAL. Debates about the teaching of reading have gone on ever since reading has been taught, and they are not likely to come to an end soon. In England, the debate has – unfortunately – become very political, to the detriment of the ways that reading is discussed and taught.

Over recent years, teachers have not been well served by official policies. The emphasis on phonics has caused confusion and the demands of national assessments have narrowed down the curriculum. With the aim of addressing some of these problems, this chapter provides a brief account of what independent readers need to do and the place of phonics within the whole picture of reading. Following this, it provides examples of ways of using learners' full language repertoires to open out reading, with case studies by Naomi Cooper and Dianne Excell. Finally, it addresses two issues that are key for multilingual and EAL learners – indeed all learners – that of understanding academic language and of developing reading for pleasure. A case study by Ali O'Grady of reading for pleasure with teenage boys closes the chapter.

These are the main sections and subsections of the chapter:

1   The processes of reading

1.1   What can independent readers do?

1.2   And what about phonics?

1.3   Reading multilingually – the power of 'identity texts'

Student teachers' experiences of literacy in primary and early years settings – case study by Naomi Cooper

Use of home language and identity texts with a reluctant English learner – case study by Dianne Excell

2   Reading across the curriculum and beyond

2.1   Academic language and literacy

2.2   Developing reading for pleasure

Reading for pleasure with teenage boys – case study by Ali O'Grady

1 THE PROCESSES OF READING

1.1 WHAT CAN INDEPENDENT READERS DO?

Reading is a complex process involving knowing and being able to do many things. Despite this, many children learn to read with ease and sometimes with very little actual teaching. This could be said about Mushtaq (Chapter 3, p. 57). I don't know how he learned to read in Bengali, but I do know that he had little explicit teaching of reading in English, as I was the one responsible for this. Mushtaq learned to read and write English himself, given some helpful resources and some time, space and lots of encouragement. Of course, this does not mean that all learners would respond like Mushtaq to the situation he was in. The first and most important point to note about learning to read is that there are almost as many ways of doing it as there are learners. This is why it is very unhelpful to insist, as official policy has done for the past few years, on one fixed model of teaching reading.

Although we cannot expect all our learners to approach the task of becoming independent readers in the same way, they all need, eventually, to learn to do the same things. Here is my list of what independent readers can do:

* They can choose the right kind language cue (e.g. graphophonic, syntactic, semantic) at the right time to decode the words in front of them (see the Research Focus below for a fuller discussion of this).

* They can use a range of 'higher-order' reading skills (inferencing, predicting, testing hypotheses, etc.) to build their comprehension of the whole text.

- They can use their personal, social and cultural knowledge of the world to make meaning with the text and construct an appropriate response.

- They can persevere and cope with uncertainty in order to achieve their goals.

- They can do all the above quickly, efficiently and simultaneously when necessary, and often without even being aware that they are doing so.

This clearly involves a lot of knowledge, and not just about language but of the wider world, including the contexts in which the text was produced and the reading that is taking place. Not all of this needs to come into play all the time, of course. I think of the independent reader like the conductor of an orchestra who knows how to make meaning with the music: when to bring in the woodwind, when to get the strings to play more quietly and just when the crucial moment is to signal to the percussionist to make her distinctive mark on the whole performance. In the same way, independent readers choose, often intuitively, from their repertoire of skills and knowledge those they need to make meaning with different kinds of texts.

Despite this complexity, the current prevailing 'official' model of reading is called the 'simple view'. It originated in the Rose Review (DfES, 2006a), was adapted in 2010 and is now embodied in the 2014 curriculum in a slightly different form. The simple view states that reading involves two processes and that the first should always come before the second:

- decoding the words;

- comprehending the whole text.

The 2014 curriculum prescribes that all pupils should be taught to decode phonically before they engage in reading meaningful texts. While not denying the importance of decoding, this is no way to develop young learners into independent, confident readers. It goes against all the research which shows that most children learn to read by making meaning with whole words, sentences and texts, not by rote learning disembodied lists of sounds (UKLA, 2010). It quickly becomes clear to anyone working with young children that, rather than being two separate, sequential aspects of reading, decoding and comprehension are intertwined and one supports the other. Sometimes a reader will only be able to decode a word once they know what it means, as well as the other way round.

- A very good way to develop understanding of the processes of reading is to listen to children reading and think about what they are doing. A form of assessment called miscue analysis offers a systematic way to do this.

RESEARCH FOCUS

Miscue analysis

Miscue analysis is an approach to making a diagnostic assessment of how children read which was devised many years ago by Kenneth and Yetta Goodman. It was used in England for a few years in the 1990s as a basis for assessing reading at KS1, where it was known as running records. A very useful short text to give you further information is Campbell (2011). The starting point for the approach is to take a positive view of the child as a reader and think that they are not just guessing but using their knowledge of language and personal and cultural experiences to read the text. In miscue analysis, the three main elements of language are known as cue systems. They are:

- graphophonic (related to the links between letters and sounds);

- syntactic (related to sentence structures and grammar);

- semantic (related to context and meaning).

A miscue occurs when a child says something different from what is written in the text. The assumption is that the child is making an informed judgement based on their understanding of the language cue systems and their knowledge of the world. The listener has to make a judgement as to whether the miscue is positive (i.e. it retains the meaning of the whole text) or negative (i.e. the meaning of the whole text is impaired). Carrying out a miscue analysis involves, essentially, listening to a child reading aloud, noting the miscues and analysing them to consider what they show about the child's strengths and needs as a reader. When a miscue occurs it is likely to be where the child has put too much emphasis on a particular cue system or has used one inappropriately. Here is an example from Robin Campbell's book:

> ... a young child reads aloud from Eric Carle's The Very Hungry Caterpillar (1969):
>
> 'One Summer's day the warm sun came out' (child's reading)
>
> 'One Sunday morning the warm sun came up' (text)

Here there are three miscues: Summer's/Sunday, day/morning, out/up. They all seem to be positive; we can see that the child has retained an overall comprehension of the text. Though not entirely correct, all the miscues are syntactically and semantically possible (i.e. they produce a meaningful sentence). They show us different things about the way the child is reading. The first one, **Summer's/Sunday**, could have occurred because the child has looked at the first part of the word and then made the wrong (but a reasonable) prediction about how the word ends. The second one, **day/morning**, suggests that the child is making meaning by predicting what word comes next and, again, makes a reasonable choice of a word to follow 'Sunday'. The final one, **out/up**, is different again; both words are syntactically correct in the sentence, and 'out' is perhaps the more common one for a young child to use to describe the sunrise. The miscues, of course, need to be corrected, but there does not seem to be much to worry about - we could conclude that this child already knows a lot about language and is using their knowledge in ways that will help them to become an independent reader and need to be supported.

ACTIVITY 5.1

Observing reading - doing a miscue analysis

If you are able to work with a pupil in primary school, you can carry out this activity which is based on miscue analysis. Or perhaps you could find a willing relative, friend or neighbour of the relevant age to be your 'target pupil'. You will need a notebook, a grid like the one shown in Figure 5.1 and a sound recorder (your phone will do). Make sure that the child and their teacher/parent/guardian know that only you will listen to the recording and then you will delete it.

1. Select a text. Your target pupil should be able to read it, but not too easily. They could perhaps help you select it.

2. Copy about 100 words of the text on to a grid like the one below, one word per cell. This will be the part on which you will do your miscue analysis.

(Continued)

(Continued)

3. Prepare some comprehension questions on the whole text, i.e. one or two literal questions and one or two inferential questions.

4. Now set up the activity with the child: find a comfortable place and explain what you are going to do, introduce the text to them and chat with them about it.

5. Switch on your recorder and begin reading the text with the child. Gradually stop reading and let the child take over, before you get to the words on your grid.

6. While the child is reading the words on the grid, use the codes to categorise their reading of each word. If you miss a word, carry on - you will hear it on the recorder later.

7. Let the child finish reading and then ask them for a brief retelling of the story so you can evaluate their comprehension. Use your prepared comprehension questions to help them if necessary. Record this conversation if you can.

Child's name:	Date:
Title of text used:	
Codes for categorising child's reading:	

✓ = correct

O = omitted

SC = self-corrected (write the word they say above the word in the cell)

M = miscue (write the word they say above the word in the cell)

/ = pause or hesitation between words

Figure 5.1 Miscue analysis grid

After the session, review your data:

8. Listen to your recording to check your coding. Note any interesting features of expression in the child's reading.

9. Analyse what you think the recording shows you about the child's strengths and weaknesses in their reading. Look at their miscues and think about what they show. Decide which miscues are positive (i.e. don't impair comprehension) and which are negative (i.e. impair comprehension) and think about which language cue system the child might have used in each case. If possible, discuss your analysis with a fellow student or teacher.

10. Note down what you might do in order to help the child develop in their reading.

1.2 AND WHAT ABOUT PHONICS?

The first point to make is that phonics is part of teaching children to read, *not* the whole thing or a separate skill on its own. If we consider the five bullet points above showing what an independent reader needs to do (p. 89), phonics can help with the first but not with the remaining four. There are, essentially, two kinds of phonics: **analytic phonics** which starts with whole words and identifies the sounds in them, and **synthetic phonics** which is about building up words from their sounds. Both are concerned with mapping the sounds in words (**phonemes**) onto the written symbols (**graphemes**). The kind prescribed in the National Curriculum is synthetic phonics and teachers are provided with a detailed set of objectives for teaching grapheme-phoneme correspondences (GPCs) through the first two years of children's schooling in Reception and Year 1. There are many commercially produced schemes for the teaching of synthetic phonics which are usually intended for whole-class teaching. They do not recognise the many different kinds of knowledge that children will bring to the classroom.

A knowledge of phonics can help readers to do various things:

- **Decode** phonically regular words, but not comprehend them as part of whole texts.

- Identify the sounds (phonemes) in spoken words, i.e develop phonological awareness.

- Recognise common letter combinations (graphemes) for each phoneme, i.e. develop phoneme-grapheme awareness.

- Blend phonemes and graphemes into whole words (useful for decoding in reading).

- Segment whole words into phonemes and graphemes (useful for spelling).

All of these are part of the processes of reading and are essential to the child's development as an independent reader but I hope it is clear from what I have already said that they will not in themselves turn children into independent readers. There is much more they need to know. Phonics does *not* help readers to do a lot of things which are essential for reading, so other kinds of knowledge and support are necessary. Phonics does not help readers to do the following:

- decode phonically irregular words – they need other language cue systems for this, such as syntactic and semantic cues;

- recognise on sight many 'high frequency' or function words, important for understanding the grammatical features of texts;

- understand the meanings of words, phrases or sentences;

- develop comprehension skills;

- develop 'higher-order' reading skills – inference, prediction, response, etc.;

- compose sentences and texts for themselves.

I hope the conclusion is clear: that, for all children, learning to read needs to go far beyond the learning of GPCs. All children need rich and diverse experiences of written language to encourage them to respond to words, sentences and whole texts, and these experiences need to begin at the earliest stages of their education.

Although the vast majority of what has been said and written about reading applies to all learners, there are some distinctive factors to consider for multilingual and EAL learners. Section 1.3 below considers issues around learning to read multilingually. In relation to phonics as part of the reading process, one of the best resources for understanding the needs of multilingual and EAL learners is Eve Gregory's book *Making Sense of Words and Worlds* (2008). Gregory provides a theoretical framework, insightful advice and many practical examples for teachers on ways to consider the teaching of phonics with their multilingual pupils. One case study (pp. 123–4) concerns Saida, a nine-year-old pupil newly arrived from Bangladesh. In her first days at school in London, Saida amazed her teacher by 'reading' correctly from a simple text. However, it soon became clear that she could not understand the words that she articulated – she was simply using the decoding strategies that she had been taught in Bangladesh. Learning to read through phonics in Bengali is actually much easier than trying to do the same in English, as the language is written in a phonically regular way. Luckily, her teacher recognised what was happening. She understood that the funds of knowledge that Saida brought to her English school included lots of knowledge of graphophonic cue systems, so she was on the way to meeting the first bullet point above (p. 89). The teacher quickly realised that what Saida needed was plenty of experience of listening to and later talking about meaningful text in English so that her strong decoding skills would become part of her repertoire of methods of engaging with the English language in meaningful ways.

From Gregory's case study, we can draw some valuable conclusions:

- EAL/multilingual learners can transfer the skills they have learnt in reading in one language to learning to read in English.

- EAL/multilingual learners are often very good at phonic decoding, though they are unfamiliar with the meanings of many words they can decode (this is borne out by the Year 1 phonics screening check, where EAL learners often do very well at decoding the nonsense words, though sometimes not recognising them as nonsense).

- Many new arrivals can decode successfully because of the ways they have been taught to read in their countries of origin and the languages in which they have learnt to read.

- Pupils with such early literacy experiences need strategies which are grounded in these early experiences to develop the full range of skills to become independent readers.

- Young, multilingual learners need rich experiences of meaningful English text in order to develop their repertoires of words they understand and to gain a 'feel' for what sounds are 'allowed' in a language.

ACTIVITY 5.2

Letters and Sounds

'Letters and Sounds' is the scheme issued by the government through the National Strategies in 2007 to teach synthetic phonics from Reception to Year 2. It is a very useful free resource and is still available online:

https://assets.publishing.service.gov.uk/government/uploads/system/uploads/attachment_data/file/190599/Letters_and_Sounds_-_DFES-00281-2007.pdf

Test your subject knowledge of synthetic phonics with the following questions. Answers are provided at the end of the chapter.

1. Complete the chart below by segmenting the words into their phonemes/graphemes:

Word	Phonemes/ graphemes	Segments
straight		
young		
four		
leopard		
thoughtful		
rainy		
broad		

2. List all the words from the chart with the phoneme /or/ (like 'for').

3. List any other words you can think of with different graphemes for the /or /(like 'for') phoneme

4. Here is a list of words:

   paste; girl; people; young; busy; find;

   spoons; bump; cart; sink; fling; wing

   Put the words that fit into a **cvcc** chart like this:

c	v	c	c

List the words that don't fit the cvcc chart, divided into their phonemes and graphemes.

1.3 READING MULTILINGUALLY – THE POWER OF 'IDENTITY TEXTS'

Reading is a social and cultural practice which takes many forms and happens in many different contexts all over the world. Indeed, for many multilingual pupils, it is more realistic to talk about 'literacies' in the plural, instead of just 'literacy', as they may have skills in reading in different languages, sometimes in different scripts. In Gregory et al.'s (2004) *Many Pathways to Literacy*, different authors present a wide range of examples of the literacy practices of young learners from diverse language and cultural backgrounds. Key theoretical principles can be drawn from this, which help us to recognise the kinds of pedagogy that will most benefit EAL learners in both primary and secondary settings:

* Multilingual learners live in 'simultaneous worlds' of language use and experience where literacies are performed in different ways for different purposes.

* Literacy learning is *syncretic* – learning to read in one language and script facilitates the learning of others and the interaction of languages and/or scripts leads to new knowledge and creativity.

* Literacy practices are social, cultural and always connected with issues of power.

These ideas resonate with the funds of knowledge concept which is discussed at different points in the book and together they point to the need to ensure that learning to read is always rooted in the learner's familiar contexts and builds on what they already know. The first essential is to find out as much as you can about the child's prior literacy learning and what they do outside school in terms of literacy, such as attending a complementary or supplementary school, place of worship and so on. A child who comes to reading in English already literate in another language is at a very different starting point from one who has never encountered literacy in any form before.

One of the most effective ways of promoting syncretic literacy learning (in Gregory et al.'s terms) is through the use of 'identity texts' (Cummins and Early, 2011). Identity texts are, in essence, developed creatively and collaboratively between teacher and pupil or groups of pupils. Everyone's home languages become 'cognitive and personal resources for learning' (Cummins and Early, 2011, p. 9). The text produced 'holds a mirror up to students in which their identities are reflected back in a positive light' (p. 30). Cummins and Early go further to argue that identity texts are a powerful means 'to promote equity for students from marginalised social backgrounds' (p. 4). They do this by recognising the power of the languages and cultural knowledge that pupils already have in the processes of becoming literate in English. The following two case studies illustrate the power of identity texts as part of EAL pedagogy. The first is by Naomi Cooper, a teacher educator. She describes the responses of different student teachers to working with EAL learners with identity texts. We see the importance of this to the students in their learning and professional development. The second, by Dianne Excell, reports on a learner in secondary school who was initially very reluctant to speak English and shows how identity texts were transformative in her learning.

STUDENT TEACHERS' EXPERIENCES OF LITERACY IN PRIMARY AND EARLY YEARS SETTINGS – CASE STUDY BY NAOMI COOPER

Student teachers need direct experience of working with pupils who have different cultural experiences from themselves. Often, this helps them to recognise the importance of the role of identity in both learning and teaching and of valuing the funds of knowledge that both teachers and learners bring to the classroom. Here I summarise conversations with student teachers Jodie Brown, Kiera Michaelis and Frances Anderson, all of whom were second-year students on one of our Initial Teacher Education (ITE) courses. All of our student teachers undertake a week-long placement in school, with the primary purpose of working with children who are learning through EAL. Schools are carefully chosen for these placements and many provide opportunities to work with a wide range of pupils, some of whom are learning English as their third or fourth language. During this placement, student teachers carry out several tasks. The first of these is supporting children to create an identity text. Students work with a small group of children to develop a story, either autobiographical or other, which includes reference to the child's family language. If the child is able and willing, the use of first language is encouraged in the creation of the story. These stories can take any form. As Cummins and Early (2011, p. 3) say:

> Students invest their identities in the creation of these texts – which can be written, spoken, signed, visual, musical, dramatic, or combinations in multimodal form.

The story should make reference to the background of the pupil, where they come from or their home language and when shared with others (school, family) should highlight in a positive light the home language and background of the pupil.

The identity text in Figure 5.2 shows Rafiq's work and clearly illustrates the varied aspects of his life so far. Rafiq was animated in the verbal account that accompanied this activity – he talked extensively about life before coming to UK and showed pride in the fact that he could write in both Arabic and English. (We acknowledge Rafiq's ownership of this identity text.)

Figure 5.2 Rafiq's identity text

Kiera reflected on what she had learnt through her experience:

> … *specific energy should be devoted to getting to know the pupils in a class and making them feel valued. [Cummins (2011)] espouses the benefits of 'identity texts', a flexible piece of work specific to individuals, as an excellent tool to develop this. Certainly, on my focused EAL placement I did a shortened Identity Text exercise which I found to be illuminating and a brilliant way to connect with the children. Initially it was a really great way to connect very quickly – almost like a shortcut to form a meaningful relationship. When discussing the result with the class teacher it became even clearer how illuminating this session was; it was clear that some of the participants had shared more with me in those 10 minutes than they had all year with other adults. I originally thought this would be a great thing to do at the start of term to help connect with any EAL learners in my class. However, upon reflection I think it might be good to wait a little longer to do this. This would perhaps challenge any preconceptions I had built about the children. Also it might give the chance for more shy children to embrace the task. An interesting side effect of the exercise for me was that I reflected more on my own identity as I did a text alongside the pupils. This self-reflection was useful in genuinely sharing my passions and heritage and (I hope) it made the children more comfortable to share openly.*

This brief insight into the child's experiences offers reminders that every child needs to be considered as a whole person who brings unique experiences to the classroom. Kiera's reflections on herself are also very interesting here; she recognises the importance of understanding her own identity and the ways it might influence her perspectives and attitudes as a teacher. This resonates with the discussion in Chapter 1 (pp. 10-11) about teachers' identities and teaching in diverse settings.

Learning about cultural sensitivity

Trainees also plan a literacy activity for their group. Jodie reflected on her observations in school. She was particularly surprised by one Year 6 lesson where the class were preparing for SATs tests. Pupils

(Continued)

(Continued)

were asked to infer information about which day of the week the story they were reading had taken place. The relevant section of the excerpt stated that a family had left church, dressed in their best clothes. In her capacity of supporting the class teacher, Jodie was able to aid children's understanding of the text through discussion, but the need to do this reminded her of the importance of planning mindfully for all members of her class, choosing texts that were culturally sensitive, appropriate and accessible by all pupils. Jodie commented that children learning through EAL may face barriers that go beyond language. She noted that the placement had given the opportunity to see this first-hand.

Jodie used many games in her pre- and post-teaching to support EAL learners within the mainstream class rather than withdrawing them for extended periods of intervention. For example, children found buried word treasures in the sand tray and put them in sequence to make word banks linked to the lesson. Pupils were given space and time to explore their own interests and, as a result, language skills were learned in a meaningful context. They invented their own games to support learning, which they could play with buddies or other members of the group. Jodie commented that these games were probably more easily accommodated in a Key Stage 1 classroom than further up the school, although she aims to use the principle of making lessons as fun as possible with every class.

Supporting the individual child

A third student, Fran, worked extensively through a longer block placement with an isolated EAL learner who spoke Polish at home, Charlie, a Year 2 pupil in a mixed Year 2/3 class. She missed a lot of days of school and when she did come to school, she looked very unhappy. Charlie didn't appear to have many friends at school and was nearly always alone in the playground. School staff were concerned about her and found it difficult to identify the cause of Charlie's unhappiness, despite their attempts to help her feel included in school life. Being in a position initially of having a little more time than the class teacher, Fran set about getting to know Charlie as well as possible, going to play with her at playtimes and observing/working alongside her as much as possible. Charlie was very behind across all areas of the curriculum and was reading books at a much lower level than the books the rest of the class were reading in literacy lessons. After taking time to begin to build Charlie's self-esteem, Fran began a daily phonics intervention with Charlie and another child. They did this instead of their daily spelling and grammar (SPAG) lessons. Fran planned this as a weekly block focusing on one or two sounds. The session was highly context-embedded at the start of the week and this scaffolding was reduced throughout the week, working through Cummins' quadrant towards low context and more challenging cognitive demands by Thursday/Friday (see p. 113 for Cummins' quadrant). In a writing intervention, which Fran and her placement partner started, activities were based on each child's interests. For Charlie this was often princesses and dogs. Sometimes *Helicopter Stories* (Make Believe Arts, based on the work of Vivian Gussin Paley (1991); see also https://helicopterstories.co.uk) were used instead of the formal intervention and Charlie grew in confidence in her storytelling throughout Fran's placement. By the end, she could contribute to sessions equally with her peers.

Planning for active learning

Trainees' plans included plenty of games, drawing, searching around school for hidden objects, use of puppets, acting, hot-seating, making videos, news reports, freeze frames, outdoor learning – all to make learning as playful as possible and give opportunities for plenty of positive feedback. Every task had two aims – to encourage friendships in school and to offer every opportunity to talk and practise speaking and writing. Charlie became more engaged; she began writing, talking and coming up with ideas. Taking the role of teacher, Charlie began to share a variety of Polish words with Fran and a few other pupils. She talked with Fran about how special it was that she could speak Polish, while at the start of placement she had seemed embarrassed to use her home language. By the end of term she would happily teach Polish to other pupils in the class. The interventions and pre-teachings which she had done with other children had helped her to make some friendships in the class and gain confidence. She became proud of her own progress, making significant strides in all areas of literacy. Fran linked this directly to Charlie's increase in self-esteem and willingness to persevere with literacy tasks.

Each trainee spoke of the importance of considering every aspect of their pupils' profiles, carefully planning and crafting sequences of work to meet the needs of their EAL pupils. They felt that the additional work involved in this planning was rewarded multiple times over with all kinds of success. It was also clear that the trainees themselves learned a lot about themselves through their close engagement with children from different language and cultural backgrounds.

USE OF L1 AND IDENTITY TEXTS WITH A RELUCTANT ENGLISH LEARNER – CASE STUDY BY DIANNE EXCELL

May came to Bradford from Saudi Arabia aged 10. After one year in primary school, she moved to secondary and was still working within the 'Early Acquisition' stage (Code B) of the DfE English Proficiency Scales (see p. 146). Her lack of English cultural vocabulary hindered her development in listening so instructions such as 'draw', 'colour' and 'tick' posed problems, as did understanding prepositions and colours. May's speaking in English was restricted to short responses using single words and phrases and her pronunciation was inaccurate. With support, she could read short pieces of text aloud, although she often reversed words and could not decode. Her writing in English was immature compared to her fluency in Arabic. She could copy words but confused 'bp' and 'bd'. With support, she was beginning to recognise some English grammar and syntax in sentences. The Special Needs Coordinator, concerned that Charlie might have learning difficulties, invited an Educational Psychologist into school to assess her. However, although she was a reluctant English learner, she achieved an A* in Arabic GCSE when aged 13. Because she had not made the expected progress in the mainstream, she was withdrawn for language support during timetabled Arabic lessons, which were too basic for her.

The EAL teacher had successfully used stories from Gordon Ward's (2007) *Racing to English* CD with previous EAL learners. Written in simple language by newly arrived children from many countries, these stories share their own experiences. Beginning with a story and picture to read and discuss, the four-sided booklets contain several enjoyable related sequential activities, moving from simple to more complex, which are of the following type:

1. Sequencing - the story cut into strips ready to re-order.

2. Key words, based on the story, which can be translated.

3. Questions requiring 'Yes' or 'No' answers (orally).

4. Questions requiring 'Yes I have' or 'No I haven't' (orally).

5. Questions requiring longer answers (rehearsed orally, scaffolding answers before the student writes them).

6. Longer writing tasks, encouraging students to write in their home language and English.

7. A wordsearch of key words.

(Continued)

(Continued)

8.   Making up questions which don't have an answer in the story.

9.   Adding to the existing story, using the new questions to add detail.

The EAL teacher had found that the 'Spider in the Shoe' story was particularly popular with students from diverse linguistic backgrounds because all had prior knowledge of spiders, so she encouraged May to read the story using gestures and illustrations to aid understanding. Afterwards the teacher and May completed activities 1 to 5 in Gordon Ward's sequence. For activity 6, May was asked whether she had ever been frightened by a spider. She said she had, so the teacher actively encouraged her to write about it by discussing the experience with her in English, using actions and prompting answers with 'who?', 'where?', 'when?' to ensure that she understood May's story. When writing her story in Arabic, May wrote quickly, neatly and fluently. After more questioning to elicit the story, the teacher scribed the 'English version' of 'Spider in the Bathroom' making the grammatical elements explicit. May was pleased with her achievement and was keen to type up the story in Arabic and English. At that stage she was reluctant to use phonics for herself so, as she typed, the teacher spelled out the words phonically and the only errors were with vowels. Later, the Arabic teacher confirmed that the English translation of the Arabic story was accurate. Figure 5.3 shows May's story.

Figure 5.3 'Spider in the Bathroom' in Arabic and English

To extend May's English cultural knowledge, the EAL teacher explained the nursery rhyme 'Little Miss Muffet' about a spider. She enjoyed the story so much that she typed it up and found illustrations on the internet. Her efforts were mounted on a wall display, which raised her self-esteem. She selected key words in the story to create her own wordsearch and solution, showing her developing independence. Her English teacher made copies for the other students in the class to solve.

May's active learning continued with 'When I Hurt My Brother', a story in Arabic and English, about a time when her parents were angry that she had fought with her brother when he took her mobile phone. Without encouragement, she was eager to follow Gordon Ward's (2007) sequence of related activities. Bernhard and Cummins (2004) explain this by saying that, by 'promoting active learning', the teacher allowed May to take 'ownership of the learning process', investing her identity in the outcome of her learning. They suggest that the resulting understanding will be deeper.

Another set of activities around an identity text was stimulated by a true BBC news story (BBC, 2009) about a sandstorm in May's home city of Riyadh – something she had experienced many times. Building on prior knowledge and supported by the EAL teacher, she read the news page and wrote a simplified version of the story in English with minimal help. She was encouraged to rehearse the sentences out loud at each stage so that they could be corrected and typed. Her ICT skills enabled her to add a few pictures from the BBC website. The booklet that followed (see Figure 5.4) included many features in Gordon Ward's sequence, such as key words, longer questions and some extra activities. It also included the Arabic version of the story. This was evidence of how much she had progressed into DfE English Proficiency Scale Code C (Developing Competence).

The Riyadh Sandstorm BBC News 08-03-2009

Some of the activities included
Please use long answers for the next questions.
14. Where is Riyadh?
15. Why did the sandstorm come to Riyadh?
16. Why did the people cover up their faces?
17. What happened at the airport when the storm came?
18. Why did the schools have to close?
19. Why were there traffic jams on the roads?
20. How many days did the sandstorm stay?

Now think of the answers to **five** questions about the sandstorm that we do NOT know the answer to. Did the buses stop running? What time did the airport re-open? Did anyone die? How can people see in the storm? What do people say to each other?

Now re-write the story about the sandstorm but include more detail to make it longer.

Figure 5.4 BBC News story activity

Bernhard and Cummins (2004) argue that students need to share identity texts with multiple audiences, such as peers, teachers, parents and grandparents. Then they are likely to receive positive feedback and affirmation of self. This certainly was the case when the finished versions were shown to May's English teacher. She asked May to teach the whole class about the sandstorm in both languages, which she did very confidently. As a consequence, all the students in the group wanted to write their own stories. The English teacher changed her lesson plans to allow the students to produce similar books and the EAL teacher supported individuals in the same way as she had with May.

(Continued)

(Continued)

Although many students only had spoken knowledge of their first language, they still managed to include relevant home language vocabulary, such as places and people's names. They used their ICT skills to integrate pictures and WordArt titles. The students took turns to teach the rest of the class about their language and culture. From Pakistan there was a Factfile which included cities, mountains, languages, currency; fashions such as salwar kameez, dupatta and chunni; foods such as naan, gulab jamun, jalebi, halwa and chapattis; flooding events which involved place names Attock, Balochistan and Turbat; and weddings with nakkah, mehndi, matai and rukasti. From Bangladesh students learned about Cyclone Sidr and Dhaka using Sylheti; also how to write Bengali letters; foods such as paratha, rasmalai, thoya, khoi, lassi, panta; and Bengali poetry. They also learned about the school day in Saudi Arabia with students such as Abdulatef, place names including Jeddah and Mecca and festivals such as Id ul-fitr. In sharing their books with their peers, they were very excited and showed great pride, in the same way as pupils described in Bernhard and Cummins (2004).

2 READING ACROSS THE CURRICULUM AND BEYOND

2.1 ACADEMIC LANGUAGE AND LITERACY

On p. 89, I suggested a list of five things that independent readers need to be able to do. This section deals mainly with the second and third of them:

- They can use a range of 'higher-order' reading skills (inferencing, predicting, testing hypotheses, etc.) to build their comprehension of the whole text.

- They can use their personal, social, cultural knowledge of the world to make meaning with the text and construct an appropriate response.

These both point to the conclusion that reading is not just something that has to be done as part of the English curriculum, but it is part of all subjects across the curriculum. Over recent years, the term 'academic language' has come into use, linked to Cummins' notions of BICS and CALP (see p. 56). In *Excellence and Enjoyment: Learning and Teaching for Bilingual Children in the Primary Years* (DfES, 2006b), academic language is characterised in two ways. First it is cognitive language, i.e. the language needed for engaging in cognitively demanding processes such as classifying, hypothesising, generalising and so on. Second, it is the formal language needed for taking part in discussions, argumentation, report writing and other academic activities. Pauline Gibbons (2009, p. 6) uses the related term 'academic literacy', which she explains in the following way:

> ... different disciplines require very different literacy skills, including the reading of different types of texts and the use of different text structures, different presentation formats, different ways of organising language, and different standards of evidence ...

She goes on to suggest (p. 7) that it is perhaps more accurate to talk about 'academic literacies' in the plural, since so much academic language is related to different subjects across the curriculum. This said, the language of different subjects has several distinctive features in common. Academic language is:

> ... more 'written like', less personal, more abstract, more explicit, more lexically dense, and more structured than the face-to-face everyday language with which students are familiar.

ACTIVITY 5.3

Academic language across the curriculum

Analyse some of the language demands of the written material you use with your pupils in different subjects across the curriculum. Choose two or three examples of sustained text from different subjects (they can be online or in printed form) and compare them with each other to see if you can identify features that may create issues of comprehension for your pupils. You could think about some of the following points:

1. Is there particular vocabulary that may need explaining and which may cause difficulties in comprehension? Remember that this is not just about long, complicated words, but sometimes words that may seem simple can cause difficulties because of their ambiguities, e.g. think of the many different meanings of words such as 'set', 'run', 'mark' and so on.

2. Does the grammar of the text seem complicated? How is it different from spoken language? Can you identify what makes it complicated? Could it be made easier without losing its meanings?

3. Is the text structured in a particular way that makes it different from other kinds of texts that your pupils would normally encounter? Does the text structure make it easier or more difficult to understand?

In Chapter 4 of her book, Gibbons provides strategies and activities 'to support student engagement with academic literacy'. Following the ideas of Leo van Leer, she argues for what she calls a 'Janus Curriculum', i.e. one which looks in two directions. First it recognises what the students bring to the classroom in terms of prior learning and knowledge of the world, and then it looks in the other direction, forward to the curriculum outcomes and goals which are the aims of the learning. The four key principles underlying the development of a Janus Curriculum are:

-   **Develop academic language on the basis of what students already know.** Build on your students' prior knowledge to make a bridge to the new learning. Dianne Excel's case study illustrates this in the way May developed her text of the sandstorm.

-   **Move from simple to complex texts.** Introduce concepts and ideas initially with simple, familiar words, building up to more complex, technical language. Use written texts that explain the ideas in simple ways: if there are too many new words and structures, your pupils will find it difficult to follow the ideas. Allow them to activate prior knowledge using their home language if this is appropriate.

-   **Model the use of academic language in your conversations with students.** Think of the learning as a 'language continuum' that moves from simple to complex and try to develop this in your classroom talk. Be aware of the language you use with your pupils and model complex language orally before you expect pupils to use it themselves.

-   **Talk about language in order to develop a metalanguage with your pupils.** This goes beyond simply naming the parts of language but is more about drawing students' attention to how languages work, e.g. by discussing the features of a particular kind of text, comparing how ideas are expressed in written and spoken forms, using relevant technical language in your classroom conversations etc.

I hope that in these principles you can recognise links with many other topics and suggestions throughout this book, especially the ideas about functional grammars in Chapter 2 (p. 32). The functional approach to literacy was actually embedded in the curriculum in England when the National Literacy Strategy was in use between 1997 and 2011, through the extensive work on text types or **genres** that it contained. The 'genre' approach to teaching about texts relates closely to academic literacy. It is based on functional grammar principles and focuses on the authentic language needed to produce different kinds of text. It offers powerful pedagogic possibilities based on the kinds of principles outlined above.

As explained in Chapter 2, the functional approach replaces conventional, prescriptive notions of grammar with the idea that grammar is a set of tools with which a speaker or writer achieves their communicative purposes. García (2009) argues that such an approach to literacy pedagogy has the potential to recognise and value the diversity of language resources which learners generally, and multilingual learners in particular, bring to their classrooms. There are many excellent pedagogic strategies in the National Literacy Strategy materials which were developed in multilingual and multicultural contexts. One, which came from New Zealand, featured the use of big books and shared reading. This proved very effective in many ways, but it has largely disappeared now from classrooms in England. It is well worth reviving some of the key approaches of the strategy, and the materials can still be accessed online on the national archives:

* http://webarchive.nationalarchives.gov.uk/20100603153934/http://nationalstrategies.standards. dcsf.gov.uk/primary/primaryframework/literacyframework

2.2 DEVELOPING READING FOR PLEASURE

In a discussion with a student teacher, eight-year-old Sarah described the importance of reading to her:

> *Reading – it is something where even though you might feel really down, a book can cheer you up, or if you are happy and need to calm down. You can make your own cliff-hangers by stopping half way through a chapter. I like that.*

Sarah has clearly grasped the importance of reading as an emotional resource and a means of pleasure and – at times – escape from the everyday world. Such aspects of reading are often forgotten in classrooms where other demands take precedence. In a very useful free resource, Atkinson (2017) relates reading for pleasure to the National Curriculum and offers much practical advice which is very relevant for EAL learners. The following case study, written by a secondary teacher, Ali O'Grady, illustrates how 'reading for pleasure' can be restored to the classroom – even for teenage boys who are often, albeit unjustifiably, seen as unwilling readers.

READING FOR PLEASURE WITH TEENAGE BOYS – CASE STUDY BY ALI O'GRADY

I teach in a very diverse secondary school, where the cohort has changed dramatically over the last seven years. Currently there are 27 languages spoken by our students, many of whom have arrived new to English. One of my responsibilities is to manage EAL, and I am also an English subject teacher.

At the beginning of the year, I was given an Alternative Curriculum lesson on my timetable – one hour a week with a Year 10 class who were taking a reduced number of option subjects. The group consisted of seven boys, with four out of the seven categorised as EAL learners. We were later joined by a new arrival, who was new to English. For the first term an outside agency was brought in to teach the group numeracy skills and I was asked to focus on literacy skills in the following two terms. The boys were clearly disengaged after the numeracy lessons, so we sat down and discussed what they wanted to do. I suggested reading a book and they were open to this. I searched for a book I thought would engage them. The boys were really sporty, in fact one of them was out of school for a day a week to train with a football club, so I looked for a novel with a sporty theme. Coincidently we had been sent six copies of *Now Is the Time for Running* by Michael Williams (Tamarind Books, 2012). After reading some reviews I decided this would be a good place to start. The novel is a story of survival that opens with a soccer match in the dusty fields of Zimbabwe. Things change when the soldiers arrive and the two brothers in the story are the only survivors. The plot follows them to South Africa and their experiences as illegal immigrants. The World Cup of street soccer features later in the novel, with some very hard-hitting and realistic themes.

We started reading the novel together. I had decided that we would discuss themes and plots, but we would not study the novel in as much detail as we would if we were studying it for GCSE. Instead, we would read the novel for enjoyment and I would not expect any formal work from the students. The students were keen that I read the novel to them and so this was what I did. I asked at various points if they wanted to read but they were adamant, as a group, that they wanted me to read to them. We discussed the novel as we went along. This started as me checking that they were not just sleeping with their eyes open as I read. I found they followed the plot with interest and had strong awareness of some of the hard-hitting themes. Some of the students in the group came from countries where they could have been exposed to violence and were happy to talk, not about personal experiences but general situations in their countries. We also talked about issues that were in the news at the time that related to the themes of the novel and I asked them to watch the news if they could so that we could all join in the discussion.

The boys enjoyed me reading the novel to them and discussing current affairs, asking questions about situations they were unsure of. The size of the group meant that they asked questions openly and without the hesitation that sometimes comes when they are part of a large group. The mix of the group and the number of EAL students meant that they were confident to ask if they were unsure of words or phrases. The English-speaking students supported by explaining meanings. This demonstrated to me the power of allowing the students to read for enjoyment. Taking away the pressure of exams or controlled assessments meant that we could take as much time as we needed, and allowed us to spend that time on discussion that really supported their English language development. I certainly feel that the students expanded their vocabulary and also their knowledge of world affairs and awareness of situations around the world. The students' engagement with the sessions was strong. We would read for the majority of the hour, quite often in the library, and various staff who walked through the library during those times commented on how the students seemed to be enjoying the experience of being read to. My decision not to do any formal work on the novel took away the stress of completing written activities and any work we did was discussion.

We read the novel over the course of a term. The students continued to enjoy reading and indeed continued to ask me to read to them. They had discussions with various members of staff who were interested in what they were doing and were very articulate in explaining what the novel was about.

When we finished the novel, they asked me to find another one to read and so I started to research similar novels. I decided to try to find one set in England as a contrast. The novel I chose was

(Continued)

(Continued)

After Tomorrow by Gillian Cross (published in 2013 by Oxford University Press). Its premise is that the banks have crashed and currency has become worthless. In the Britain of this novel, families go hungry and live in fear of armed raiders. The answer for some people is to leave Britain and this is what the family in the novel do. They go to France and end up in a refugee camp, facing similar problems that we see on the news about refugees and asylum-seekers.

Again this was a novel that engaged the students. They were keen to understand how banks could crash and what the impact would be. The idea of currency being worthless fascinated them, as the novel talked about how the prices for fresh food rocketed. The shortages of food and the lawlessness fascinated them, especially as it was set in this country. They could also relate the experiences of the refugee camps to what they saw on the news. This allowed us to discuss the plight of people in camps, fleeing their countries for whatever reason. These discussions led nicely to some discussion of current affairs and also fitted nicely into the SEAL themes of empathy and thinking about others. Those students who were more aware of world issues, maybe because of personal experiences, were keen to share their knowledge and others were keen to learn. Culturally it was a very mixed group from a number of different countries with very differing experiences and they were very keen to learn from each other. In this context reading allowed us to share personal experiences, and learn about the very real experiences of others.

My brief had been to work on literacy skills with the students and I feel this approach benefited them, especially the EAL learners. They enjoyed reading the books in a small-group environment without the pressure of GCSE exams. They asked about vocabulary they didn't understand and so developed their vocabulary. They were exposed to books they perhaps would not ordinarily have read in the English language, and their confidence in speaking English certainly developed. For some of the students, the social and emotional aspects of the work were really important and helped them develop relationships with other students. I was lucky to have the time and opportunity to read with my group without the formalities of studying for an exam. I believe that reading for enjoyment is vital, especially for EAL students, and being read to can improve the experience. If there are opportunities to read for pleasure I would highly recommend this approach – indeed I feel it should be an element of the curriculum for EAL learners.

CHAPTER SUMMARY

There are four learning outcomes for this chapter. They each focus on a different dimension of reading, both in a general way and in relation to the needs of EAL learners. Reading is presented as a complex set of processes and skills that need to be orchestrated by the individual reader. The debates about phonics were raised in the chapter, with a discussion about the ways in which phonics can and cannot help children to become independent readers. This is an aspect of reading you will have to think carefully about, reflecting on the ways in which phonics might help or hinder your own pupils in their development as readers. Finally, the importance of reading for pleasure is illustrated by means of a case study with teenage boys.

Self-assessment questions

1.   What issues do you think you might face in developing independent reading with EAL learners? Try to think about this in relation to some pupils that you know.

2. In what ways do you think the debates about phonics have either helped or hindered teachers in meeting the needs of EAL learners? How do you think you will resolve some of the issues around phonics in your own teaching?

3. How do you think the principles underpinning identity texts could be brought into different subjects across the curriculum?

4. Do you allow yourself enough time to read for pleasure? If so, how do you communicate the value of this to your pupils? If not, has reading the chapter given you the incentive to begin reading for pleasure?

FURTHER READING

Cummins, J. and Early, M. (eds) (2011) *Identity Texts: The Collaborative Creation of Power in Multilingual Schools.* **London: Trentham Books/Institute of Education Press.**

Cummins and Early relate the notion of identity texts to pedagogy. Their ideas are illustrated by case studies written by teachers and students from different countries. The emphasis is on the ways that such approaches can promote empowerment and transformational learning for students from diverse backgrounds.

Gregory, E. (2008) *Learning to Read in a New Language: Making Sense of Words and Worlds.* **London: Sage.**

This book is one of the very few which focuses on children who are learning to read in a language different from their mother tongue. It argues that plurilingualism should be at the centre of literacy tuition and offers a practical approach to teaching, based on sociocultural theory, which can be used with individuals, small groups and whole classes. Gregory argues that reading must make sense to children; there is no common method, but rather a shared aim to which they aspire, that of making sense of a new world through new words.

STUDYING AT MASTER'S LEVEL

Critical reading:

Read Chapter 4 'The Context of the Mind', in Eve Gregory's' book:

Gregory, E. (2008) *Learning to Read in a New Language: Making Sense of Words and Worlds.* **London: Sage.**

In this chapter, Gregory argues that reading is 'a mental and linguistic process' and that new learners need to 'situate' themselves in 'the context of the mind' as they make sense of reading. These ideas come from sociocultural theory. Gregory gives us many examples of the ways that young children make sense of learning to read, and what is striking with the multilingual learners she describes is the way in which they naturally and creatively make links between what they know in one language with the new language they are learning.

(Continued)

(Continued)

After reading Chapter 4, consider the following questions, ideally in discussion with colleagues:

1. Gregory uses Vygotsky's example of a broom handle to show how young children begin to symbolise. What point does she make, and how does she relate this to the processes of learning to read?

2. Gregory characterises learning another language as learning that labels cannot be 'stuck' to objects. What does she mean by this and what is its significance for learning to read?

3. What are the essential contrasts between the 'bottom-up' and the 'top-down' theories of learning to read as Gregory describes them? Which do you find more helpful for understanding what children do when learning to read?

4. On p. 112, what conclusions does Gregory report from the systematic review of phonics teaching carried out by Greg Brooks and the group at Sheffield University in 2006? How far do these conclusions resonate with your own experience of teaching reading, especially to multilingual and EAL learners?

5. What does Gregory argue to be the key issue for young readers like Husna, Naseema and Lina, who she describes towards the end of the chapter? How do their experiences differ from Nicole, who appears at the start of the chapter? What aspect of language does Gregory see as key to the development of young multilingual and EAL children as independent readers?

REFERENCES

Atkinson, P. (2017) *Promoting Reading for Pleasure.* Free resource available at https://ukla.org/downloads/Reading_for_Pleasure.pdf (accessed 19 September 2018).

BBC News (2009) *Powerful Sandstorm Hits Riyadh.* Available at http://news.bbc.co.uk/1/hi/world/middle_east/7935689.stm (accessed 19 September 2018).

Bernhard, J. K. and Cummins, J. (2004) *Cognitive Engagement and Identity Investment in Literacy Development among English Language Learners: Evidence from the Early Authors Program.* English Language Learners Conference, National Center for Culturally Responsive Educational Systems, Scottsdale, AZ, November.

Campbell, R. (2011) *Miscue Analysis in the Classroom,* 3rd edn. UKLA (United Kingdom Literacy Association). A substantial extract is available online at: https://ukla.org/extracts/Minibook_32.pdf (accessed 19 September 2018).

Cummins, J. and Early, M. (eds) (2011) *Identity Texts: The Collaborative Creation of Power in Multilingual Schools.* London: Trentham Books/Institute of Education Press.

Department for Education and Science (DfES) (2006a) *Independent Review of the Teaching of Early Reading* (Rose Review). Available at http://dera.ioe.ac.uk/5551/2/report.pdf (accessed 19 September 2018).

Department for Education and Science (DfES) (2006b) *Excellence and Enjoyment: Learning and Teaching for Bilingual Children in the Primary Years.* Available at https://www.naldic.org.uk/Resources/NALDIC/Teaching%20and%20Learning/pri_pubs_bichd_213306_015.pdf (accessed 19 September 2018).

García, O. (2009) *Bilingual Education in the 21st Century: A Global Perspective.* Chichester: Wiley-Blackwell.

Gregory, E., Long, S. and Volk, D. (eds) (2004) *Many Pathways to Literacy: Young Children Learning with Siblings, Grandparents, Peers and Communities.* London: RoutledgeFalmer.

Gibbons, P. (2009) *English Learners, Academic Literacy and Thinking: Learning in the Challenge Zone.* Portsmouth, NH: Heinemann.

Gussin Paley, V. (1991) *The Boy Who Would Be a Helicopter*. Cambridge, MA: Harvard University Press.

United Kingdom Literacy Association (UKLA) (2010) *Teaching Reading: What the Evidence Says*. Available free at https://www.teachers.org.uk/files/UKLATeachingReading%5b1%5d.pdf (accessed 19 September 2018).

Ward, G. (2007) *Racing to English*. Over 300 language activities available at http://www.racingtoenglish.co.uk/ (accessed 19 September 2018).

ANSWERS TO ACTIVITY 5.2

1.

Word	Phonemes/ graphemes	Segments
straight	5	s/t/r/aigh/t
young	3	y/ou/ng
four	2	f/our
leopard	5	l/eo/p/ar/d
thoughtful	6	th/ough/t/f/u/l
rainy	4	r/ai/n/y
broad	4	b/r/oa/d

2. four; thoughtful; broad.

3. au – autumn; aw – saw; or – for; al – walk; augh – caught; oor – floor; ore – more; etc.

4.

c	v	c	c
p	a-e	s	t
p	eo	p	le
f	i	n	d
b	u	m	p
s	i	n	k

5.

g/ir/l
y/ou/ng
b/u/s/y
s/p/oo/n/s
c/ar/t
f/l/i/ng
w/i/ng

6
PLANNING FOR LEARNING ACROSS THE CURRICULUM FOR MULTILINGUAL AND EAL LEARNERS

LEARNING OUTCOMES

This chapter will help you to achieve the following learning outcomes:

- develop understanding of how to plan to promote content and language learning across the curriculum;

- gain strategic knowledge of ways of working with colleagues to meet the needs of multilingual and EAL learners;

- gain greater understanding of the importance of speaking and listening for learning generally and for multilingual and EAL learners in particular.

INTRODUCTION

This chapter provides a framework for planning and strategies to promote multilingual and EAL pupils' English language and content learning across the curriculum. They are all based on the theories about language, multilingualism and learning discussed in Chapters 2 and 3, and the principles listed at the end of Part 1 of the book. Cummins' ideas relating to the common underlying proficiency (CUP), basic interpersonal communication 'skills' (BICS) and cognitive academic language proficiency (CALP) underpin section 1 as they help you to think about planning for progression in different subjects across the curriculum. The case study by Oksana Afitska closely analyses the talk in a KS2 science lesson and so highlights the important role of talk in learning. Section 2 focuses on the ways that subject teachers and EAL specialists can work together in planning and teaching, mainly in secondary contexts. The two case studies, by Pete Ruse and Linda Sadler, illustrate planning and partnership teaching strategies. Section 3 focuses on the role of talk for learning, and ways of working with new arrivals. It contains two case studies, the first by Catherine Porritt on the Talking Partners programme and the second by Ana Korzun on planning for a new arrival in a secondary classroom. Throughout the chapter, there are discussion points and activities to help you think about the ideas you are reading about. There are some suggestions for further reading at the end of the chapter along with guidance for Master's level study.

These are the sections and subsections of this chapter:

1 PLANNING ACROSS THE CURRICULUM

1.1 STARTING POINTS – DEVELOPING PLANS

Developing medium-term plans or units of work and short-term plans or lessons to promote the learning of multilingual and EAL pupils is complex. Do not be tempted simply to depend on plans you find on the internet or in published schemes of work. They may give you some starting points and resources, but they do not have your pupils in mind. You need to spend time thinking about your own pupils and their particular needs. This will also help you understand much more fully what you need to teach and why. Your lessons will be much better, as will the learning and behaviour of your pupils. You will also build up a stock of ideas and strategies that you will be able to use over and over again in your career.

For pupils who are at the early stages of learning English, there are always two strands involved in their learning. They need to learn:

•   the curriculum content;

and they also need to learn

•   the English language in increasingly academic ways.

Of course, this is true for all pupils, but it is clearly more important for many EAL learners who often need to catch up with their peers in terms of their knowledge and use of English. Some EAL learners may be ahead of their classmates in their understanding of the concepts and content in particular curriculum subjects, but they lack the English vocabulary and grammar to show you what they know. This is often the case with mathematics. It can be very frustrating if such pupils are given tasks to do that are far below their academic capability in a subject. It is very important that you find out whether your 'new to English' pupils have been to school in their countries of origin and try to get some idea of what they may have learnt. There are some ideas in Chapter 8 (p. 189) that can help you to do this.

The functional model of language and grammar introduced in Chapter 2 will help you to clarify the language demands of the subjects you are teaching. It reminds us that we need to be clear about two important language-related elements in planning, which are:

- what we are expecting our pupils to be able to *do* with the language they are learning;

- the *kinds* of language they will need in order to do these things.

This means that we have to go beyond thinking about just the key vocabulary that our pupils need in order to understand concepts and content in different subjects across the curriculum. We also need to think about how to help them become familiar with the ways the language is organised grammatically and textually – in other words, the kinds of spoken and written texts (or genres) they will be using and constructing in their learning. For example, in science, they will no doubt be following instructions – as well as making up their own – and perhaps writing reports; in history and other humanities subjects they will be taking part in discussions and debates, writing narratives and so on.

Remember that texts can be spoken as well as written. We now feel very familiar with the idea in literacy of teaching the different text types pupils need to know for their writing, but the suggestion that we can also teach them the different ways in which they need to use language in speaking is a fairly new one. This will be discussed further when we introduce the Cummins' quadrant.

ACTIVITY 6.1

Text types for learning

Create a table like that below showing the main different kinds of text that pupils will come across in school. Remember that the text types occur in different subjects. In the second column, list the subject areas for which you think each text type is most relevant. In the third column, list some of the different kinds of texts that you have used with pupils in different subjects across the curriculum. Include spoken as well as written texts. There are some examples to start you off.

Text type	Curriculum area	Example of text
Reports	Science History	• A written report of a 'fair test' that the pupils have conducted. • An oral role play of warriors reporting to their chief what happened in a Viking raid on a Northumbrian village.
Discussion texts		
Reference texts (explanations)	Geography	• A weather forecast as part of a radio or TV programme.

Text type	Curriculum area	Example of text
Persuasive texts		
Recount		
Instructions		

Relating different kinds of text to areas of the curriculum in this way helps us to think about the language demands of all the different subject areas and of the particular tasks we are asking our pupils to do.

1.2 THE CUMMINS' QUADRANT

Cummins' ideas about the CUP, BICS and CALP are explained fully in Chapter 3. They have important implications for your planning in three dimensions, namely:

- conceptual development;

- language development;

- progression.

Cummins' concept of the CUP emphasises the importance of *all* the knowledge of any and all languages that pupils bring to their classrooms and how this can be seen as a resource to support their learning of any subject. We need to find ways to tap into the full repertoire of our pupils' language resources.

The BICS and CALP concepts have many implications for medium-term planning and also for lesson planning. Pupils need to progress in their learning from context-based, cognitively less demanding activities that mainly use informal language (BICS) to the more academic and cognitively demanding tasks that require more academic language (CALP). We need to start with activities at the level where pupils can use their BICS-related language skills, and gradually move into activities which are more demanding cognitively and where CALP-related language capacity and knowledge come into play. This will scaffold pupils' academic learning and help them to develop deep and rich conceptual understanding of the subjects they are learning. At the same time, they will be developing confidence as speakers and writers of English in a wide range of ways.

Figure 6.1 shows the Cummins' quadrant. Each axis can be thought of as a continuum, with contextual support on the horizontal axis and cognitive demand on the vertical. The horizontal axis, moving from left to right, helps you to sequence your activities from context-embedded learning with lots of hands-on activities and artefacts to activities which are less dependent on the immediate context. The vertical axis relates to the degree of cognitive demand in a task, linked to the language demands. Moving upwards goes from tasks that are not very demanding to increasingly cognitively challenging activities.

Good planning will ensure that pupils always move from activities with strong contextual support to less contextually supported ones which are more dependent on linguistic cues and the pupils' own knowledge of language. The following vignette, in mathematics, gives an example of progression through the quadrants.

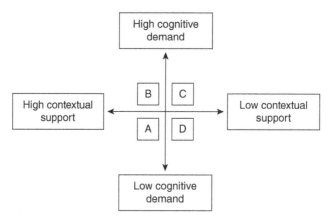

Figure 6.1 The Cummins' quadrant

VIGNETTE

Progression in mathematics in Reception

If you are teaching children in Reception or Year 1 about the properties of different shapes, the progression from activities with low cognitive demand and high contextual support to activities with high cognitive demand and low contextual support and how they fit into the quadrants may look something like the following.

- *Quadrant A* - activities which involve pupils in touching and handling plastic shapes, talking about them, making patterns and pictures with them, describing, matching and beginning to compare them.

- *Quadrant B* - activities which move pupils to seeing and talking about the shapes as visual representations, such as matching shapes to pictures, finding objects in the classroom which are particular shapes, talking about what is the same, similar or different about a collection of shapes or pictures.

- *Quadrant C* - activities which encourage pupils to think and talk (and perhaps write and draw) about the shapes without immediate visual or concrete support, such as answering questions (or making up their own questions) about a square and how it is different from a triangle, making a chart about the similarities and differences of shapes, drawing shapes following instructions given by the teacher or other adult, or their peers.

- *Quadrant D* - there should be no activities in this quadrant as they would not promote the pupils' learning.

The kinds of activities that can fit into each quadrant, defined by their conceptual and language demands, are categorised in Figure 6.2.

At all stages, talk remains a key vehicle for learning. It is equally important for activities in quadrants A, B and C. As you progress, you need to plan activities for your pupils to use talk in more sophisticated and adventurous ways, at the same time as supporting them in trying out ways of speaking

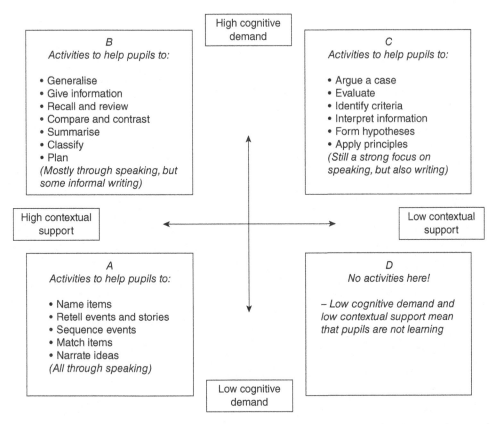

Figure 6.2 Planning for learning using the Cummins' quadrant

which may not be familiar to them. Pauline Gibbons (1998) talks about the 'teacher-guided reporting' stage of teaching. This equates to quadrant C, when pupils will be talking in much more formal, discursive and analytic ways than they were at the start of the activity. This helps them both to develop confidence as speakers of English and to think about and learn the new concepts in the subject you are teaching. Thus their understanding of the content is enhanced and they are also using the language they will need for writing. The principles of **dialogic talk**, developed by Wolfe and Alexander (2008; see Chapter 8, pp. 176–177) and the list of functions of language will also help you think about progression in planning your activities.

To illustrate this, here is an example of planning for a set of story-based activities in literacy, relevant for both primary and secondary pupils. The key learning objectives are to have pupils write their own version of a story and write from a particular character's viewpoint. A sequence of activities based on the story that helps pupils to progress through quadrants A, B and C might look something like Figure 6.3. The pupils may not actually get down to any formal writing at all in the first three or four lessons of the sequence, but when they do come to the task of writing, they will have a rich stock of words, structures, ideas and understanding of the story to bring to it.

Hall et al. (2001) have some examples of planning using the Cummins' quadrant which show the progression of activities in science.

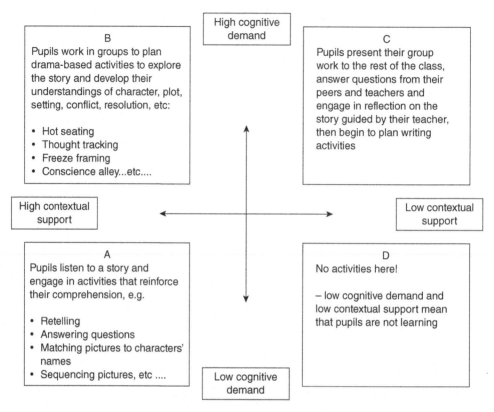

High cognitive demand

B
Pupils work in groups to plan drama-based activities to explore the story and develop their understandings of character, plot, setting, conflict, resolution, etc:

• Hot seating
• Thought tracking
• Freeze framing
• Conscience alley...etc....

C
Pupils present their group work to the rest of the class, answer questions from their peers and teachers and engage in reflection on the story guided by their teacher, then begin to plan writing activities

High contextual support

Low contextual support

A
Pupils listen to a story and engage in activities that reinforce their comprehension, e.g.

• Retelling
• Answering questions
• Matching pictures to characters' names
• Sequencing pictures, etc ....

D
No activities here!

– low cognitive demand and low contextual support mean that pupils are not learning

Low cognitive demand

Figure 6.3 Cummins' quadrant and literacy planning

ACTIVITY 6.2

Planning for progression

Using the Cummins' quadrant and the ideas and diagrams above, look at some of your planning in a particular area of the curriculum. See if you can identify which activities might fit into each of the four quadrants, and consider whether you could re-order the activities to build in better progression or whether you need more activities in any quadrant.

1.3 FOCUSING ON LANGUAGE DEMANDS

The Principles for Planning for Multilingual Learners (p. 73) emphasise the importance of speaking and listening and of hands-on activities to provide pupils with rich opportunities for learning that can meet individual needs in a range of ways. Equally important is the need to think carefully about the language demands of the activities you are planning for your pupils. This means asking two key questions of your activities.

1.   What key vocabulary and grammatical structures are involved in the particular concept and/or content that is the objective of the learning?

2. How can pupils be supported through the activity in developing their understanding and capacity to use the language independently?

Key vocabulary refers to the words that underpin the concepts pupils are learning, and grammatical structures are those words in context, as part of whole texts. Learning key vocabulary is not always simple – many words in English have different meanings in different contexts. This can be confusing for all pupils (and many adults), not just EAL learners. Think of the meaning of the word 'relief' in a geography lesson or on the label of a bottle of cough medicine. Think of the word 'materials' in a science lesson or in a dress shop. Think of words that we use every day in particular phrases that can seem contradictory – 'running fast' is about moving quickly, but 'sticking fast' is about staying still. Many words have everyday meanings that pupils will be familiar with, but then very particular meanings when they are used in school subjects.

RESEARCH FOCUS

The meanings of 'half'

One of the early KS1 mathematics SATs questions (for seven-year-olds), set in 1997, was about children having soup for lunch. On the test paper, there was a simple picture of four children sitting round a dining table with bowls of soup in front of them. The question read something like:

Half the pupils had chicken soup and half the pupils had tomato soup. Draw a circle round half the pupils.

The examiners were surprised to find that almost 70 per cent of the pupils who took the test got this problem wrong, as mathematically it was not difficult. When the scripts were analysed, it was found that many pupils had drawn a circle round half of each child in the picture, rather than two out of the four pupils. It was clear that the people setting the test had one meaning for the word 'half' while many of the children had another.

(Example from an examiners' moderation meeting)

All pupils develop semantic strength and agility by having the opportunity, in a language-rich environment, to play with words, to encounter words in a range of contexts and texts and to make their own connections in word meanings. Here are some simple activities and ideas that can make your classroom a language-rich environment and encourage your pupils to be enthusiastic, curious and analytical about words and their meanings.

- ***Displays.*** Find as many ways as possible to have vocabulary related to the concepts you are teaching on display round the classroom – word mats, word walls, labels, word banks and so on. Change them regularly to maintain pupils' interest. From time to time, mix up the labels and have pupils sort them out. Use multilingual lists and labels whenever you can. Ask your multilingual pupils to provide equivalent words and encourage your class to compare the words in different languages for particular things and ideas.

- ***Washing lines.*** This is a good activity to reinforce pupils' understandings of words and develop awareness of shades of meaning. Prepare sets of words that show different degrees of meaning, e.g. size (minuscule, tiny, small, middling, big, huge, gigantic); volume (whisper, mutter, mumble, grunt, shout, scream, screech). Other categories could be heat, probability, speed and so on – choose categories that link with what pupils are learning across the curriculum. Pupils in groups put the words in order, discussing and justifying their choices. Then they stand in line so the class can see the words, and explain their decisions. Finally, the words are pegged on a washing line strung across the classroom so that everyone can see them and use them in their speaking and writing.

- **Odd one out**. This activity is based on sets of three or four words, which all have something in common, but there is always a feature shared by two but not all three. The point is that pupils make their own decisions and justify them. Here are some examples:

  o   Sea, river, canal: they are all bodies of water, but 'sea' is the odd one out because it has three letters; 'canal' is the odd one out because it is man-made; and 'river' is the odd one out because it has a 'v' in it.

  o   Knight, sword, stone: they are all from traditional stories, but 'knight' is the odd one out because it does not begin with 's' and 'stone' is the odd one out because it does not have a silent letter.

  o   Bird, fly, feather: they are all to do with birds, but 'feather' is the odd one out because it has four phonemes and the others have three; 'bird' is the odd one out because it ends in a consonant sound and the other two end in vowel sounds.

As you can see, there can be a range of answers to do with phonics, spelling, meaning or grammar. Groups of pupils can be given sets of words to discuss and come up with their own answers, then the same words can be given to another group. One of the benefits of this game is that it encourages pupils to think of meanings above individual word level, and this helps to develop their understanding of texts.

WORDS, SENTENCES AND TEXTS

As we saw in Chapter 2, words cannot be fully understood in isolation. Key vocabulary in lists is not enough to help pupils develop the deeper understandings that are needed to promote the academic language required for real, powerful learning and achievement. Pupils need rich experiences of words used in a wide range of authentic **texts** (both spoken and written) in order to develop as capable speakers, readers and writers. They need to analyse texts in order to understand how they work and how to make the right choices in their own writing. The '5Ws' questions introduced in Chapter 2 are helpful in analysing the language demands of the concepts and content that pupils are learning across the curriculum.

A very useful strategy here is to take a cross-curricular approach to teaching literacy. For example, you can use topics for writing in literacy for which your pupils already have practical experience and knowledge from their learning in other subjects. This will help to make their writing meaningful, authentic and purposeful. For example, after studying electricity in science, pupils could write instructions to make a circuit in their literacy lesson. After finding out about the Vikings in history, they could write a newspaper report about a raid on a village.

In a language-rich learning environment, analytic activities can help pupils develop academic language and independence as readers and writers. **Graphic organisers** (or key visuals) are a visual way of helping pupils understand text structure, how ideas are linked in texts, and how to report, explain, justify, discuss and argue about the concepts they are learning. They can be used to illustrate cause and effect, processes, cycles and so on. Pupils could complete them after a science task with the information they have learnt, or after reading a non-fiction text in a particular genre. Examples of graphic organisers can be found at: https://ealresources.bell-foundation.org.uk/teachers/great-ideas-graphic-organisers.

Text reconstruction activities (sometimes called **DARTs** – directed activities related to texts) are all about getting pupils to think beyond word level when they are reading. Pupils are expected to put back together a text that has been disrupted in some way. It can be cut into sections, and pupils have to work in a group to agree on how to reconstruct it. Or pupils can be given the first part of a sentence and then asked to choose the correct ending from a selection on the interactive whiteboard. Again, the emphasis needs to be on their explaining and justifying their choices. DARTs provide excellent opportunities for discussion as an introduction to writing. Examples of DARTs activities can be found at: https://ealresources.bell-foundation.org.uk/teachers/great-ideas-darts.

ACTIVITY 6.3

Content and language

Choose a short non-fiction text from a topic you are planning to teach or a book or other resource you are using in your teaching. Using the 5Ws (see p. 29), analyse the type of text it is and consider what language demands it places on EAL learners. Prepare a graphic organiser that would help pupils analyse and understand the text.

If possible, try your ideas out with a group of pupils. Review and adapt this for use in a future lesson.

The following case study is taken from a dataset of 20 lessons collected in five primary schools in Sheffield, South Yorkshire as part of the EAL Science Project (a collaborative project between the University of Sheffield and Sheffield City Council, 2013–15). Lessons were observed and recorded and the transcripts were then analysed to identify the strategies the teachers used to integrate science and language learning.

TEACHING SCIENCE TO EAL LEARNERS AT KS2 – CASE STUDY BY OKSANA AFITSKA

The 'Keeping Warm' science lesson reported here was observed in a Year 4 class in a school where 90 per cent of pupils are categorised as EAL. It lasted 90 minutes and included many examples of effective teaching strategies that could be used in both primary and secondary settings. The lesson began with a warm-up activity where the pupils were asked to put word cards into two separate categories, the names of which were not provided. As the teacher gave the instruction she used gestures alongside her verbal instruction to reinforce the points of the task. For example, as she said:

... two separate categories, please

she stretched out two fingers. This supported those pupils who might not be familiar with English numbers and also reinforced the instruction. She kept using this strategy throughout the lesson.

(Continued)

(Continued)

The pupils completed the card-grouping activity and identified that the two categories were 'hot' and 'cold'. The teacher then asked them to come up with their own words to be put into the 'hot' and 'cold' categories. The words underlined emphasise how she did this:

> I want you to think of any words or any vocabulary related to keeping warm that you might know ... it does not matter whether you got one word two words twenty words ... I want you to talk to the person sitting next to you ...

In this way, the teacher was achieving the following teaching and learning objectives:

- activating further the pupils' existing knowledge and vocabulary on the topic;

- identifying any possible gaps in their knowledge prior to introducing the new topic;

- using the paraphrasing technique to increase the chances of pupils understanding her instruction (and also expanding their vocabulary repertoire);

- reinforcing the idea that it doesn't matter how much or little learners say, thus putting beginner and less confident EAL learners at ease;

- encouraging peer support in learning.

The pupils spent 16 minutes doing peer-work activities during the 90-minute lesson. This allowed them to try out their 'new' linguistic knowledge (for example, a word from their passive vocabulary) and 'scientific' ideas. The teacher also had an opportunity to monitor individual pupils' responses more closely and provide them with targeted one-to-one help where needed.

Having completed the activity in their pairs and discussed a few examples with the teacher, the pupils called the words out one by one and the teacher clarified, exemplified and put them into context as needed to support the pupils' comprehension of these words. The following extracts illustrate this classroom interaction. The words underlined show the actions the teacher performed along with her talk:

Monitoring peer-work, eliciting specific vocabulary items from the learners (Freezing episode)	Plenary work, collecting pupils' responses, clarifying and exemplifying the answers (Chilli episode)
T: What's the word? Hot ____ P3: Boiling T: Boiling, lovely [...] T: Cold - what's the word for cold [Teacher wraps herself with her hands and makes a movement as if she is shaking] ... you are cold, you are ___? P4: Freezing T: Freezing ... write it down.	P5: Chilli T: Chilli. Do you mean chilly as in cold? You are chilly [teacher wraps herself with her hands as if trying to make herself feel warmer] or do you mean chilli as if you eat and it is hot? [Teacher makes a movement pretending that she is eating something.] P5: Hot T: Hot, hot chilli that you might eat ... sensation, heat. OK.

Throughout the lesson the learners produced different kinds of written language, starting from simply copying the lesson topic from the board into their books and drawing spider diagrams using single words, to gradually progressing to writing their own questions in full and instructions in the form of bullet point lists. Whenever the learners were asked to produce written language, the teacher gave them an example or two of what to write and how to write it. For example, in the following extract the teacher reminded the learners to use sentence starters to help them construct their sentences.

Sentence starters episode

T: I want you to think of five questions that you might want to find the answer to, so you can use the sentence starters to help you - who, what, which, how, does or when. [...] You might ask a question like erm ... how do we measure heat or how do we measure temperature, OK? You might ask a question like erm ... what happens when we leave an ice cream out in the hot weather, OK?

Once the learners finished writing their questions, the teacher elicited a wide range of responses, providing extensive feedback to the learners on their questions and inviting them to elaborate on their responses further, both linguistically and conceptually in relation to science, as is illustrated in the following example:

Elicitation of responses and provision of teacher feedback

P1: How do you measure the heat?

T: How do you measure ___?

P1: Heat

T: Heat. How do you measure heat? OK. P2?

P2: How does the [inaudible]

T: How does the sun ___?

P2: How does the snow melt

T: Ah, how does the snow melt? or Why does snow melt? Excellent. Well done.

[...]

P5: How does temperature grow?

T: How does temperature grow? or What makes temperature rise? OK. Anybody else got a question, P6?

P6: Does the ice cream melt?

T: Does ice cream melt? Where? Be a bit more specific. Does ice cream melt ___ ... Where?

P6: ... in a ... in a ...

T: Does ice cream melt when you are in an igloo? It may be different than when you are in a sun. OK. [...] P7?

P7: What would happen if you left an ice cream in a sun?

T: Good. What would happen if you left ice cream in the sun? P8?

P8: Why does the chocolate melt in the sun?

T: Why does chocolate melt in the sun?

The teacher accepted responses that had already been given by other learners in the class just as readily as the original ones and acknowledged them as equally valid contributions. For less confident EAL learners, the simple act of uttering a sentence in an unfamiliar language in front of the whole class is a major achievement and contribution to the lesson, and they learn a great deal from listening to their more advanced peers.

Having elicited and discussed the learners' questions, the teacher invited them to think about and explore their ideas about certain scientific facts. As she elicited the pupils' responses she encouraged them to produce answers in full sentences. In this way, she maintained the dual focus of her science lesson - teaching scientific concepts and supporting learners' English language development.

(Continued)

(Continued)

Full sentences episode

T: P1, what happens when the ice cream is left out in the sun?

P1: It melts.

T: Right. Full sentence please.

P1: When you leave an ice cream <u>outside where it is boiling weather</u> it melts.

T: OK. It melts. Anyone else can answer this question. P2, full sentence please.

P2: Ice cream – What happens when an ice cream is left in the sun? [P2 reads this question from the board] Ice cream – When you leave ice cream in the sun it will melt <u>into a liquid</u>.

T: OK. Anybody else got an answer?

P3: When you em ... leave ice cream em ... <u>outside</u> in <u>a really</u> hot weather it turn into a <u>really runny</u> liquid.

T: OK. Right. Second question then [...]

This example also shows how creative pupils can become in forming their full sentences, sometimes providing fuller syntactic structures in their answers than are actually needed (e.g. P1 and P3's responses).

As the lesson progressed, the teacher spent some time eliciting specific vocabulary items from the learners. This practice is linked to **formative assessment** in that it allows teachers to probe their pupils' knowledge, identify gaps in it and instantly adjust their teaching, where needed, to address the needs of the class. Here are two examples. The words underlined show how the teacher focused on vocabulary.

Temperature episode	Thermometer episode
P1: The decking will feel very cold or cold because at night it will be very windy and colder than in the day.	T: What do you think this bit of a thermometer might be called? Make a guess.
T: ... OK <u>I am looking for one word in particular</u> let's see if anyone can get it into their sentence, P2?	P1: It might be top
	T: Top. Could be. Now you should all know the answer to this. <u>What is this bit called</u> [points to the body of the thermometer]? Make the link to maths. What is this bit called?
P2: It will be cold or very cold because the sun erm ... got erm ...	P2: Value
Class: down	T: No, not value
P2: and then the moon will come and it won't be hot	P3: Length
T: OK	T: What would it be in maths?
P3: the temperature [inaudible]	P4: Scales
T: Um? [referring to P3's utterance]	T: Scales. Scale part of the thermometer. <u>Does anybody know what this bottom part is called?</u> I'll give you a clue. The gardeners at the moment are planting them in the garden in the school.
P3: the temperature will [go down]	
T: Excellent. Good boy. The temperature changes at night-time. What happens during the night-time?	P5: Soil
	T: It's not called soil.
P3: The temperature goes down.	P1: Bottom
T: Yeah, the temperature falls [teacher makes a hand movement downwards] at night-time.	T: Bulb. Its called bulb. It's like a flower that has a bulb. A flower. Same name but different meaning. This is called a bulb of a thermometer.

Thoughout the lesson, the learners actively enquired about unknown or unclear words as they came to their attention. This practice is very important for EAL classrooms and demonstrates the learners' active and meaningful engagement, and that the teacher was able to create a classroom environment where her learners felt safe to raise questions. In this class, learners also felt free to provide help to their peers not only in group work but also in plenary sessions, as is evidenced in the 'Temperature' episode above, demonstrating yet again the level of their concentration and the extent of their engagement with the activity.

At certain points in the lesson, the teacher chose not to probe the learners' knowledge but to provide them directly with the explanations of specific vocabulary items, perhaps to save the lesson time for the discussion of more 'important', fundamental scientific concepts related directly to the topic. She did so in two ways: implicitly, by rephrasing her utterance, or explicitly, by providing contextual synonyms and actually showing what the item meant.

Occurring episode
T: Something is happening, the change is occurring ... it is either heat is added or heat is taken away from something
Decking and tarmac episode
T: Decking, so the decking is here [shows], the steps [...]
The tarmac - which means the concrete [makes a hand movement parallel to the floor]

Finally, the teacher made extensive use of the whiteboard throughout the lesson to provide visual clues to support the learners in:

- learning new vocabulary items;

- reading in the target language;

- comprehending instructions and core lesson information in the target language.

Learning new vocabulary and subject-related concepts
T: OK, most of you agree that temperature means whether something is hot or cold. OK, let's find out. [Teacher reveals the definition on the board] Temperature is a measure, right, well done who said this, of how hot or cold something is.
P1: Thermometer
PP: Ah, that's what I was gonna say!
T: Shh! We measure temperature with the thermometer. And those who do not know, this is just one example of a thermometer [teacher reveals a picture of a thermometer on the board]
Comprehending instructions
T: OK, so, question - What happens when an ice cream is left in the sun? Question number two - How are ice cubes made? Talk to the person next to you, see if you can come up with the answer straight away.
T: Can anybody think of another example when heat is either added or taken away from something?
Reading in the target language
T: OK, reading the thermometer. Eyes on board. [...] Right, at the moment these one, two, three, four, five, six statements are all mixed up [statements are written on the interactive whiteboard]. This is how to read the thermometer properly. What I'd like you to do with your partner is read them. We will read them together. And I want you to shuffle them in a right order [...] [Teacher reads the statements one by one and learners follow.]

(Continued)

(Continued)

Labelling

T: This is a thermometer. We have to label the thermometer. Scale - is this bit [teacher writes label on the picture on the interactive whiteboard]. Stem - the big long part [teacher shows the stem and labels it].

P1: Stem

T: And a bulb

P7: is at the bottom.

P2: Bulb

T: Bulb. Stem [shows]. You have to imagine - like the way the flower grows - bulb is at the bottom, stem is the bit that comes up [shows]. OK.

Notice how in the 'labelling' excerpt, the learners repeat the names of parts of the thermometer to themselves after the teacher. This behaviour suggests that 'noticing' and active learning are taking place. The teacher ends the lesson by implementing a quick **summative assessment** procedure to monitor the extent to which the learning objectives were achieved.

Summative assessment episode

T: What is temperature, P7?

P7: Temperature is ___

T: What is the definition of temperature?

P10: Temperature is it measures hot or cold.

T: Good. Temperature measures how hot or cold something is. OK. What do we measure temperature in?

PPs: Celsius

T: Celsius degrees and ___?

PPs: Fahrenheit

T: Good. What instrument measures temperature?

P2: [no response]

T: What do you handle? What have you been learning about all afternoon?

P2: Thermometer

T: Good. Thermometer measures temperature. Full sentences please [...]

---

2 WORKING WITH COLLEAGUES – SKILLS FOR EAL SPECIALIST TEACHERS

2.1 THE IMPORTANCE OF JOINT PLANNING

In many schools, there are teachers and Higher Level Teaching Assistants (HLTAs) who have specific responsibility for EAL learners. It is essential that they have time to work together with subject coordinators, subject teachers in secondary schools and class teachers in primary schools to develop joint planning which meets both the language needs and curriculum needs of pupils. This takes time, but the benefits are considerable. The following case study, written by a subject coordinator and an EAL teacher in a secondary school, shows how this can be done.

PLANNING AN RE LESSON – CASE STUDY
BY PETE RUSE AND LINDA SANDLER

The head of EAL in one secondary school negotiated planning to fit in with whole-school priorities related to literacy development. The focus for the lessons would be talk as a rehearsal for writing in RE. Given the critical importance of exam results to the school, it was decided that Year 11 would be the priority. A group was selected that included some International New Arrivals (INAs) (i.e. those with fewer than four years in the UK), some of whom were at an early stage of acquiring English language. The head of EAL was already supporting this group. The language priority identified was writing answers to GCSE exam questions that required an extended response. The topic to be covered in the weeks that fitted in with the project timetable was 'The Causes of War', using Darfur, Sudan as a case study, a part of the 'Peace and Conflict' module of Edexcel GCSE RE.

The chosen Year 11 group consisted of 11 boys and 18 girls. One learner had a statement of special educational needs. Learners had a range of attainment from a predicted F grade to a B. Nine learners were INAs, five of whom were in the early stages of English language development. Three of these were at very early stages and of these, two had had full schooling in their country of origin and had good academic skills in their first languages (L1). In a planning meeting, the two teachers (RE teacher and EAL teacher) decided on groupings that supported language development and encouraged talk for learning. The criteria taken into account were:

- mixed levels of English language development;

- target grade;

- gender;

- friendship (or not);

- previous engagement with content.

The two early-stage EAL learners had high target grades, reflecting their academic competence in their L1s, and were grouped accordingly – the teachers were very aware of the dangers of placing new arrivals in lower ability groups because of their limited English.

This grouping represented a departure from usual practice in the RE teacher's classroom, where the early-stage INAs were usually together at the front of the classroom so that the EAL support teacher had easy access to them. As an outcome of the project, this subject teacher has now reconfigured her teaching space to facilitate group work and talk for learning. Joint planning naturally led to joint lesson delivery, building on existing ways of working in a more considered and explicit process than is generally possible in the bustle of daily life in a busy school. Both teachers felt that this further deepened their teaching partnership. This resulted in a stronger voice for the EAL practitioner, which led to a clearer language focus in the curriculum generally. Both agreed that pupils' learning behaviour improved as a consequence, with the early-stage EAL learners working more independently and all learners being more engaged.

The first lesson in the sequence had the following learning objectives (notice how they include both curriculum and language knowledge):

- to identify reasons why countries go to war;

- to analyse reasons behind a recent conflict;

(Continued)

(Continued)

- to reflect on your own view and to explain whether you think that war is the best way to solve conflict;

- to become more confident in using PEEL in an extended answer question (PEEL is a model paragraph structure – **P**oint, **E**vidence, **E**xplanation, **L**ink back to question – used by the English Department – see Figure 6.4);

- to unpack models of appropriate academic language;

- to use the four language skills (listening, speaking, reading and writing) in context;

- to practise academic language in both speaking and writing (explanation and analysis).

The first phase of the lesson activated learners' prior knowledge of the topic. The task was to select four possible justifications for war from eight possibilities, which included some red herrings. This involved reading for meaning, having a purpose for talk and engaging with good models of spoken and written English in a supportive group dynamic. It introduced subject- and topic-specific vocabulary in context as well as formal academic English language and grammar patterns.

The main phase of the lesson involved reading a case study of the conflict in Darfur, Sudan and identifying four causes of conflict. There was a clear purpose for reading and less confident readers were supported by more confident ones. The text itself provided a good model of academic English and was challenging enough to generate talk about what it meant. Texts made accessible by stripping them of more complex language structures deny learners experience of the kinds of language they need to achieve highly. Learners were given an empty grid of four rows, each representing a paragraph, and four columns, one each for Point, Evidence, Explanation and Link back to the question. As differentiation, early stage EAL learners also had sentences on cards to fill the grid with. Put together correctly, this resulted in a model text of four paragraphs (see Figure 6.4).

Evidence sentences all start with 'for example'; explanation sentences all start with 'thus' and link back to the question sentences, which all start with 'therefore'. This 'filling a grid' activity enabled early-stage EAL learners to move bits of text around and try them out in various places in the process of deciding what goes where. The minimal production demands allowed focused engagement with text instead of the pressure to fill the grid with writing, which might distract early-stage EAL learners into copying chunks of text. More advanced learners had the opportunity to fill the grid with their own notes.

This activity generated lots of task-focused talk among the pupils. The two teachers could circulate and listen in to each group to identify individual and common issues, such as issues with words and expressions. 'Plagued by' and 'drought' were two notable examples in this lesson. This Assessment for Learning (AfL) strategy resulted in the early-stage EAL learners being encouraged to use their bilingual dictionaries to look up words they had identified as key words. This allowed them to make connections with their L1 and access the content of the text efficiently, especially where vocabulary was not concrete. There was also discussion about what reading strategies learners were using. Encouraging a 'meta-stance' on their learning in this way helps learners to identify what they are doing and enables them to get better at it.

The main phase of the lesson was concluded with a self-assessment activity, which encouraged learners to evaluate what they had done and how confident they felt about it and to consider the next steps they might take to make progress. The final phase of the lesson was writing an answer to an extended answer question, giving learners the opportunity to use the text structure and language that had been modelled in the lesson. The resulting texts provided the 'grist for the mill' for the next lesson.

Explain the causes of a recent conflict. (8 marks)

A conflict is ....

There are several reasons why countries and communities go to war.

	POINT	EVIDENCE	EXPLANATION	LINK BACK TO QUESTION
Firstly	Historical conflicts between countries or communities are sometimes left unsolved and lead to war or civil war.	For example, in Sudan during the conflict of 2003–7 the government was accused of persecuting non-Arabs.	Thus, religious and ethnic issues and disagreements were deepened and made worse.	Therefore, non-Arabs were involved in the conflict in Darfur because they were persecuted by the Sudan government.
In addition	Some countries or communities go to war to protect their own natural resources, or are attacked so that others can take control of their natural resources such as oil or land.	For example, in Sudan in 2003–7 there were food and water shortages because of drought and people were forced to move to different areas and start new lives.	Thus, the original people living in these new areas had fewer resources because there were more people.	Therefore, because people in Darfur were unhappy with this happening they felt forced to fight back to protect their land and fight against the government for allowing it to happen.
Furthermore	Some countries or communities go to war because they feel they need to protect their interests and identity.	For example, in Sudan in 2003–7 the people living in the west were segregated and felt they were being treated unequally by the government.	Thus, the people of the western districts wanted to be independent of the Sudan government and set up their own state.	Therefore, people in Darfur being segregated and marginalised led to conflict because they felt they had to fight to protect their interests and identity.
Finally	Some countries or communities go to war because of conflict between different groups battling for power and status.	For example, in Sudan in 2003–7 some ethnic groups were armed by the Sudan government and encouraged to attack other ethnic groups and take their land.	Thus, many people were unable to defend themselves and were killed or displaced into refugee camps, where they remain.	Therefore, some groups being armed and supported by the Sudan government at the expense of other groups caused conflict in Darfur.

Figure 6.4 PEEL grid for RE lesson

(Continued)

(Continued)

Both teachers valued the way that having language objectives for the lesson as well as content objectives organised the lesson. Learners had the opportunity and support to engage in task-focused talk that prepared them for engaging with a challenging text that modelled the type of writing demanded by the curriculum. The two teachers noted how the organisation of the classroom and the nature of the activities had a positive impact on learning and language development. For example, embedding the use of appropriate sentence starters for specific purposes (e.g. 'thus' for explanation) allowed the teachers to use them as prompts for eliciting appropriate sentences.

The pre-planning in the RE lesson clearly resulted in a more equal teaching partnership. The teachers' care with organising groupings reminds us that, alongside planning the content and progression of the teaching activities, we need to think carefully about ways of organising classes and groups of pupils to facilitate their learning. This is the focus of section 3 below.

2.2 PARTNERSHIP TEACHING

As the case study above shows, one of the essential skills in EAL pedagogy is the ability to work with colleagues to plan and implement teaching that allows pupils the opportunities to learn both the concepts of the subject being studied and the English language required to think, talk and write about the subject. This is especially important in secondary schools, but applies also to primary schools. In the 1980s and 1990s, there was much research and development of the concept of partnership teaching (NALDIC, 2017). This showed, among other things, that time spent by subject and 'EAL specialists' working together in careful planning was always of benefit to the quality of the pupils' learning and always time well spent. If one of the colleagues is bilingual or multilingual themselves, the partnership can be even more beneficial. The following case study, written by a secondary EAL specialist teacher, illustrates the benefits of subject and EAL teachers working together.

PARTNERSHIP TEACHING IN GEOGRAPHY – CASE STUDY BY PETE RUSE

I work as an EAL support teacher part-time in a number of schools. I see building partnerships with subject teachers as a core part of my practice and strive to create a balance between supporting learning directly within lessons and, outside of lessons, having an impact on the curriculum they experience so that it is more organised with language development objectives in mind. Explicitly and implicitly acting to increase subject teachers' knowledge and skills in this area is a fundamental aspect of this, especially as new teachers join the profession.

In a school where I was working on a temporary basis, I was timetabled to support a Year 10 geography class for one lesson a week, taught by the Head of Geography, who had extensive experience of working with EAL practitioners. Circumstances dictated that while she knew I was going to turn up, we did not have a chance to have a conversation before the lesson. On arriving in her classroom, she invited me to sit down and look through a pile of test scripts that the class had completed the lesson before. She was particularly concerned about their answers to extended answer questions in that many learners seemed not to have grasped what the questions were asking of them.

Reading carefully through the scripts, I was able to tune into the class and the teaching and learning dynamic in the classroom. Having all chosen geography as an option, all the learners seemed motivated and engaged. They had a range of attainment from predicted 'A*' to 'E' grades at GCSE. There was one International New Arrival (INA) who had been in the UK for three years and who was able to communicate in English verbally quite effectively, though his written English was at a much earlier stage of development. From his test script, he clearly had problems identifying what the questions were asking him to do.

I negotiated with the geography teacher that I would prepare a lesson on reading exam questions for the following week. This seemed to be a good place to start. I knew that the class had had lots of practice doing exam type questions so I tried to think of another way to approach the matter. I decided to 'reverse engineer' a test, where I would supply a set of answers and the activity would be to write the (possible) questions. I calculated that this would really focus learners on close reading of answers (a useful model) and generating an appropriate form of question for that answer. If you can write something you can read it.

The starter activity – to match terms with their opposites – introduced the concept of an 'anti-quiz':

	The Antarctic
A cyclone	
	An anti-quiz
A syncline	
The Arctic	
	An anticline
A quiz	
	An anticyclone

Then a quick anti-quiz – what are the (possible) questions to these answers:

1. Name of school
2. 11 o'clock
3. 1,050 m
4. 250 miles
5. A corrie

This further established the idea of making up the question to match the answer. Then, some real-life geography GCSE examples: first some one-mark questions, for example:

1. Study **Figure n** on the insert, a 1: 50 000 Ordnance Survey map extract of [a river in England].

a) ....

a. 18–22m

b) ....

Possible answers:

- There is a confluence.

- A tributary joins the [river].

(Continued)

129

(Continued)

- It meanders.

- A bridge crosses it.

The real question to a) being:

What is the approximate height of the [river] in grid square xxxx?

And to b):

What happens to the [river] at [grid reference] xxxxx?

Followed by some two-mark questions. For example:

- 5 ....

- Weather is the day-to-day variation of features such as rainfall, temperature and wind, while climate represents the average weather conditions over a long period of time – at least 30 years.

The real question being:

- What is the difference between weather and climate?

There was some animated discussion during the activity, followed by feedback and unpacking some of the language issues, focusing on the links between the structures of the questions and the structures of the answers.

For me, this example shows how, as staff, we both created some space for ourselves. The geography teacher had room to reflect on the class and their learning from a different perspective, and I had room to put together an activity that focused learners on useful language development objectives. Best practice would involve collaborative planning to embed language development objectives in schemes of work, as well as the production of suitable learning materials and activities presented collaboratively. Real-world constraints on time and opportunity mean that this is not always possible. Producing materials for other teachers to use and taking lessons are useful strategies for EAL specialist teachers, enabling them to put language development on the agenda. Showing subject teachers that it is possible (and desirable) to build language development objectives into curriculum content lays the foundations for more collaborative planning and joint delivery of lessons.

3 ORGANISING TO PROMOTE LANGUAGE AND CONTENT LEARNING

3.1 PLANNING FOR COLLABORATIVE TALK

If you want to provide as many opportunities as possible to promote talk for learning, you need to have flexibility in organising both the classroom space and the grouping of your pupils, as Pete Ruse and Linda Sandler's case study shows. In this section, we will consider ways of grouping pupils for talk. But simply placing pupils in groups around tables does not mean that they will somehow automatically engage in learning through talk. Your activities need to be structured so that you progressively build your pupils' understandings of the content and concepts they are learning. The kinds of talk that your pupils need to do should become increasingly complex as they move through the activities.

They should be able to talk in increasingly well-informed, thoughtful and independent ways about the topic, and to engage in increasingly sophisticated discussions with their classmates. The activities you plan need to provide pupils with clear aims and purposes for their talk, clear structures to guide their work and clear outcomes so that they know what they are expected to achieve. The following vignette illustrates this.

▬ VIGNETTE ▬

Planning for progression in oral activities

Figure 6.5 shows part of a medium-term plan developed by a student teacher on the popular classic narrative poem *The Highwayman*, designed to be carried out over two weeks with a Year 5 class. Notice how the key learning objectives are in terms of pupils' understanding and knowing, and how they are linked with the assessment/outcome activities, which are in terms of what pupils will be able do (at different levels, of course) at the end of each set of activities. Notice also how there is a strong focus on oral work, and a mix of whole-class and group activities across the plan.

Key learning objectives	Main activities	Resources	Assessment/ outcomes
Understand the structure and key features of narrative poems and ways of performing them	• Introduce *Highwayman* poem with pictures and artefacts – focus on setting, events, characters (mainly whole class, some group work) • Develop performance of whole poem, in groups	• Story sacks, artefacts from poem, pictures on IWB • Audio or video recorder to record performance	All pupils take part in performance of poem
Understand the differences between literal and figurative language	• Pupils in groups explore different characters in poem (using drama techniques) • Pupils in groups explore literal and figurative language used to describe characters, and write prose description of their own character • Pupils consider main events in the narrative from a range of viewpoints and write narratives from different viewpoints	• Large cut-outs of different characters from poem, thesauruses, dictionaries, simple props for role-play work	All pupils produce a piece of narrative writing based on the poem

Figure 6.5 Medium-term planning for The Highwayman

Here are two examples of talk from the lessons on *The Highwayman*. Read them and then reflect on them using the questions in Activity 6.4 (see below). The first example comes from the first lesson the student teacher taught. She was introducing the poem to her class and began by discussing the history of roads and stagecoaches and the ways that highwaymen held up coaches. After this, she showed her pupils pictures of the characters and setting of the poem (the pictures by Charles Keeping are excellent) and then read the first section to them. She wanted her pupils had to remember the main facts of the poem, so she led a whole-class discussion.

Teacher: Who do you think is the main character in the poem?

Child 1: The highwayman.

Teacher: That's right ... who are the other important characters?

Child 2: Bess, the black-eyed daughter.

Teacher: That's right, and who else?

Child 3: Tim, the ostler.

Teacher: Who can tell me what an ostler is?

Child 1: Someone who looks after the inn.

Teacher: Not quite ... he works in the stables, so he looks after the ...

Child 4: Horses.

Teacher: That's right. Who can find a simile to describe Tim the ostler?

Child 3: Hair like mouldy hay.

Teacher: That's right.

The second example of talk came in the middle of the second week of work. The class had rounded off the first week by carrying out a performance of the whole poem, which had been videoed and which they enjoyed very much. Following this, the pupils had been divided into mixed-ability groups and each group was given a different character to study. They did **hot seating** activities in their groups to explore the decisions made by their characters in the poem. Following this, the teacher reorganised the groups so that each group included pupils who had studied different characters (this is called **jigsawing**). Each jigsaw group was given a different section of the poem to discuss from the viewpoints of the different characters, in such a way that the whole poem was covered. Then the class came together to review their findings about the different characters. This was to be followed in the next lesson by a writing task – each pupil was to plan a piece of writing where they wrote a narrative from the point of view of one of the characters in the poem: Bess, the landlord's beautiful daughter, Tim the ostler, King George's men or the highwayman himself. Here is part of one jigsaw group's discussion – they were talking about the end of the poem, after King George's men had killed the highwayman.

Child 1: I don't think the highwayman should have come back for her, he should have known he would get killed.

Child 2: But how was he to know that King George's men would come to the inn and set a trap for him?

Child 1: It was really sad when he died ... they shouldn't have killed him.

Child 3: I think he deserved to die, highwaymen killed a lot of people ... It shows you about Dick Turpin in York Museum and how he killed people on the roads.

Child 1: But he really loved Bess, and he made a promise to her.

Child 3: He should have realised that they would be out to get him.

Child 2:   They shouldn't have killed Bess the black-eyed daughter as it wasn't her fault.

Child 4:   They should have got Tim with the tatty hair.

ACTIVITY 6.4

Planning for collaborative talk, understanding *The Highwayman*

When you have read the two examples of classroom talk, think about the following questions.

- Which quadrant in the Cummins' framework do you think each example fits into?

- What do you think are the teacher's objectives in the first discussion?

- What roles do the pupils take in this discussion?

- What do you think the teacher did in order to prepare the pupils to take part in the second discussion?

- What role does the teacher take in this discussion?

- What roles do each of the four participating pupils take in this discussion?

- What are some of the differences between the kinds of language the pupils use in each extract?

- Do you think the second discussion is successful? Why?

In the *Highwayman* activities, there were several different kinds of group work:

- *whole-class*, with a teacher-led question-and-answer session;

- *mixed-ability groups*, where pupils were sharing ideas about something they all knew about;

- *mixed ability (jigsaw) groups*, where pupils had to share knowledge about different parts of the poem.

At other points in the *Highwayman* plan, the pupils would be engaged in different kinds of group work in order to complete different tasks:

- *talking partner (pairs)*, for recalling and reinforcing knowledge and sharing ideas quickly at different times;

- *friendship groups*, for the oral performance;

- *ability groups*, for the writing task, so that support could be provided to meet the different needs of the pupils.

Other ways of grouping your pupils could be as follows.

- ***Pair to four***. Pupils are given a task to do in pairs, and then join up with another pair to make a group of four to share their findings – this can be a good way to form mixed-sex groups by having the pairs same-sex, then joining pairs of boys with pairs of girls.

- ***Listening triads***. Three pupils work together. Child A and child B carry out a task, which could be following instructions, telling a story, etc. Child C's role is to be the observer. They have to make careful notes of what is said, then report back to the rest of the class in the plenary part of the lesson.

THE TALKING PARTNERS PROGRAMME – CASE STUDY BY CATHERINE PORRITT

After describing the Talking Partners programme, which was developed in Bradford, I illustrate how Talking Partners as an intervention was introduced into one primary school and the results that were achieved. All adult partners, teachers, TAs and so on need to understand the rationale behind the programme as well as the methods and successes of past work, joining in the activities to experience the programme first hand. The role of the adult in a Talking Partners activity is to model language, and also to ask questions to extend children's responses, reframe what the children say and introduce alternative words and structures. Examples of this are given in the extracts from the activities around *The Pirates Next Door* below. Ideally, staff work collaboratively to plan.

Talking Partners comprises a range of talk-related activities in which the key aim is to provide opportunities for pupils to hear, use and rehearse meaningful language in supportive contexts. The demands for performance are deliberately reduced to enable students to experiment and extend the repertoires of English language structures that they understand and use. Comprehension is supported through the use of concrete objects, artefacts, puppets, high-quality images or short extracts of selected text. In this supportive context, and through careful modelling of the target language, the pupils hear and rehearse language, developing and extending beyond the known into the unknown. For each activity the cognitive challenge is designed to remain high while the language becomes increasingly demanding as confidence in English grows. This progressive development follows the Cummins' quadrant, from context-embedded to context-reduced learning.

Small group work is an essential element of the programme, where the Talking Partner (TP) works with groups of three pupils to scaffold and encourage more sophisticated uses of language. Three is judged to be the optimum group size allowing enough chance for rehearsal and practice while maintaining interest, as no child has to sit and listen for extended periods without the chance to interact. Three 25-minute sessions are spread across the week. Here are some typical activities, with examples of the talk generated.

Picture Talk

In *Picture Talk*, the pupils work with their partner to build a group description of the selected picture. In this example, a group of Year 2 pupils is working on a Picture Talk activity based on an illustration from *The Pirates Next Door* story (Duddle, 2012), showing a pirate ship parked outside a house.

TP: Let's look carefully at this picture. There is Tilda, riding her bike, and then look, she sees that pirate ship! She is surprised! What else can you see?

Ch. 1:   It's got wheels.

TP: Oh yes, the pirate ship is on a trailer with wheels.

Ch. 2:   There's a shooter, it's got ... um ... um ...

TP: Yes, on a ship there are big guns, they are called cannons, and they shoot cannon balls like those (pointing to illustration). Do you want to say that?

Ch. 2:   Cannons, the ship got cannons ...

TP: Who is this in the picture?

Ch. 3:   Um ... he is up ...

Ch. 2:   He is Jim lad.

TP: Yes, it's Jim, the pirate and he's up the ladder.

The discussion continues for a few minutes until everything in the picture has been considered.

Character role play stage 1

A group of Year 2 pupils (who are all advanced bilingual learners) is working on *The Pirate Next Door*, exploring character. They are taking the role of the neighbour telephoning complaints to the council. The children and TP together develop ideas of the imagined problems caused by the pirates and formulate one or two as complaints to the council. With a telephone prop, the pupils take turns to ring up the council officer played by the TP, who responds in role, clarifying and agreeing with their complaints and modelling back the complaints to be addressed.

Ch 1:   They got swords, big swords.

TP: Oh, they are carrying swords, I see, they are carrying sharp swords, that could be dangerous.

The next child is invited to make a complaint, either on the same sword issue or another. Such interaction encourages precision, differentiation of the scaffolding provided and allows TPs to consider each child as an individual. For this group, the priority is increasing the range of vocabulary used; other groups may focus on language structures. The same materials can be used for pupils to develop curriculum-relevant spoken language and comprehension in parallel, small-group activities. This provides ideal opportunities for pre-teaching the vocabulary and language structures that will be necessary to allow pupils full access to the cognitive academic language necessary for the whole-class lessons.

The range of possible activities is wide and covers the spoken language demands of the English curriculum, focusing on the functions of the language. Here are some more examples of activities:

- **Same and Different** - the group identifies the features that two objects or images share, and compare and contrast the differences.
- **Question Circles** - the group collaborate to produce long lists of questions that could be asked of a picture, character or expert.
- **What is it**? - a picture sequencing activity.
- **Barrier games** - children work in pairs: one describes a picture or diagram in detail and the other attempts to draw it.

The Bell Foundation is developing an excellent bank of teaching resources, many of which would be appropriate for Talking Partners sessions (e.g. **Collaborative Activities**: https://ealresources.bell-foundation.org.uk/teachers/great-ideas-collaborative-activities and **Barrier Games**: https://ealresources.bell-foundation.org.uk/teachers/great-ideas-barrier-games).

Introducing Talking Partners into one school

This section describes how the programme was introduced into one primary school to address three particular needs: firstly to help the recently arrived EAL pupils move beyond the very early stages of

(Continued)

(Continued)

English; secondly to support the significant number of pupils in the school with speech, language and communication needs; and thirdly to address the need across the school to help all pupils to learn to speak and listen to each other more effectively.

In the first term, an LA specialist EAL teacher visited the school for a morning each week. The oracy coordinator was trained to support and advise the teaching assistants during the programme delivery and assist in the initial and final assessments. Following a three-week training period, the teaching assistant partners spent an additional morning together with their oracy coordinator, planning the first few weeks of their programme and sourcing support materials. These included images relevant to the curriculum to be studied, picture sequences to illustrate scientific or story sequences, artefacts, puppets and small world figures for story-building activities, and texts rehearsing academic language vocabulary that would need explanation and modelling. The oracy coordinator liaised with class teachers to ensure the plans and resources would support the topics to be studied in each year group.

Each group of three pupils was selected to contain at least one EAL child, someone each child could build a relationship with, a possible friend and a child who may have an additional speech language and communication need for whom additional rehearsal was necessary. The intervention consisted of three sessions a week covering six different activities, each selected to rehearse a different aspect of language. The week typically included news telling, story telling, describing and comparing, question circles, character study and reporting. The teaching assistants reported that the pupils really liked the variety of activities. Pupils really enjoyed going out on a regular basis in their little groups of three with an adult. Frequently, visitors would overhear pupils asking teaching assistants 'Is it Talking Partners today?'

There was a staged model of introduction for each activity, initially with high levels of support through modelling, concrete artefacts and pictures to describe, gradually reducing stage by stage as pupils built confidence and language skills. In this way, dependency on the adult partners was reduced. The adult role gradually changed to one of formative assessment and recording. Activities which pupils could do independently were reported, along with those for which they needed support and how frequently. The colour-coded record indicated clearly where the pupils were developing and where more support was needed. The teaching assistants commented on the simplicity of the recording system. Teaching assistants leading the groups began to notice changes in the children quite quickly, and during the course of the programme class teachers and parents frequently became aware of their child's increased confidence in experimenting with spoken English.

Evidence of progress was collected with examples of pre- and post-intervention speech and responses to class activities. Responses from the beginning and from the end of the programme showed clearly the children's progress. Here are two examples:

A picture showing a mother about to remove wellington boots elicited the question, 'What is the mother going to do?' At the beginning of the programme, a reception class child answered, 'Off your shoes'. At the end, her response was, 'taking girl's shoes off, no boots, they off'. Where initially her response was telegraphic, using single words together with phrases collected from the classroom to convey meaning, by the end of the programme she had learned how to nominate people, how to indicate possession, she knew some different verbs and parts of verbs, she had an increasing range of vocabulary and was self correcting.

The child was shown a picture of a man climbing a ladder to rescue a cat and asked, 'What is the man doing?' She replied initially, 'Up cat, tree up'. At the end of the programme, her answer, 'Man getting cat down on up the house', shows she is now able to nominate people, use prepositions, use appropriate participles of verbs, knows positional vocabulary and has an increasing vocabulary.

Statistical data collected in the pre and post assessments confirmed the TPs' observations. All pupil groups made good progress when on the intervention, and it is interesting to note that they continued to make good progress after they had completed their course of Talking Partners.

3.2 INCLUDING NEW ARRIVALS IN YOUR LESSONS – BUDDIES AND MENTORS

One of the main decisions that a teacher needs to make when a new-to-English pupil arrives in their class is what ability group they should join. Many teachers feel intuitively that new arrivals will be best placed in a low-ability group, perhaps because they feel they will be supported by additional staff and the activities will not be too demanding. But new arrivals are not necessarily of low ability and, as Pete Ruse and Linda Sandler suggest in their case study (p. 125), they may be hampered in their learning by being placed in a group where they are not given interesting things to do which provide some cognitive challenge. They may also feel that their prior knowledge and experiences are not valued. It is often better to place new arrivals in a middle-ability group so that they can begin to tune into the discussions taking place and pick up models of classroom language.

As they settle into school and their social English begins to develop, new arrivals need to hear academic English being used fluently and competently. It is often a tricky balance to provide new arrivals with cognitively demanding activities at the same time as supporting them in understanding and using the language involved. This means that new arrivals must never be assigned to a group permanently. Their progress needs to be constantly monitored to make sure they are being challenged and moved to a different group if it helps. They must also have the opportunity to mix with other pupils and engage in activities with different levels of language challenge.

It is often helpful to team a new arrival with a buddy or peer mentor. This could be a child who speaks the same home language and is more fluent in English and can therefore communicate readily as well as translate, or it may be a 'monolingual' child who is confident and curious and willing to assume responsibility for someone else for a while. The buddy's role could be shared by different pupils. For example, a 'language buddy' may be someone who shares the same first language as the child and who can act as an interpreter. If there is no other child in the class who can do this, the language buddy could be from another class or even a sibling or other relative who does not attend the school, but who comes in from time to time. Then there may be a 'school buddy' who helps with getting to know the routines of the school, where things are, when things happen and so on. There may be a 'learning buddy', or different buddies for different lessons or areas of the curriculum. The kinds of things buddies can do include:

*   help familiarise the new arrival with where things are such as toilets, cloakrooms, dining hall, assemblies;

*   explain who's who in school and what they do, e.g. secretaries, dinner ladies, TAs;

*   support the new arrival in making friends;

*   introduce the new arrival to other members of the school.

3.3 PLANNING FOR NEW ARRIVALS

The final case study in this chapter illustrates the way a pupil arriving in school with no English was gradually incorporated into the life of the class over the course of a year, while being given opportunities to use the knowledge and experience he brought to the school to support his learning of the class's curriculum.

PLANNING FOR ONE EAL LEARNER IN SECONDARY SCHOOL – CASE STUDY BY ANA KORZUN

Kristof arrived in the UK from Poland at the end of Year 6 with no level of English. In September, when he started his secondary school joining the other English-speaking Year 7 students, he seemed very withdrawn and did not participate in his lessons. In October a teaching assistant, Mrs T, started supporting Kristof in his English lessons and he began to come out of his shell, but with Mrs T only. By the time she left the school six months later, Kristof was still very withdrawn.

In March I started supporting Kristof in his mainstream English lessons. At that time, he also had individual EAL tuition twice a week with a Polish-speaking family support worker. His English vocabulary was expanding and one of his favourite exercises in English lessons was labelling pictures. Kristof, as much as the other pupils in class, enjoyed having a complete final product at the end of each lesson.

March

In March all Year 7 pupils were studying *Macbeth* in English. Kristof could not participate in the lessons without differentiated work, which I provided for him. When the whole class was asked to write a paragraph imagining being present in the castle, Kristof copied out the story of Act 2 of *Macbeth* filling in the blank spaces with words from a list. He produced some vivid labelled drawings of the play, which showed his strong engagement with it (see Figure 6.6). He began to translate the key words into Polish using his bilingual dictionary.

Figure 6.6 Kristof's drawing of Macbeth

April-May

In April Kristof was more fully engaged in his English lessons and demonstrated a great ability in critical thinking. He was introduced to writing in PEE (Point, Evidence, Explain) paragraphs, which he seemed to understand. With some help from a teaching assistant, Kristof managed to produce some excellent paragraphs. Most of the differentiation was based on using writing frames and completing them with the information from a list or particular book pages. Kristof could successfully complete comprehension-based tasks but still was not able to write independently, which is why writing frames worked really well. Then the class read the Roald Dahl story called 'A Lamb to the Slaughter' which Kristof read together with the whole class, and which he also read in Polish at home. After that Kristof wrote a diary entry in Polish, based on the events in the story. This was translated into English with the help of a Polish-speaking family support worker. At first, he was confused about why he was asked to write in Polish, but then he found it helpful and enjoyed writing in his home language (see Figure 6.7). He said that it was 'great writing in his home language' because he could write everything that he thought and also because he loved Polish.

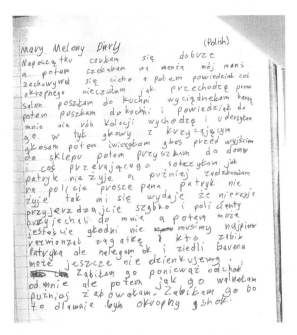

Figure 6.7 Kristof's Polish diary (a retelling of the Roald Dahl story 'A Lamb to the Slaughter')

June

In June, Kristof demonstrated continuous improvement in his independent writing. He read the Scottish tale 'Selkie's Wife' in English and used a Google translator to translate it into Polish, showing later a very strong understanding of the story. He re-read and translated the tale in his own time independently and managed to answer in English all the questions given to the whole class (in writing). He showed his understanding of the story, again labelling and storyboarding as well as drawing some key images from the story. Kristof did not have any new differentiated tasks but was very confident with what he was doing on a regular basis at that time. He immediately looked up the key words, used the translator or a dictionary and kept writing in Polish, which did not stop him from

(Continued)

(Continued)

writing in English. By this stage, Kristof's confidence had grown a lot he was doing well in his main-stream lessons even without a teaching assistant. He put his hand up when he knew the answer and even performed reading a poem out loud in front of the class.

July

In July, Kristof was able to analyse poems and write in simple PEE paragraphs if the writing frame was provided for him. For example, the teacher asked him to use sentences such as: 'In this poem, the poet describes ... as ... This suggests that ...' Using these sentence frames, Kristof produced the following PEE paragraph:

> In this poem, Island Man, the poet describes London as 'grey and metalic'. This suggests that London is not beautiful and the island man does not like.

He wrote all his PEE paragraphs without using his dictionary and did not pre-write in Polish. Kristof was proud of the writing that he was producing and even asked if he could take his book home to show to his parents. His class teacher and I were very happy with the progress that he had made over the year and he seemed to be a different boy compared to the one he was when he started. Kristof's rapid progress over a period of a few months was very pleasing.

■— CHAPTER SUMMARY

The three learning outcomes for this chapter are all to do with linking the theories you read about in Chapters 2 and 3 to your thinking about the kinds of strategies and resources that will promote learning for your EAL and multilingual learners. You may be able to take some of the specific ideas described in the chapter into your own planning, but it is more likely that you will use your professional judgement to adapt them to your own classroom setting and the pupils you are teaching.

Self-assessment questions

1. Analyse some of the lessons you have planned in different areas of the curriculum to identify their language demands.

2. In what ways could you make sure that speaking and listening are emphasised in your teaching across the curriculum?

3. Do you work with other colleagues in your classroom? If so, can you think of ways in which you could make your work more collaborative?

■———— FURTHER READING

Creese, A. (2005) Teacher Collaboration and Talk in Multilingual Classrooms. Bristol: Multilingual Matters.

This book looks in detail at the interactions between subject and EAL teachers in multilingual class-rooms and shows their importance for learning in secondary schools. It also shows how policy statements and multilingualism ideologies position teachers and learners in particular ways. Different chapters consider the links between languages, different pedagogic approaches and teacher identities in secondary classrooms.

Gibbons, P. (1998) 'Classroom talk and the learning of new registers in a second language', *Language and Education*, **12 (2), pp. 99–118.**

This article, along with other material written by Pauline Gibbons, gives very clear examples of the ways that concept learning and language learning go side by side, and how teachers can scaffold children's learning through oral activities across the curriculum.

STUDYING AT MASTER'S LEVEL

Critical reading:

Sandoval-Taylor, P. (2005) 'Home is where the heart is: planning a funds of knowledge-based curriculum module', in N. Gonzalez, L. Moll and C. Amanti (eds), *Funds of Knowledge: Theorizing Practices in Households, Communities and Classrooms.* **New York: Routledge, pp. 153-65.**

In this chapter, Sandoval-Taylor, a teacher in Arizona, USA, describes how she planned, implemented and assessed a learning module based on the theme of house construction for her second-grade bilingual education class (5-6 year olds).

After reading the chapter, there are some reflection questions that you could think about (p. 165). Also, consider the following questions, ideally in discussion with colleagues:

1. On p. 154, Sandoval-Taylor writes: 'I wanted the children to make the decisions and negotiate the curriculum.' From your reading of the chapter, discuss how she did this. How far do you think this approach might be possible in your own classroom or classrooms you have worked in?

2. On p. 155 and then on pp. 159 and following, Sandoval-Taylor describes the assessment processes she developed for the module. How effective do you think they were and how far might you be able to use such approaches formatively in your own teaching?

3. Sandoval-Taylor provides the plan for her module on page 156, and then gives a revised version of the Day 7 activity on p. 158. How did the work she planned make links with the children's communities?

4. What possibilities and constraints do you think there are in your own school, or a school you have known, for promoting a funds of knowledge approach to planning in different areas of the curriculum?

REFERENCES

Duddle, J. (2012) *The Pirates Next Door*. London: Templar Publishing.

Gibbons, P. (1998) 'Classroom talk and the learning of new registers in a second language', *Language and Education, 12* (2), pp. 99–118.

Hall, D., Griffiths, D., Haslam, L. and Wilkin, Y. (2001) *Assessing the Needs of Multilingual Pupils: Living in Two Languages*, 2nd edn. London: David Fulton.

National Association for Language Development in the Curriculum (NALDIC) (2017) *CPD Through the Power of Partnership Teaching*. Available online at https://naldic.org.uk/httpsealjournal-org20170220cpd-through-the-power-of-partnership-teaching/ (accessed 4 November 2018).

Wolfe, S. and Alexander, R. J. (2008) *Argumentation and Dialogic Teaching: Alternative Pedagogies for a Changing World*. Available online at http://www.robinalexander.org.uk/wp-content/uploads/2012/05/wolfealexander.pdf/ (accessed 4 November 2018).

7

ASSESSING MULTILINGUAL AND EAL LEARNERS ACROSS THE CURRICULUM

LEARNING OUTCOMES

This chapter will help you to achieve the following learning outcomes:

- understand the differences between standardised, summative assessment of attainment, assessing achievement and assessment for learning (formative assessment);

- understand the issues involved in assessing the attainment of multilingual and EAL learners using standardised assessments;

- understand the importance of assessment for learning for multilingual and EAL learners;

- gain knowledge of some practical strategies for assessing the strengths and needs of EAL and multilingual learners.

INTRODUCTION

In Chapter 3 (pp. 52–53), some issues connected with developing an inclusive approach to assessment were raised. The National Curriculum requires us to assess all pupils according to the same standards. This has its value, but if it is the only way in which they are assessed, the diversity of our pupils' experiences, knowledge and skills will not be recognised and understood. We may never find out about the things that individual pupils can do, which may be crucial to their ongoing development, learning and future attainment. In order to plan the best opportunities for learning for multilingual and EAL pupils, it is important to get to know them as individuals and to recognise and value the full range of their experiences, knowledge and skills. Official assessments are briefly discussed in this chapter, but the main focus is about how you can learn about your pupils so that you can best meet their needs in the classroom.

The chapter begins by offering some key principles for assessing multilingual and EAL learners, taken from the QCA (2000) document *A Language in Common*, which is still the most definitive official statement about assessing multilingual and EAL learners. Following this, issues are discussed which relate to the official, standardised assessment tools, including the 'Proficiency in English' scales, introduced in 2016 but now not statutory. In the third section of this chapter, there are suggestions for practical strategies to assess the learning and achievements of multilingual and EAL learners, and for using the outcomes to support their future learning. There is an illustrative case study by Dianne Excell, who describes how she developed a range of assessments for secondary pupils from Year 7 to GCSE.

The final section of the chapter deals with the need to understand the views of those most directly involved in assessment, the pupils, their teachers and their parents. This includes a case study by Pete Ruse and Linda Sandler on pupil voice in secondary schools. This is followed by suggestions for ways of consulting with the parents and families of multilingual and EAL learners about their pupils' achievements and attainments.

Throughout the chapter, there are discussion points and tasks to help you think through the ideas you are reading about, and there are some suggestions for further reading at the end of the chapter, including a text for Master's level study.

These are the main sections and subsections of the chapter:

1   Principles for assessing EAL and multilingual learners

2   'Official' assessments of attainment

2.1 Issues in national assessment procedures for multilingual and EAL learners

2.2 The 'Proficiency in English' scale

2.3 Language need or learning need?

3   Assessment for learning – formative assessment

3.1 Profiling and sampling

Assessing multilingual and EAL learners across the curriculum in a secondary school – case study by Dianne Excell

3.2 Observing as a tool for assessment

3.3 Pupils' views

Learner voice – case study by Pete Ruse and Linda Sandler

3.4 Consulting with parents

1 PRINCIPLES FOR ASSESSING EAL AND MULTILINGUAL LEARNERS

The SATs (Standard Attainment Tests), the national tests of attainment in England, were first introduced in the mid-1990s. At the time, there was a great deal of discussion about how to assess pupils who did not have English as their first language. It was recognised that, for pupils new to English, it could be difficult to find out what they already knew and to assess their understanding of concepts in different subjects without placing demands on their knowledge of English. It was also recognised that the content of the tests could never be culture-free and so there could be difficulties with comprehension or with the fairness of the tests. Certain content or ideas might be strange to pupils from different cultural backgrounds, or open to different interpretations. Given what we know about the importance of contextual support for pupils' learning and for multilingual and EAL learners in particular, this presents something of a paradox – in trying to provide contextual support in assessment, we may actually be making things harder for some pupils. There are clearly sensitivities in this aspect of testing, and care must be taken not to make assumptions, which could lead to unwitting stereotyping or even racism. Zaitun Varian-Roper illustrates this beautifully in her chapter about mathematics in Gravelle (2000, p. 70). Joshua, a child from Uganda, was asked the following question as part of a mathematics test:

I ate half an apple and half of it was left. What was left?

Joshua's written answer was 'seeds', but he later asked the teacher, 'But what is an apple, Miss?'

These issues will never be fully resolved and must always be taken into account in interpreting the results of SATs and other kinds of summative assessment. It also has to be remembered that assessment instruments such as the SATs are developed by professional testers and commercial testing agencies in order to provide a final, externalised measure of attainment. There are many other reasons and purposes for assessment and these are the main focus of this chapter.

A Language in Common was produced in 2000 by the Quality and Curriculum Authority (QCA). It provides an excellent general overview of the language issues underpinning formative assessment for EAL and multilingual learners. It also makes suggestions for ways of taking their levels of language development into account. It begins by stating some principles for all teachers to consider (QCA, 2000, p. 8):

- Be clear about the purposes of the assessment, distinguishing summative, formative and diagnostic aims.

- Be sensitive to the pupil's home language(s) and heritage culture.

- Take account of how long the pupil has been learning English.

- Assess in ways that are appropriate for the pupil's age.

- Focus on language, while being aware of the influence of behaviour, attitude and cultural expectations.

- Recognise that pupils may be at different levels of attainment in speaking, listening, reading and writing.

The first principle is crucial – it is vital to remember always to be clear about the reasons why you are assessing pupils and what you intend to do with the outcomes. The remaining principles stress in different ways the importance of understanding about pupils' knowledge of other languages, and also their community and cultural contexts. They recognise that, for many multilingual and EAL learners, their learning of their new language of English will not be progressing in the same ways as for pupils whose first language is English. As Cummins' BICS and CALP concept shows, pupils learning English as an additional language may quickly become competent and confident speakers while their reading and writing may take much longer to develop. But for some, particularly older pupils, their reading and writing may be much better developed than their speaking. In assessing multilingual and EAL learners, no matter what the subject area, always bear in mind their language experiences and prior knowledge.

2 'OFFICIAL' ASSESSMENTS OF ATTAINMENT

2.1 ISSUES IN NATIONAL ASSESSMENT PROCEDURES FOR MULTILINGUAL AND EAL LEARNERS

SATs are designed to test pupils' attainments in very specific ways. The 'fair test' cartoon in Chapter 3 (p. 53) raises issues about having one such universal means of assessing the attainment of every pupil at each stage of school. Not only does it mean that some pupils (like the fish or the seal in the cartoon) simply cannot do whatever the test might demand, but – just like the fish and the seal – they may have skills and expertise which the test simply ignores. It is crucial not to assume that because a multilingual or EAL pupil cannot do the standardised task, they cannot understand or do not know the concepts being tested. Over the years since the SATs were introduced, a wide range of intervention and assessment procedures have been developed, aimed at supporting the assessment of multilingual and EAL learners. These are sometimes attached to funding arrangements in the same way as special needs assessments and the process of statementing. As Safford's (2003) paper clearly demonstrates, such assessment procedures can be very difficult and time-consuming to manage. And the outcomes may not always be very helpful for the pupils or their teachers.

ACTIVITY 7.1

Language and testing

Get hold of some old SATs papers on any subject. You may find some in school, or download some from the free SATs website (https://www.sats-papers.co.uk/ks1-sats-papers; https://www.sats-papers.co.uk/ks2-sats-papers).

Think about the language demands of the tests. Here are some points to consider.

1. Does the layout of the papers help or impair comprehension?

2. Are the instructions clear? Note down any you think may be difficult to interpret and think about how you might re-word them.

3. Is the wording of the questions clear? Are there any possible ambiguities or confusions?

4. Is the content of the questions appropriate? Can you identify any cultural issues or possible ambiguities that may cause problems?

5. Are the illustrations clear? Do they support the understanding of the questions or make them more difficult?

2.2 THE 'PROFICIENCY IN ENGLISH' SCALE

In 2016 the government introduced a new data collection item in the schools' census (DfE, 2016). This is a five-point scale for assessing proficiency in English in EAL learners. There were concerns about the purposes of the scale, as it was linked with the requirement to collect data about pupil nationality, two issues which, as NALDIC and others strongly argued, should be kept separate (NALDIC, 2017). This said, the proficiency scale was seen to offer a potentially useful tool for formatively assessing EAL learners' levels of English. Confusingly, the government has recently removed the mandatory requirement on schools to report on the English proficiency of their EAL learners using the scale. This decision has been met with dismay by most professionals who work with multilingual and EAL learners. Peta Ullman, Chair of NALDIC, wrote (Ullman, 2018, p. 11):

> Our ability to provide a high quality inclusive education for all pupils requires accurate EAL proficiency data for planning and teaching purposes. Data about the performance and progress of pupils with special educational needs is collected to meet the requirements of the Equality Act. Pupils with English as an additional language deserve the same attention and focus in accordance with equalities legislation.

Indeed, it could be argued that the proficiency scale is potentially more valuable as a tool for internal school use without the imperative to report the results. Here are the five levels in the scale:

A: NEW TO ENGLISH – *May use first language, remain silent, copy/repeat words; may understand everyday English but have minimal or no literacy in English; needs considerable EAL support.*

B: EARLY ACQUISITION – *May follow social communication and take part in learning with support; understand simple instructions, follow narrative/accounts; have developed some reading skills, subject-specific vocabulary; needs significant EAL support.*

C: DEVELOPING CONFIDENCE – *Increasing independence; able to express self in English; grammatical inaccuracies; needs ongoing support for literacy; may be able to follow more complex written English; needs ongoing EAL support.*

D: COMPETENT – *Successful engagement across the curriculum; understand a wide variety of texts; occasional errors in structure of written English; needs support to develop abstract vocabulary and nuances of meaning; needs occasional EAL support.*

E: FLUENT – *Can operate across the curriculum comparably to English L1 pupil; operates without EAL support.*

The Bell Foundation have produced a detailed assessment framework based on the proficiency scale, which includes support strategies and tracking tools so that teachers can monitor and record the progress of their EAL learners (Bell Foundation, 2017). You can download this free by registering on the Bell Foundation website.

2.3 LANGUAGE NEED OR LEARNING NEED?

Since the Education Act of 1981, there has been a requirement that pupils who speak other languages besides English at home must not be categorised per se as having special needs (SEN):

> *A child is not to be taken as having a learning difficulty solely because the language (or form of language) in which he [sic] is, or will be, taught is different from a language (or form of language) which has at any time been spoken in his home.*

Despite this, EAL and SEN are often confused in assessment. Language needs can become interpreted as learning needs. EAL in itself can become constructed as a learning difficulty, which – of course – it is not.

Pupils who speak other languages besides English at home or who arrive in school from another country, new to English, are often at earlier stages of acquiring English than 'monolingual' pupils of the same age. They often very quickly develop confidence and skill in conversational language (BICS), but their capacity to understand and use academic language (CALP) takes much longer to grow. Of course, it is also true that young 'monolingual' pupils are at the early stages of developing CALP too. But, because their acquisition of English is usually more advanced, they can move ahead more quickly in a classroom where English is the only means of communication and of learning.

If these aspects of language development are not well understood, there is a risk that the multilingual or EAL learner is assessed as having learning needs or special needs, whereas in fact they more accurately have language needs. There may also be cultural factors that are affecting their learning which the school is not aware of. The answer to providing for their needs and promoting progress in their learning is *not* to set them to do cognitively simplified tasks and give directed teaching of simple English. It may instead be much more helpful to ensure that they have the opportunities and the support, including using their home languages, to engage in increasingly cognitively challenging activities in contextually supported ways, as is suggested in the discussion on planning in Chapter 6. It may be helpful not to rush to intervene in any way, but simply to spend a bit of time in observing the child and thinking about his or her behaviour, as the following vignette, taken from Gregory (2008, pp. 20–1), illustrates.

■ VIGNETTE ■

Tony - EAL and/or SEN?

Tony, a Chinese-heritage child who lived with his parents and grandparents, was very bright and eager when he joined the Reception class of his local school at the age of 4 years 10 months. For a while, all went well. He was very alert and constantly asked, 'What's that?', pointing to things in the classroom. This amused the teacher and made her think of him as a much younger child. He loved to draw, and spent a long time carefully and methodically copying the covers of books. After a while, Tony changed. His enthusiasm seemed to evaporate, and he would wander round the classroom aimlessly. His constant 'What's that?' worried the teacher, who began to think he lacked ability or was not getting encouragement from his family. A researcher who was studying Tony's literacy development visited his home. She was surprised by the frosty reception she received from Tony's grandfather, who showed her an exercise book with pages filled with rows of immaculately written Chinese characters. This was the product of Tony's work at the Chinese Saturday class he regularly attended. The grandfather compared this with a drawing Tony had done on the back of a shop advertisement, where he had written his name in the corner in poorly formed English letters, some capital, some lower case.

At his Saturday class, Tony was clearly a capable and assiduous pupil, who could sit for long periods, carefully copying characters until the strokes were perfect, which is very important in Chinese calligraphy. At his mainstream school, he seemed unable to pay attention for a few minutes, and the work he produced often looked careless and messy. In discussing the home visit with the researcher, Tony's teacher began to understand that he was a very intelligent and hardworking child who needed to have the space to learn in different ways from the other pupils in the class, who were mostly 'monolingual'. Placing him in a special needs group would not help him develop to his full ability.

■ ACTIVITY 7.2 ■

Reflection - EAL or SEN?

Consider the issues raised in the vignette above about Tony. Think about pupils you have worked with who may have been identified as having SEN and pupils categorised as EAL. Use these open questions to reflect on the possible confusions between EAL and SEN.

1. From what you read above, how would you have assessed Tony's capabilities when he began school?

2. What might have helped the teacher to understand Tony's behaviour when he began school?

3. Why do you think Tony's grandfather was unhappy when he met the researcher?

4. What does the vignette tell you about the ways that multilingual pupils might learn literacy and how does this relate to the theories you read about in Chapter 3?

5. What does the vignette tell you about the links between home and school?

6. If you were Tony's teacher, what would you do, now that you know something about his experiences of literacy learning in his home community?

3 ASSESSMENT FOR LEARNING – FORMATIVE ASSESSMENT

3.1 PROFILING AND SAMPLING

In essence, assessment for learning is the process of making informed, diagnostic judgements about the pupils you teach in order to decide what to do next. To help them make progress in a particular area of their learning, you need to know what your pupils can and cannot do. Collecting the information you need to make these judgements takes thought and time. Profiling and sampling are important strategies in formative assessment. With multilingual and EAL learners, the first and most essential kind of profiling you need to do should take place as soon as – or even before – they enter school, whether as a new pupil in Nursery or Reception or as a new arrival further up the school. Hall et al. (2001) suggest the information that schools need to know about pupils' languages and cultural backgrounds, and they provide a useful photocopiable form (pp. 76–7), which could be used for the purpose. Ideally, this kind of information should be collected as part of normal, everyday whole-school routines and made available to teachers. If this is not the case in your school, you could collect it in your classroom. Here is a slightly adapted version of Hall's list:

1. Name child is called at home

2. Name to be called in school (if different)

3. Place of birth

4. Arrival date in UK

5. Family members who the child lives with

6. Length of previous schooling (in country of origin and elsewhere, including UK)

7. Religion and festivals observed

8. Languages spoken at home to:

   a. Mother

   b. Father

   c. Siblings

   d. Grandparents

9. Languages used by family members to child

10. Languages other than English that child can read/write

11. Is the child right- or left-handed?

12. Does the child attend any school or class in the community:

    a. Supplementary/complementary school

    b. Religious school

    c. Any other?

13. What languages are used and taught here?

14. Contact name(s) and details for the organisation(s)

15. Is an interpreter needed for the teacher to talk to the parents?

16. If so, who and how can they be contacted?

Another aspect of profiling is the sampling of progress through the work that pupils produce. This can be done for any subject across the curriculum. The aim is to collect evidence of pupils' achievements at different stages of their learning of a particular topic or concept. Their development in speaking, listening, writing or reading can also be evaluated in this way to help you decide what to do to help them to make progress.

For example, to assess a child's progress in writing, samples of their written work are collected over a set period of time. Then they are assessed according to criteria that recognise what they can already do and indicate what might be done next to promote learning.

The vignette below (taken from Edwards, 1995) shows the rapid progress that can be made by a multilingual learner in a supportive classroom environment where he is allowed to use his literacy in his first language to support his development in English.

▬ VIGNETTE ▬

Shahed's writing

Shahed was ten years old when he arrived in England from Iran. He had a high level of literacy in Farsi, the official language of Iran, but very little English. For the first few months of his time in England, he was given the opportunity to write in Farsi while the other pupils in the class were doing their normal literacy activities. The teacher was able to find out what he wrote about with the help of his father. Figure 7.1 is an example of one of his early Farsi texts.

In common with many other biliterate pupils, Shahed is using his knowledge of different scripts to express his meanings in his writing. After six months in the school, Shahed was still writing in Farsi, but his writing in English was developing fast. Figure 7.2 is taken from his writing journal.

Three months later, he was taking a full part in most lessons, and literacy was one of his favourites. In a lesson where the pupils had been looking at picture books in order to write a story for younger pupils, *Not Now Bernard* by David McKee was a favourite. Shahed wrote a letter to Bernard's parents (see Figure 7.3).

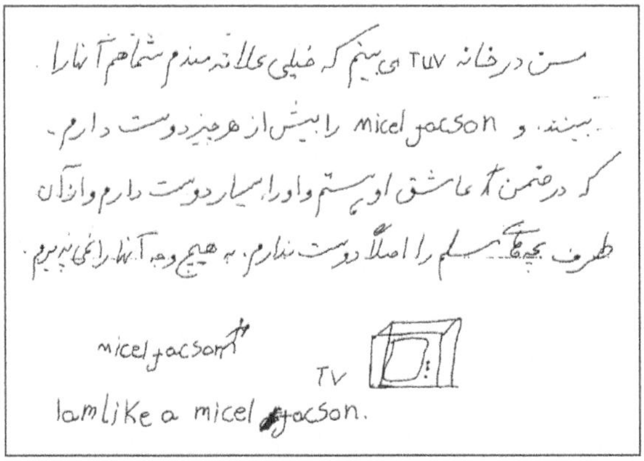

Figure 7.1 Shahed's Farsi writing

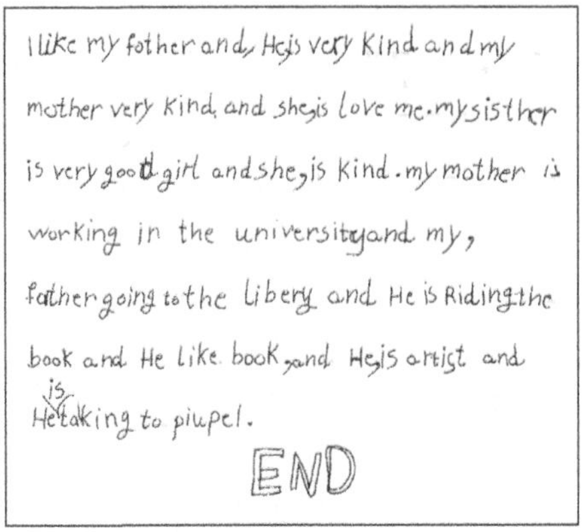

I like my father and, He is very Kind and my mother very Kind, and she is love me. my sisther is very good girl and she is Kind. my mother is working in the university and my, father going to the Libery and He is Riding the book and He Like book, and He is artist and He is taking to piupel.

END

Figure 7.2 Shahed's writing, six months later

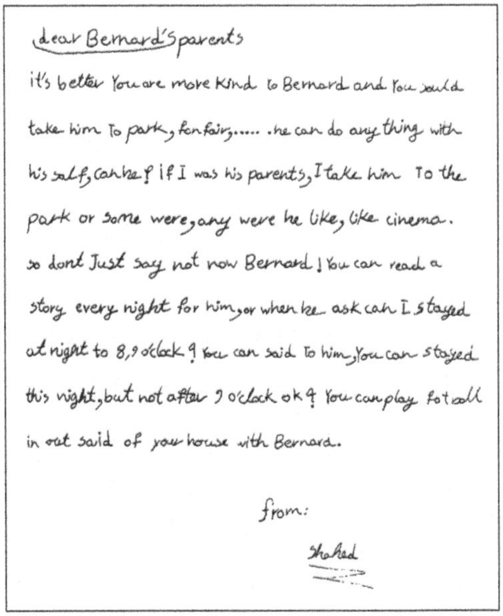

dear Bernard's parents

it's better You are more Kind to Bernard and You sould take him To park, fonfairs...... he can do any thing with his salf, can he? if I was his parents, I take him To the park or some were, any were he like, like cinema. so dont Just say not now Bernard, You can read a story every night for him, or when ke ask can I stayed at night to 8,9 o'clock? You can said to him, You can stayed this night, but not after 9 o'clock ok? You can play fot ball in out said of you house with Bernard.

from:

Shahed

Figure 7.3 Shahed's writing, three months later

ACTIVITY 7.3

Assessment for learning and writing

Here are some statements (taken from the National Literacy Strategy) which can be used to assess KS2 writing.

1. Write imaginative, interesting and thoughtful texts.

2. Produce texts that are appropriate to task, reader and purpose.

(Continued)

(Continued)

3. Organise and present whole texts effectively, sequencing and structuring information, ideas and content.

4. Construct paragraphs and use cohesion within and between paragraphs.

5. Vary sentences for clarity, purpose and effect.

6. Write sentences with technical accuracy of syntax and punctuation in phrases, clauses and sentences.

7. Select appropriate and effective vocabulary.

8. Use correct spelling.

Using these statements, analyse Shahed's two pieces of writing in English. Think about what he can do in each piece, and also what he seems to be trying to do. Think about these questions:

1. What progress do you think he shows in the three months from the first piece to the second?

2. What do you think are Shahed's strengths and weaknesses?

3. If you were his teacher, what would you do to help him make further progress in his writing?

The following case study is written by a secondary school teacher who works in a school with pupils with a very diverse range of languages.

ASSESSING MULTILINGUAL AND EAL LEARNERS ACROSS THE CURRICULUM IN A SECONDARY SCHOOL – CASE STUDY BY DIANNE EXCELL

Before the end of the summer term, secondary schools usually receive the SATs results of those pupils who will be joining them in September. These provide useful information but more is always needed. At the beginning of the autumn term, reading tests are often used as a baseline assessment to provide more specific information about each student. But it is not clear whether these standardised tests give a clear indication of ability for students learning English as an additional language (EAL). The observations shared here are the result of many years of experience in trying to overcome the issues which can create a barrier to achievement for EAL students in these tests.

At one girls' secondary school in inner-city Bradford most students have ethnic origins in Pakistan but were born in Bradford. Additionally, a few students each year arrive from a wide variety of countries such as Algeria, Bangladesh, Egypt, Greece, Hong Kong, India, Iraq, Japan, Jordan, Libya, Saudi Arabia, Spain, Sudan and Tanzania. Some speak three or more languages and have little experience of English in their home environment. Most have been taught in education systems where English is the medium of instruction for at least six years. Many students are literate only in English. When the students arrive in Year 7, most are competent and confident communicators (BICS), but are at different stages of developing CALP. They may not even have been entered in the SATs because their reading and writing skills were below the level of the tests.

Baseline reading tests

Until 2011, the school used a published reading test for baseline assessment to test understanding. I observed that there was often a discrepancy between student reading ages (RAs) derived from the test and their SATs results; many students who had achieved Level 4 in the KS2 English SATs had RAs at least two years behind their chronological age (CA). This risk of underachievement could apply even to students who achieved a good Level 5. Also, some students gained lower scores at the end of the year than at the beginning (and from one September to another). Many recent arrivals could achieve only a few correct answers and a low RA, even though they appeared to have good oral skills. There was a danger that this could be misinterpreted as that they had special educational needs (SEN) and lead to their being wrongly placed in the lowest set, with lower expectations and a risk of perpetual underachievement. At the end of the year, EAL students may still have a low RA even though they had significant progress in other curriculum areas and there should be no cause for concern – for example, a student with only two years of English language experience achieved Level 5 in science at the end of Year 7 but her RA in September Year 8 (6.05) was over a year lower than in Year 7 (7.06).

When analysing 40 tests one year, I found only five words which were almost always correct. Problems were caused by a range of factors, such as:

- lack of general, specialist or cultural knowledge (words such as: bolt, gale, saddle, theatre, tulip);

- idiomatic language ('raced' in a non-literal context);

- homophones (knot/not);

- prepositions ('to' instead of 'from');

- wrong word association (for example 'chemist' confused with 'clinic' for buying toothpaste and 'tiles' being associated with floors rather than 'roofs');

- unusual/old-fashioned polysyllabic words (fruit being sold from a 'barrow'; confusion of department/apartment, praise/price/prize).

I therefore concluded that the published test was only appropriate for testing monolingual English speakers because most sentences assumed prior cultural knowledge.

Development of alternative reading tests

In an attempt to eliminate cultural bias, I developed an Alternative Reading Test for the end of Years 7 and 8. Although it was not standardised, it was probably fairer than the published test because it was based directly on what had been taught in the curriculum of Year 7 and 8. Subject colleagues were asked to provide six key words from their scheme of work (ranging from basic to advanced), which all students had experienced at some stage in the year. I produced a test in a similar format to the published one by fitting the words into sentences and giving multiple choices for the answers (see Alternative Year 7 Reading Test at the end of this chapter, p. 161). I used the 'Collins KS3 Word Bank Dictionary' to create some sentences if the key word was listed. Word choices were made in such a way as to ensure that the students had to use a wide range of knowledge about words in order to select the correct answer, e.g.

- homophones (write, white, right, light);

- similar sounding words (pleasure, leisure, treasure, measure);

- words from the same context (pilgrim, journey, pilot);

- words with similar combinations of letters (digits, fidgets, gadgets);

- same beginnings (obligation, obedient, obstruction, objective).

(Continued)

(Continued)

The test was challenging for most students and seemed to be useful for identifying students who were gifted and could remember what they had learnt across the curriculum throughout the year. Pupils who gained low scores sometimes had learning difficulties or poor attendance. Others were new to English and making good progress; their errors highlighted areas still needing further support in their English-language acquisition. A final group who scored poorly were new to English and making less progress than expected, suggesting perhaps that they needed support. Moreover, the tests could also identify the words and concepts across the curriculum that were causing most difficulty. Subject colleagues were informed of the results so that appropriate adjustments could be made in succeeding years.

I marked all the Year 7 to Year 9 papers and analysed the results of the two top set English groups in Years 7 and 8. I found that in both groups two of the students only got 50 per cent of the answers correct, although some in Year 8 got over 90 per cent of the marks and in Year 7 over 80 per cent. Many students throughout KS3 had RAs which were well below their chronological ages. Another interesting result was that the Year 7 student who had the highest KS2 English SATs result (Level 5c) achieved the lowest RA (9:03) and one of the brightest Year 8 only got 52 per cent correct answers – with an RA two years below her previous year's! However, there were some students who achieved better than expected scores. Overall some achieved RAs two or three years above their CA and some two or three years below ... or more.

These results are shared with all colleagues so that strategies to compensate can be planned. The needs of individual students are also shared in order to ensure that able EAL students are not assumed to have special educational needs just because they have a low reading age. For example, in her initial assessments, one new arrival of Libyan heritage was able to write copious amounts of Arabic in mature language which showed the correct use of connectives, punctuation, verb tenses, punctuation as well as feelings and opinions. Although she produced less English writing on the same subjects, it was also correctly formed with some knowledge of sentence structure and grammar. However, her RA was seven years and six months and her spelling age was seven years and three months. There was a danger of the student being placed in the bottom set because it was thought she had speech, language and communication difficulties (SPLD), which is clearly not the case.

3.2 OBSERVING AS A TOOL FOR ASSESSMENT

In Chapter 3, section 2.1, p. 51, I mentioned the importance of observation for understanding the behaviour and learning of multilingual and EAL learners. It is particularly important to take as many factors into account as you can in your professional judgements, to ensure that you decide on the right provision to help pupils make progress. This is often the case when you are trying to assess the knowledge and understanding of multilingual and EAL learners. If a child is at an early stage of acquiring English and so has a limited capacity to produce spoken English, they may show their understanding of an instruction, an idea or a concept non-verbally. For example, watching carefully how young children place magnetic letters while trying to spell a word or how they physically write on a whiteboard can reveal a lot about what they understand about letter sounds and symbols. In the same way, in maths, children may not be able to count in English. But watching how they count using their fingers or concrete resources such as blocks and counters can tell you a lot about their understanding of numbers and number bonds. More broadly, watching how a child interacts with other pupils, in the playground and in other settings besides the classroom at different points in time, can show you a lot about their overall language development, self-confidence and identity as a learner.

In many ways, observing is a key professional skill for all teachers, and you will quickly find that you are constantly making a mental note of things you observe or notice about a child. If you get into the habit of writing down things that strike you as significant, it can help you understand your pupils as individuals and their strengths and needs. As discussed in Chapter 4, in many Early Years classrooms this is part of the routine, but it is not so common once pupils move through primary and into secondary schools. It is something you could introduce in your own class. As well as this kind of spontaneous observing and recording, it is useful to arrange more focused observations from time to time in order to collect evidence about a particular child's progress or evaluate a specific approach or strategy in your teaching.

Remember that in observing, as in any form of research, you must always act ethically and be sure to take account at all times of any ethical issues connected with the activity and the pupils involved. This is particularly important when you are a trainee, as you are working always under the guidance of others who will take ultimate responsibility for your actions. Here are a few ethical points to consider when carrying out observations.

- Always seek 'informed consent' before beginning an observation by making sure that pupils know you are observing them – teachers have responsibilities for protecting their pupils.

- Be aware of legal considerations and child protection issues.

- Make sure that confidentiality is maintained.

- Interpret and analyse – don't judge!

- Think about how you will use your findings – always be clear about the purpose of your observations.

- What do you do if you observe something inappropriate or dangerous – intervene or not intervene?

The last point has clear links to safeguarding and it is a good idea to check with your class teacher beforehand if there might be any sensitive issues related to a child you plan to observe. If anything did emerge during the course of the observation, for example inappropriate behaviour or comments that come up in conversation, your role as a trainee teacher is to pass them on immediately to your class teacher and then withdraw from the situation. Any resulting action may need to be kept confidential and, as someone who is in the school for a limited period, you must not be involved.

ACTIVITY 7.4

Observing

During your next school placement, if possible arrange to spend 20–30 minutes observing a multilingual or EAL learner in their classroom in order to gain a sense of how they behave and participate in the classroom. Have a brief conversation with the child before you begin so that they are aware of what you are doing. Here are a few 'dos and don'ts' to think about in setting up your observation.

1. Do remember to record contextual features - layout of classroom, organisation, lesson topic, resources used, etc.

2. Do set up a specific focus for your observation, e.g. a particular child, teacher's use of questions as a teaching strategy, etc.

(Continued)

(Continued)

3. Don't judge - only write down what you see and hear.

4. Don't observe for long periods of time - usually ten minutes at a time is enough, then break for a minute or so, and then continue.

5. Do recognise your own biases and viewpoints - no observation is neutral.

3.3 PUPILS' VIEWS

Another important aspect of assessment is finding out the perspectives pupils have on the ways they experience school and how they are taught. This can indicate ways in which teaching and general school routines and practices can be improved to enhance outcomes for pupils and even raise attainment. In the following case study, the authors show how they explore their pupils' views on their experiences in school.

━ LEARNER VOICE – CASE STUDY BY PETE RUSE AND LINDA SANDLER ━

At one secondary school, the EAL department conduct annually a series of exit interviews with Year 11 pupils who have arrived at the school as early-stage EAL learners. The outcomes of these interviews are collated and used for a variety of purposes - training, informing governors of the department's work (a highly significant purpose as it is not always obvious) and feedback for the department and pupils. Over the years, this exercise has informed developments in practice, such as deploying dedicated teaching assistant support for international new arrivals (INAs) and prompting staff generally to smile at pupils and be welcoming. This year the interviews were video recorded. The pupils were asked about their experiences when they first came to the school. Here are the responses of four pupils:

Dj: I was scared. Didn't know how to speak [English]. Sometimes girls you didn't speak their language they talking to your name and you didn't understand what they saying. Every day I cry when I went home 'cos I doesn't know how to speak English.

[In maths lessons]I didn't know the numbers. I was embarrassed ... I am good in maths but first time I didn't understand him to tell me the numbers. I just have in my brain ... I can't say it. It's too difficult. It was so hard.

A: I was afraid to say something - it came out wrong so I didn't say anything.

I thought I knew English. I could understand what people said [in Africa]. What didn't help was English accent because I was used to American accent in Africa.

D: [In English lessons] ... I was not able to speak properly. I was nervous inside and can't fully [get] out the words.

The school like so hard 'cos I didn't understand the English. And then to make a new friend. For to understand what the teacher is saying in the class.

M: I was the only one who could speak my language [Ndebele]. Like D has friends who can speak Portuguese and I am on my own. Even if I went to google translate it would not let me because my language is not there.

And about their previous experiences of education:

Dj: My worst subject was English in Africa. I doesn't like English. In my school in Portugal every time I get lowest grade in English and I cry a lot in my class. And then my mum say – you going to England to study the English. When I'm coming here I didn't want to come in England but I didn't have any choice. I think to myself I want to learn English and then I can do what I want to do. This school very different from Portugal. How to learn and how to teach is very different.

The thing I think is if at first I understand the English is when I gonna be a good student here, get good grade, because the [indistinct] in Portugal is hard … Harder than here … because … if they give you a test, every two weeks, you do your tests, you didn't get to do your plan like you do here, to do your plan or something [she is talking about revising]. You need just to do it in your hair [pointing to head].

M: [School here] is different. This school is big. And, like, our lessons that were different. Like, when I'm going to English it's just down there, but to go to English in my class [in Zimbabwe] I have to walk a long distance.

D: This school is big, like, in Portugal school is middle size. More pupil in the school.

And about what helped them:

D: The first people see, the first Portuguese people see was A, in science, then I said to her 'do you speak English, ah, do you speak Portuguese?' Then says 'yes' then I was happy … 'Cos he can help me as well …

[EAL lunchtime] homework club help me with homework … good friends, they help me as well, with the homework.

[Outside lessons] Got friends quickly. They say: 'what's your name?' and I say: 'D', then they say: 'what lesson you got next?' and I say: 'science or maths'. You [EAL teacher] help me. EAL teachers help me … help me to get good grade … yes, to understand. You give me dictionary to see what it means. That's help me.

Dj: [Meeting others with the same L1] Yes, really helpful to show me my class … So hard to talking with girl who talking English.

M: I come [to EAL lunchtime club] for help, like read book … Like watched TV and my dad helped me with the accent because he's been in this country a long time.

A: I had some students help me … Teachers … people from reception helped me.

And plans for the future:

M: I want to be a nurse. I applied in college for Health and Social Care. I have done my interviews and I'm waiting for my grades. I have to have good grades to go there.

Dj: My intention is to be a doctor. But now I think I'm not gonna do it this year. You need good grades in English. You need to get Cs and 5 GCSE to get in college or sixth form. It's 'A' level but I'm not worry about this. I'm doing retailing.

When I was in Portugal I get good grades in my own GCSEs. I just have less level in English. All my grades was good. I chose to be a doctor but now I think I'm not gonna do it because I don't have a good level for my GCSE. Now I'm doing retailing. [Happy?] Yes, I'm happy for that.

(Continued)

(Continued)

A: I will be study travel and tourism in college because I'm studying French and I want to, like, work in a sort of a hotel that I can translate French into English or any other language that I can learn.

D: I wanna be a football player. I got grades to do football in college ... football academy. For football academy you need to get D so I think I'm gonna get D in some things.

And advice for school (with respect to early stage EAL learners):

Dj: More time in lessons to do their work.

A: To be nice to them and smile and just try to help them as much as they can.

One recurring positive feature mentioned in exit interviews is the EAL lunchtime homework club, where pupils develop cross-year and cross-language friendships based on their common experiences as international new arrivals. It is a forum that allows them to support each other and draw on each other's experience. Here, they are in a space that values their use of their home languages and this has allowed EAL practitioners to encourage learners to use their home languages in classrooms to learn, to make notes in home language, for example.

This year's exercise has prompted thinking among staff about how to better support pupils' progression from school, including college applications and interviews. It has prompted thinking about how to make space for learners to talk about their aspirations earlier in their school careers so they can become clearer about where they want to go and how they might get there. One development already planned is to establish a series of themed EAL homework club lunchtimes around different topics and issues. Life goals might be one, interview practice another. What came across really strongly, though, is how significant a life event it is for these learners to come to another country with another language environment. We can forget how scary that can be and it is a good thing that as education practitioners we are reminded of it.

3.4 CONSULTING WITH PARENTS

Tony's story above (see the vignette in section 2.2, p. 148) reveals a great deal about the importance of finding out about a child's home and community experiences of learning and of literacy, a point that has been emphasised many times throughout this book. In terms of assessment, it can help you interpret what the child does in school in much more holistic ways and lead to much better informed decisions about what to provide for the child. As part of the assessment cycle, teachers also have the responsibility of reporting pupils' achievements to their parents and providing an opportunity for them to discuss their child's progress. As a trainee, you may be involved in this and you need to gain some experience in this area. An important issue in relation to multilingual and EAL learners is the need to make sure that the arrangements for reporting and consulting meet the parents' needs, which may differ according to their language and cultural backgrounds. In some families, it is not the parents who take the responsibility for communicating with the school about the child's education: it may be an uncle or aunt or even an older sibling. There may be the need for an interpreter, which might be someone working in the school or someone from the community.

CHAPTER SUMMARY

The four learning outcomes for this chapter are about developing your understanding of the different purposes and types of assessment as a whole, as well as specific issues related to EAL and multilingual learners. The chapter also introduces you to some practical ways in which you can use assessment processes to support and promote learning for your multilingual and EAL learners. Thinking about school-based experiences you have had in general and with EAL and multilingual learners in particular, reflect on the learning outcomes using the questions below.

Self-assessment questions

1. What are the key differences between assessment *for* learning and assessment *of* learning? What are the general issues related to each in assessing the achievements and attainment of EAL and multilingual learners?

2. Why do you think it is important that learning needs are not confused with language needs for multilingual and EAL learners?

3. Why are assessment for learning strategies, such as profiling and sampling, particularly important for multilingual and EAL learners? What specific issues have you faced (or might you face) in sampling the work of a child who is relatively new to English?

4. What factors may make consulting with parents of multilingual and EAL learners about their pupils' achievements and attainment different from consulting with the parents of 'monolingual' pupils, and how is it the same?

FURTHER READING

Briggs, M. (2011) 'Assessment', in A. Hansen (ed.), *Primary Professional Studies*. Exeter: Learning Matters, pp. 184–203.

This chapter provides a full overview of assessment and introduction to assessment for learning and assessment of learning in primary classrooms.

Hall, D., Griffiths, D., Haslam, L. and Wilkin, Y. (2001) *Assessing the Needs of Multilingual Pupils: Living in Two Languages*, 2nd edn. London: David Fulton.

This short book provides very clear guidance on assessing multilingual and EAL pupils, avoiding the pitfalls of conflating EAL with SEN.

STUDYING AT MASTER'S LEVEL

Critical reading:

Hopewell, S. and Escamilla, K. (2014) 'Struggling reader or emerging biliterate student? Reevaluating the criteria for labeling emerging bilingual students as low achieving', *Journal of Literacy Research*, 46 (1), pp. 68-89.

(Continued)

(Continued)

In this article, Hopewell and Escamillia call into question the official ways of assessing multilingual and EAL learners in the USA, which are very similar to those in the UK. They argue that official frameworks disadvantage multilingual learners. They prove their case by interpreting one set of data according to two different frameworks, leading to very different outcomes. They make positive suggestions for changing the system. The article makes quite extensive use of statistics, but do not worry if you are not familiar with how they work - keep reading so you grasp the main ideas.

After reading the chapter, consider the following questions, ideally in discussion with colleagues:

1.   Why do you think that the authors suggest (on p. 69) that the history of assessment in the USA is 'dubious'?

2.   What is the 'Matthew effect' and how do you think it applies to the assessment of multilingual and EAL learners?

3.   According to Hopewell and Escamillia, what is 'parallel monolingualism'? How does it contrast with 'holistic bilingualism' and why is it unhelpful in assessing multilingual and EAL learners?

4.   On p. 82, the authors characterise the tailored instruction provided in Colorado for pupils labelled 'low ability'. What are its key features, and how does it *not* meet the needs of multilingual and EAL learners?

REFERENCES

Bell Foundation (2017) *EAL Assessment Framework*. Available at https://www.bell-foundation.org.uk/eal-programme/teaching-resources/eal-assessment-framework/ (accessed 31 August 2018).

Department for Education (DfE) (2016) *Education Data Division – Request for Change Form for CBDS*. Available at https://assets.publishing.service.gov.uk/government/uploads/system/uploads/attachment_data/file/509299/RFC_875_-_new_data_item_for_proficiency_in_English.pdf (accessed 5 December 2018).

Edwards, V. (1995) *Writing in Multilingual Classrooms*. Reading: University of Reading, Reading and Language Information Centre.

Gravelle, M. (ed.) (2000) *Planning for Multilingual Learners: An Inclusive Curriculum*. Stoke-on-Trent: Trentham Books.

Gregory, E. (2008) *Learning to Read in a New Language: Making Sense of Words and Worlds*. London: Sage.

Hall, D., Griffiths, D., Haslam, L. and Wilkin, Y. (2001) *Assessing the Needs of Multilingual Pupils: Living in Two Languages*, 2nd edn. London: David Fulton.

National Association for Language Development in the Curriculum (NALDIC) (2017) *School Census Returns: NALDIC's Position Statement*. Available at https://naldic.org.uk/assessment/eal-assessment-schools/school-census-returns/ (accessed 31 August 2018).

Quality and Curriculum Authority (QCA) (2000) *A Language in Common: Assessing English as an Additional Language*. Sudbury: QCA Publications. Available at https://webarchive.nationalarchives.gov.uk/20100205230820/http://www.qcda.gov.uk/5739.aspx (accessed 5 December 2018).

Safford, K. (2003) *Teachers and Pupils in the Big Picture: Seeing Real Pupils in Routinised Assessment*. Reading: NALDIC. Available at http://www.naldic.org.uk/eal-publications-resources/Shop/shop-products/op17 (accessed 28 October 2014).

Ullman, P. (2018) 'Withdrawal of EAL proficiency data from the Schools census returns: a response from NALDIC', *EAL Journal*, Summer, pp. 10–11.

ALTERNATIVE YEAR 7 READING TEST

Name: _____ Form: _____ Date: _____

Raw Score: _____ Percentage: _____ RA: _____ CA: _____

Read each sentence carefully. Look at the list of words. Choose one word from the list which completes each sentence best. Underline the word.

1. The school rounders _____ won the game.

    term; team; time; tear

2. At the theatre they saw a _____.

    plea; pray; poem; play

3. He changed the _____ to make the text look clearer.

    font; fund; front; formula

4. We belong to the _____ race.

    boat; sports; human; humour

5. The _____ of cricket are complicated.

    runs; rules; role; routine

6. The players ran onto the _____.

    field; file; fiend; fierce

7. A _____ angle is 90 degrees.

    write; white; right; light

8. She read the _____ carefully before beginning her project.

    brief; birth; breathe; breadth

9. The number 1492 contains four _____.

    fidgets; digits; gadgets; minutes

10. They gave a _____ account of the war.

    battle; based; biased; beside

11. She crossed the _____ on a camel.

    desert; develop; design; deserve

12. She _____ so well that we won the match.

    blow; below; bowled; boiled

13. Is this _____ of information fact or opinion?

    source; sauce; sores; scarce

(Continued)

(Continued)

14. We tried to _____ what the story was about.

    point; portrait; phrase; predict

15. They were better at _____ than bowling.

    knitting; writer; painter; batting

16. You can relax in your _____ time.

    pleasure; leisure; treasure; measure

17. Muslims fast in _____.

    religion; rebellion; Ramadan; remember

18. The _____ went to Makkah for the Hajj.

    journey; pilot; personal; pilgrim

19. She studied a _____ language at school.

    foreign; French; forget; forward

20. The paper came out of the _____ with the words on it.

    product; private; printer; pointer

21. The south of France has a warm _____.

    climax; climber; migrate; climate

22. The _____ displayed what she had typed.

    mouse; monitor; motor; module

23. _____ can be odd or even.

    names; letters; cucumbers; numbers

24. The Norman _____ was in 1066.

    connect; conquest; conscience; construct

25. Who _____ the best package?

    deserving; described; desire; designed

26. There was new _____ on her computer.

    software; sometimes; solution; source

27. She knew where all the letters were on the _____.

    knowledge; kilometrer; kitchen; keyboard

28. I used a _____ to write my History homework.

    computer; connection; consequence; component

29. There is no _____ to support this idea.

    escape; estimate; evidence; evaluation

30. A faithful Muslim is _____ to the will of Allah.

    obligation; obedient; obstruction; objectives

31. _____ Geography is the study of mountains and rivers.

    physical; psychology; philosophy; photocopy

32. Look at the records on the school's _____.

    library; classrooms; database; lessons

33. They _____ the results of the experiment.

    apparatus; anniversary; approximately; analysed

34. Three quarters is a _____.

    fraction; fiction; fashion; friction

35. There was an attractive leaflet to _____ people to come.

    person; parade; persuade; permission

36. Who did you vote for in the ____?

    education; edition; electricity; election

37. They measured the _____ of the field.

    perimeter; centimetre; percentage; kilometre

38. The magician is a clever _____.

    charity; chapter; challenge; character

39. Bradford has a large Asian _____.

    commandment; committee; communication; community

40. Britain is a _____ where people elect their government.

    democracy; demonstration; dictionary; dependency

41. There are several _____ in an experiment.

    vegetables; valuables; variables; varieties

42. After the experiment her _____ was that water boils at 100°C.

    condition; competition; concentration; conclusion

43. This _____ began in Roman times.

    settlement; sentence; statement; section

44. Myths and fables are _____ stories.

    triangular; typical; traditional; thesaurus

45. Looking after the environment is good _____.

    commandment; civilisation; circumstances; citizenship

(Continued)

(Continued)

46. The _____ of the project was set out clearly.

   significant; specification; spectacular; secretary

47. _____ is measured with a rain gauge.

   precipitation; punctuation; prediction; preparation

48. Her _____ told the truth about her life.

   anthology; alliteration; autobiography; antonym

Mark scheme:

1. team	2. play	3. font
4. human	5. rules	6. field
7. right	8. brief	9. digits
10. biased	11. desert	12. bowled
13. source	14. predict	15. batting
16. leisure	17. ramadan	18. pilgrim
19. foreign	20. printer	21. climate
22. monitor	23. numbers	24. conquest
25. designed	26. software	27. keyboard
28. computer	29. evidence	30. obedient
31. physical	32. database	33. analysed
34. fraction	35. persuade	36. election
37. perimeter	38. character	39. community
40. democracy	41. variables	42. conclusion
43. settlement	44. traditional	45. citizenship
46. specification	47. precipitation	48. autobiography

8

PROMOTING INDEPENDENCE: USING HOME LANGUAGES AND CULTURES IN LEARNING

---- LEARNING OUTCOMES ----

This chapter will help you to achieve the following learning outcomes:

* develop awareness of the importance of promoting independent learning in your pupils;

* gain knowledge of practical classroom strategies that promote independence in learning across the curriculum, using pupils' funds of knowledge;

* gain understanding of some strategies through which families and communities can become involved in their children's learning.

INTRODUCTION

This chapter provides practical examples of strategies and resources to promote multilingual and EAL pupils' independent learning across the curriculum, grounded in the theories about language, multilingualism and learning discussed in Chapters 2 and 3, in particular the concept of 'funds of knowledge' and the importance of talk for learning. In Chapter 3 'funds of knowledge' was introduced as a theoretical concept to explain the links between your pupils' home and family learning experiences and their success in school. The most important funds of knowledge for EAL learners are, of course, the languages they speak and write in other contexts besides mainstream school. With this in mind, in section 2 of this chapter there is a discussion of the community-based learning contexts that many multilingual pupils attend.

The use of home languages in mainstream classrooms is gaining popularity but is still a controversial area. There is no recognition or support for the use of home languages in learning in current official policy. Many secondary schools, and some primaries, have 'English only' policies in their classrooms. But, as I have argued at several points in this book, there is a great deal of research that supports the idea of bringing home languages into learning in mainstream classrooms. Research, such as Cummins' work described in Chapter 3, has for many years shown the cognitive benefits for learning when pupils are allowed to access their full language repertoires in classroom activities. This is discussed further in section 3.1 of this chapter where there are two case studies. The first, by Charlotte Wood, gives an example of using language repertoires as funds of knowledge in science in a secondary school. The second case study is by Shila Begum, and describes learning to count in home and family contexts.

Throughout the chapter, there are discussion points and activities to help you think about the ideas you are reading about, and there are some suggestions for further reading at the end of the chapter.

These are the main sections and subsections of the chapter:

1 PROMOTING INDEPENDENT LEARNING

1.1 PRINCIPLES FOR INDEPENDENT LEARNING

The theories introduced in Chapter 2 help us to recognise the active and dynamic nature of learning. Learners are not merely 'empty vessels' waiting passively to be filled with knowledge – they are active participants in the processes of interaction through which learning happens and new knowledge is constructed. This view of learning, particularly in relation to language learning, is supported by such theoretical ideas as Vygotsky's ZPD (p. 36) and Cummins' linguistic interdependence hypothesis (p. 56). Unfortunately, one major and potentially very dangerous effect of developments in initial teacher training and CPD over recent years is that we now tend to see teaching and learning as two separate activities. Instead of promoting understanding of the subtle relationships between the two, much initial training is about teaching methods, strategies and activities, which is only one part of the picture. CPD has largely come to be seen as packages of 'training' to be delivered in pre-digested chunks to waiting audiences of teachers, often by commercial companies. It could be argued that there is an unrealistic aim embedded in many government initiatives, that of finding the infallible, 'perfect' methods of teaching that will always work with all pupils and have guaranteed success. Such methods do not exist. The onus on targets and results feeds into this, putting pressure on teachers and schools to predict with certainty what their pupils will attain. This is particularly so in secondary schools, but primary schools are equally held hostage to their targets.

Once they get to know their pupils, teachers may be able to predict outcomes to a certain extent, but they cannot possibly be expected to predict with 100 per cent accuracy what results their pupils will attain, nor even what their pupils will learn from the activities they provide. The negative implications of the 'universal model' of assessment for EAL learners are spelt out in Chapter 3 (section 2.1, p. 52). There are many examples in this book which show how pupils interpret what teachers ask them to do in creative and sometimes surprising ways, often coming up with new and inventive interpretations. Teaching and learning are always in dialogue, and the practical implications of this are explored in the next section. One of the essential skills of an effective teacher is the ability to construct the kinds of 'safe spaces' which offer the best opportunities possible for their pupils to learn through using their personal knowledge and experience to achieve deep understanding of the new content being presented (see Chapter 2, section 1.2, p. 30). In this way, teaching is more productive, learning is stronger and – perhaps even more importantly – pupils are developing the skills which help them to become confident, independent learners.

Allwright and Hanks (2009) argue eloquently that learners should be regarded as 'key developing practitioners' (p. 2), in just the same way as teachers are regarded as practitioners whose skills and understanding continually develop (hence the existence of books such as this). They go on to introduce 'five propositions about learners' (pp. 4–7), which are worth repeating here as they sum up what I think are essential elements in being and becoming independent learners. Here, re-worded slightly, are Allwright and Hanks' propositions:

- Learners are unique individuals who learn and develop best in their own ways.

- Learners are social beings who learn and develop best in a mutually supportive environment.

- Learners are capable of taking learning seriously – they are motivated to learn.

- Learners are capable of independent decision-making.

- Learners are capable of developing as practitioners of learning – in other words, they can learn how to become independent learners.

Allwright and Hanks' writing is based on their research and practice around the world with language learners of different ages, beginning in Brazil in the 1990s. Their conclusions are relevant for both primary and secondary pupils in England. They link with ideas that have been around in the education system in England for many years, such as the need for high expectations, both by teachers and by the demands of the system itself. They also stress the importance of recognising learners' identities and link with various theoretical ideas I have introduced in this book, such as the ways that language, culture and identity are connected in learning (see Chapter 2, section 1.2, p. 30). Sonia Nieto's vital point is that everyone is capable of learning, but we learn best in our own individual ways. The risks of categorising EAL learners as needing to be taught alongside SEN pupils (see Chapter 3, section 2.1, p. 51) or in so-called 'low ability' sets are many. In the next section, I explore a range of strategies to promote independent learning, based on another important way of thinking about teaching and learning which benefits from 'the power of talk' – **dialogic teaching**.

ACTIVITY 8.1

Understanding independent learning

Read through the following two teaching and learning episodes and think about them in relation to the two questions below. Discuss them with colleagues or fellow students if you have the opportunity. The pupils in both episodes are in Year 6.

(Continued)

(Continued)

- Which of the two episodes gives a better example of independent learning? Explain your reasons for your choice – what specific aspects of the activities will promote independence?

- How might you develop the activities in the other episode, to promote more opportunities for independence?

Episode 1

In the last lesson in a set of literacy lessons on narrative poetry, the teacher's aim is for his pupils to provide some evidence of their responses to a long narrative poem they have been working on. After a whole-class introduction where he uses questioning to make sure the pupils can recall the story and understand the messages underpinning the poem, he organises them into groups according to their ability in reading. He gives each child a photocopy of the poem and each group a different set of questions to discuss, written on a big card. He informs them that he expects each pupil to write their own responses in complete sentences to the questions by the end of the lesson. There is a teaching assistant on hand to help those pupils who find writing difficult. The pupils set off on their task: there is little talk between them in the groups as they mostly concentrate on producing their written responses. Towards the end of the lesson they are largely working in silence.

Episode 2

In a history lesson, the teacher's aim is for her pupils to understand the experiences of children being evacuated during the Second World War. They already have quite a lot of subject knowledge about the war, including the reasons for the evacuations, how they were organised, how many children were involved and so on. There is a collection of reference books available in the classroom, as well as computers with relevant websites accessible. After a short whole-class introduction to review their prior knowledge about the Second World War through question and answer, the teacher asks her pupils to organise themselves into small groups and then sets them the task of writing a letter from a child evacuee to their parents at home the day after they have been evacuated. Each group is to work together to produce one letter, to be read out to the rest of the class at the end of the lesson. They are allowed to refer to any of the books and websites as they wish. The lesson becomes a bit noisy at times, but by the end, each group has more or less finished the task.

1.2 PRACTICAL STRATEGIES TO PROMOTE INDEPENDENT LEARNING

The notion of 'safe spaces' for learning, raised in the previous section and in other parts of the book, has practical implications for teachers working in multilingual classrooms. It links with Wolfe and Alexander's (2008) concept of 'dialogic teaching'. In this section, I explain briefly what these two ideas mean for teaching, and why they are important in developing independence in learning, particularly for EAL pupils. Activity 8.2 provides some practical examples of activities that have the potential to promote independent learning across the curriculum. They are the kinds of activities that can be adapted to different ages and subject areas.

The idea of 'safe spaces' comes from cultural studies. It is not really about physical spaces, though these, of course, are important. It is primarily about the kinds of relationships that need to develop between teachers and pupils in order to promote mutual respect, trust and the willingness of both parties to take risks. A major factor in this in multilingual classrooms is in the use of home languages. I have argued strongly throughout this book that languages are resources for learning and that multilingualism is a rich resource. I understand fully that teachers take a big risk when they allow their pupils to use languages that they do not understand in their classrooms: perhaps they will say rude words or abuse the trust invested in them in other ways. Also, how on earth do you assess something that you do not understand yourself? In using their own languages, pupils also take a risk: perhaps they will be laughed at, or they may not be very confident speakers of their home language, as is the case with many second- or third-generation multilingual pupils. But, in the right kind of 'safe space', allowing pupils to use their full language repertoires can open out opportunities for learning, leading to meaningful interactions which promote critical thinking and deep understanding of the issues being discussed.

In the same way, the kinds of dialogic talk advocated by Wolfe and Alexander can lead to interactions that both support pupils' understandings of the concepts they are being taught and help them to develop the cognitive skills they need to succeed as learners, in a wide range of ways. But there is no package of 'dialogic activities' that teachers can take off the shelf and deliver to their pupils. Developing a dialogic approach is more about the ways that things are done, the relationships that are constructed and the attitudes and values behind the activities. Wolfe and Alexander suggest five 'teaching principles' that help teachers to think about how to plan activities that are genuinely dialogic. They say that teaching is more likely to be dialogic if it is:

- **Collective**: participants work together.

- **Reciprocal**: participants listen to each other and consider alternative viewpoints.

- **Supportive**: participants express their ideas freely without fear of embarrassment and help each other to common understandings.

- **Cumulative**: participants build on each others' answers to develop coherent lines of thinking and understanding.

- **Purposeful**: the classroom talk is open and dialogic, but also planned and structured with specific learning objectives in view.

They also provide a useful checklist of the kinds of 'things' (i.e. functions – see Chapter 2, section 1.3, p. 32) that pupils need to be able to do with language and which promote independent learning and real understanding. This list begins with the simpler functions, moving to the more complex:

- Narrate
- Explain
- Analyse
- Speculate
- Imagine

- Explore
- Evaluate
- Discuss
- Argue
- Justify

These two checklists are very useful for your planning. They have many parallels with Cummins' quadrant (see Chapter 6, section 1.2, p. 113). You could incorporate the 'function words' into your learning objectives in subjects across the curriculum to remind you of the kinds of language your pupils need to use in the activity and of what they are learning to do with language.

ACTIVITY 8.2

Activities to promote independent learning

Below, there are eight examples of activities designed to promote independent learning through dialogic talk (they are not complete lesson plans). Using Wolfe and Alexander's list above, think about which functions of language and kinds of talk and thinking they entail and help to develop. They all entail more than one kind of talk, and are the kinds of activities that can be used with pupils of different ages. Choose three or four activities and do the following for each activity:

- Decide which language functions (using the list above) each activity would help to develop.

- Write two learning objectives, using relevant function words, for each activity.

Activity 1

In science, before beginning their first lesson on a new topic related to living things, pupils in **Years 5 or 6** are given five minutes to write down as much as they can about what they already know. They are told that the writing is just for them; the teacher will not look at it. They can write in any language they wish. After the five minutes, they have two minutes to share and compare their ideas with their talk partner (see p. 133). After this, the class comes back together for a brief plenary before they start the lesson.

Activity 2

Pupils in **Years 7 or 8** have been studying the First World War over several lessons. They are told that they are to have a visiting speaker who they will be able to interview on the causes of the war. Then they are organised into groups of four and given ten minutes to come up with five questions to ask the visitor. Following this, the pupils are organised into pairs to practise asking and answering questions. While this is going on, the teacher collates all the questions and the activity finishes with the class deciding which are the best questions to ask the visitor.

Activity 3

In maths, pupils in **Years 1 or 2** have been learning their times tables up to 6x. As a consolidation activity, they are organised into mixed ability groups and each group is given a set of tables sums on small cards (see Figure 8.1). In their groups, they have to organise the cards correctly (there may be some incorrect answers). Following this, the group is given a set of blank cards and asked to write any missing correct answers, then come up with questions of their own to ask another group, which they write on the cards.

Activity 4

Years 3 or 4 pupils are beginning a new topic on the location of different countries in the world, as well as the ideas of latitude, longitude, the tropics and so on. The teacher works from a blank map of the world on the smart board, and asks pupils to come up in turn to point out countries they know or have visited, countries their families came from, countries where they have relatives and so on. After this, the teacher marks in the equator and the Tropics of Cancer and Capricorn, and the class checks whether any of the countries they have discussed is between the tropics. The teacher sets the pupils a task for the next lesson, which is to find out what they can about the words 'latitude' and 'longitude'.

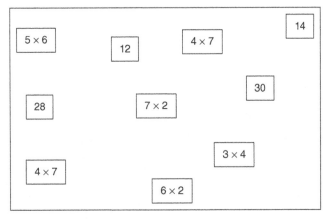

Figure 8.1 Activity 3: Times tables check-cards

Activity 5

In literature, **Year 11** pupils are working in groups to revise their knowledge of *Romeo and Juliet* in preparation for a written assignment. Each group has copies of the play and is working on a different scene. They have a chart to fill in where they need to write details of characters, main events and closing actions, as in Figure 8.2. When they finish their charts, two pupils from each group move to another group, who give them a quiz on their scene.

Act:	Scene:	
Characters	**Main events**	**Closing actions**

Figure 8.2 Activity 5: Romeo and Juliet scene summary chart

Activity 6

In maths in **Years 9 or 10**, two pupils who have recently arrived from Poland are told in Polish what the new topic of study is going to be and are given the opportunity to write down what they already know about it and then explain (all in Polish) how they studied the topic previously in Poland. NB: this could happen in most classrooms and in other subject areas.

Activity 7

In design and technology, **Year 8** pupils are evaluating the plans they have made for designing a garden for people with sight impairments, following a set of specifications. Working in pairs using different-coloured highlighters, they are checking each other's plans against the specifications. Some pairs of pupils share the same home language. The teacher has asked them to devise their own way of coding the plans to show which specifications they meet and which they do not and has said that

(Continued)

(Continued)

they can use their home languages if they wish. After completing the task, they have to report back in a whole-class plenary.

Activity 8

In French, which is the Modern Foreign Language (MFL) that all the class are studying in **Year 5**, multilingual pupils are invited to share the ways they say things in their own languages about the topic they are studying. The teacher builds up a comparison chart on the whiteboard and then invites everyone in the class to point out any similarities or differences between the words.

2 INVOLVING FAMILIES AND COMMUNITIES IN LEARNING

2.1 THE WORK OF SUPPLEMENTARY/COMPLEMENTARY SCHOOLS

Many EAL pupils go in the evenings or at weekends to community-based schools to learn to speak, read and write their home languages and to learn about their home cultures. Such schools have existed in England for as long as different languages have been part of our society. Most commonly called **supplementary schools** in the past, they are now often known as **complementary schools**, which acknowledges the ways in which they can complement learning in mainstream schools and contribute to educational success. In most major cities in England, there are many such schools – sometimes up to 50 or 60. They meet in rented mainstream school premises, people's homes, community centres or places of worship. Some have been functioning for over 50 years: in Bradford, for example, there is a Polish Saturday school which has been running since the 1960s, attended by children from all over West Yorkshire. Complementary schools have a variety of aims and purposes, depending on the hopes and aspirations of the communities that establish and nurture them. Maintaining heritage and home languages and cultures is a very important aim, but there are others. Making up for the problems faced by pupils in mainstream schools can be a big motivating factor – such is the case for schools set up by African-Caribbean parents in the 1970s, who felt that institutional racism in the education system was affecting the chances of their children.

Complementary schools take a big role in the teaching of modern languages that are not available in mainstream schools. Indeed, mainstream schools benefit from this in that pupils taught in complementary school can then take the GCSE or 'A' level exam in the language they have been learning, thus boosting the school's results. Many different languages are taken at GCSE in this way. Polish is an interesting example – it is now fifth highest on the list of languages taken at GCSE, with a high level of success, but all the teaching takes place outside of mainstream settings.

Until very recently, complementary/supplementary schools were a hidden aspect of education in England, hardly known about and largely ignored. The Swann Report (DES, 1985) can take some responsibility for this, with its strong recommendation that, on the grounds of 'equal opportunities', the teaching of community languages should have no place in mainstream education and should entirely be the concern of the communities themselves. But in recent years, research is beginning to open out the wide range of ways in which complementary schools operate (e.g. Conteh et al., 2007) and to reveal the advantages of communication between complementary and mainstream schools, to the benefit of the pupils who attend them, their teachers and their families.

ACTIVITY 8.3

Finding out about community-based learning

- Look on the website of the National Resource Centre for Supplementary Education (http://www. supplementaryeducation.org.uk) to find out about the supplementary/community schools movement and whether there are any such schools in the area in which you live or study.

- Talk to the pupils that you teach to find out whether they take part in any out-of-hours learning and, if so, what form it takes. If you can, try to arrange a visit to a supplementary/complementary school and observe one or two lessons. Even if you cannot understand the languages being taught, you can get a sense of the approaches taken by the teachers, and the responses of the children.

- Think about the ways they are similar to or different from the approaches taken in other schools that you know.

2.2 BRINGING HOME LANGUAGES AND CULTURES INTO SCHOOL

The first point to emphasise in this section is that, while it is certainly very helpful if you can speak even a little of the home languages of the pupils you teach, it is not really a disadvantage if you can't. It is much more important that you have a positive attitude towards the language diversity of your pupils, and that you understand something of the ways that languages work and of how knowledge of other languages influences the learning of English. The theories discussed in Chapters 2 and 3 should give you some starting points in this. This said, if you can say a few words in some of the languages spoken by the pupils in your class, it will promote a positive and welcoming classroom ethos – even if you just say 'hello' in a child's language it will make their face light up and make them feel included in the class. The 'monolingual' pupils in your class also benefit from such a welcoming approach to other languages. Awareness of the language diversity of their communities is a very valuable way to break down barriers and promote social cohesion.

Language and cultural diversity can become a feature of your classroom through interactive displays, through the stories you choose to read and study with your pupils, through the choices of content you make in different areas of the curriculum, and in many other ways. Time can be found in PSHE or other times in the day to allow the pupils to bring in news and information about family and community events and about family in other parts of the world. The school and classroom can visibly reflect the diversity and global connections of the community in which it is situated. One school I worked in had clocks in the reception area and in the classrooms set to the times of the countries of origin of the pupils' families. If pupils go on visits to extended family in their countries of origin, this can be turned into a positive aspect of their education by asking them to find out information to tell the class on their return and to bring back artefacts, if possible.

Once back at school, they can be encouraged to bring in photos and to talk about where they went and what they did. Having a map available of the country visited can be very helpful, so that routes can be traced and places identified. If proficiency in English is an issue, a family member could be invited into the class to support the child in talking about their visit, or questions could be written down and taken home for parents to answer. This can lead to fascinating discussions, such as the one described in Conteh (2003, pp. 42–4) about an unusual medical treatment witnessed by a Year 3 child on a visit to Pakistan. Zofia Donnelly's case study (see Chapter 3, p. 47) illustrates the way that much richer discussion can be generated by allowing pupils to talk about their family experiences in their home languages.

Simple routines, such as doing the register in different languages, can promote awareness of language diversity; the pupils can respond to their names with a greeting in any language they know. If a child brings a new language to the class, they can be asked to teach their classmates the greetings. This can be reinforced with a poster showing *How many ways can we say hello?* which is regularly reviewed and updated. I once visited a Year 3 class where a boy, keen to find a new greeting to add to the poster, met me at the door and asked, 'Miss, can you speak any languages?' As well as greetings, other simple language features can be brought into the class as part of whole-class routines and in sharing times, possibly during PHSE. Primary pupils find counting in different languages fun and interesting. Start off by introducing a way of counting up to five in another language and then find out what languages the pupils themselves can count in. This can be surprising, as they may have been taught to count in their home languages by their grandparents or other family members. This project can grow and become an ongoing subject of interest, involving parents, research on the internet and a working wall display. In secondary classrooms, activities like this can take on a more research-focused approach, where pupils are set off to find specific information on the internet or from others in the school, and are then developed into quizzes, PowerPoint presentations and so on.

Another excellent activity, which links to literacy, geography and RE, is finding out about the pupils' names and their origins. This can be done with pupils of any age. The following vignette illustrates an activity with Year 1 children.

▬ VIGNETTE 1 ▬

Name tree

Lisa, a trainee on her final placement in a Year 1 class in a multilingual school, decided to make a 'name tree' as part of her literacy work. She began by making a large cut-out tree shape (without leaves) for the classroom wall. Then she introduced the activity by showing the pupils a photo of her own daughter and telling them what her name meant and why she was given it. After this, she gave each child a letter and a leaf cut out of green paper to take to their parents. The letter, which was available in different languages, gave brief information about the project and asked the parents to help their child to write their name on one side of the leaf, in their own language as well as English if possible, and a sentence about what the name meant and why they were given it on the other. The parents were enthusiastic about the project, and the leaves soon began returning to the classroom, along with positive comments from parents, who noticed the name tree sprouting leaves (Figure 8.3). Lisa organised her literacy lessons over a couple of weeks to allow each child to stand up, show their leaf, give a brief explanation of their name and then attach it to the name tree. The teacher, TA and other adults in the class added their own names. When all the names were on the tree, Lisa invited the parents to come and see the completed name tree. She also prepared a presentation with the pupils about the project for a whole-school activity.

Figure 8.3 A name tree on display in a classroom

Using family and community funds of knowledge in your teaching makes the learning engaging and meaningful for all your pupils, not just those who are multilingual or EAL learners. It can be done across the curriculum, not just in literacy. There are some excellent examples of topic work which allow pupils to explore their own communities' histories while achieving learning objectives for geography, history, RE, science, ICT, literacy and other subjects on the Multilingual Learning section of the Goldsmith's Department of Educational Studies website (https://www.gold.ac.uk/clcl/multilingual-learning/).

VIGNETTE 2

The Rag Trade

The Rag Trade project, details of which can be found on the Goldmsith's website as part of the 'Complementary-Mainstream Partnerships' project, is a particularly powerful example of how home languages and cultures can be brought into school. It was carried out with Years 5 and 6 pupils in Tower Hamlets in East London, and linked both with the community's history and the current situation in Bangladesh, where most of the pupils' families had relatives.

The work began with finding out about the tailoring industry in the East End of London, which was in decline as a result of being increasingly outsourced to Bangladesh, exploiting cheap child labour. Factories in London, which in the past had employed many of the pupils' grandparents, were closing down. In one activity, the pupils in London thought of questions to ask the child workers in Bangladesh. They decided to translate the questions into Bengali so the children could understand them. This is what they came up with.

(Continued)

(Continued)

Questions to send to children in Bangladesh

- Do they make clothes for themselves? (*Ora ki nijeder jonno kapor banai?*)

- Do they get enough money? (*Ora ki poriman poisha pai?*)

- If they don't get their work done do they get beaten? (*Ora jokhon kaj shesh korte pare na oderke ki mare?*)

- How do the pupils know how to make the clothes? (*Bachara ki bhabe kapor shilai korte jane?*)

- Why are the pupils doing the work when there are so many adults to do it? (*Boro manush thakte bachara keno kaz kore hoi?*)

- Where do the pupils live? (*Ei bachara kothai thake?*)

- How do the pupils feel about working? (*Bachader kemon lage kaz korte?*)

- What happens to the people when they get hurt while they are working? (*Kaz korar shomai betha pele manushra ki kore?*)

- How many minutes break do they get? (*Ora koto shomoier jonno birotipai?*)

- Is this happening now? (*Egolo ki ekhon hoche?*)

- How can we help them? (*Amra oderke ki bhabe shahajjo korte pari?*)

The questions were sent to Bangladesh and the responses built into further topic activities.

These questions constitute a powerful, authentic written text in themselves. They demonstrate not just the pupils' understanding of the topic they were studying, but their strong emotional engagement and empathy with the people whose lives they were studying. Such work offers rich opportunities for pupils from all cultural and language backgrounds to be experts in particular aspects of knowledge and learning.

ACTIVITY 8.4

Reflection on funds of knowledge for learning

In a small group, reflect on one of the case studies you have just read, either about the name tree or about the Rag Trade. The following questions can help you think about and discuss it.

1. What do you think made it effective as an opportunity for promoting independent learning?

2. What literacy learning objectives do you think the pupils achieved in the activity?

3. What language functions from Wolfe and Alexander's list do you think pupils would use in the activity?

4. What are the implications for planning activities such as these as part of your teaching (look back at the principles for planning in Chapter 4)?

5. Think of similar activities you could do in your class, using your pupils' funds of knowledge as a resource for their learning. If you can, plan and carry out a simple activity for your class to promote awareness of language diversity. If you are on placement, consult your class teacher about what might be a good starting-point.

ACTIVITY 8.5

Diversity across the curriculum

Choose a topic from the history, geography, RE or science curriculum and think of ways in which you could develop activities which key into pupils' funds of knowledge, starting either with a significant object, picture or a local issue. Look back at the principles for planning in Chapter 4 and devise two or three activities which could be the starting-point for teaching the topic. You could do this activity with a small group of colleagues, each taking a particular curriculum area and discussing the outcomes.

2.3 PROMOTING LANGUAGE AWARENESS THROUGH HOME LANGUAGES AND CULTURES

The following case study shows the value of regarding language diversity as a positive feature of school life and a resource for all pupils, using many strategies that follow **language awareness** principles. Essentially, language awareness is about understanding how language underpins all subjects across the curriculum, as well as the subjects which overtly deal with language, such as English and Modern Foreign Languages (MFL). It is about understanding the ways in which language is used in every situation in which learners find themselves, understood through the functional approach to grammar explained in Chapter 2 (p. 32). Datta and Pomphrey (2004) provide many ideas for promoting language awareness in children. They show how young children often have a natural fascination with languages, and there is more about this in Chapter 5, EAL in the Early Years. The relevant point here is that such positive attitudes to language can be promoted through language awareness, and feed into making learning an optimistic experience for all.

The following case study is about an extra-curricular activity in a primary school which puts into practice many language awareness principles. It reports work done in a school with a high number of multilingual pupils, but similar work can easily be done in schools where most pupils are monolingual, though it would need to be organised in a different way. Indeed, the important messages about language diversity that the case study illustrates are even more important in such settings.

THE LANGUAGES CLUB IN A PRIMARY SCHOOL – CASE STUDY BY ANITA CONRADI

Context

I work as a part-time EAL teacher in a primary school in south-east London: almost half of our 450 pupils are from ethnic minority families. I have counted 27 languages spoken by the families, who

(Continued)

(Continued)

come from at least 38 different countries. Although in the course of every year some pupils arrive at the school who are new to English, many of our multilingual pupils have lived most of their lives in the UK and the majority have done all their schooling in English.

Our school was relatively successful, but I felt that many of our multilingual pupils had the potential to achieve even more. With the introduction of the new primary curriculum in 2014, with its emphasis on the teaching and memorising of facts, I was concerned that there would be even fewer opportunities for class teachers to draw on the vast linguistic experiences of our pupils, or to raise the profile of multilingualism in their classes, even though research has shown what a positive impact this can have on pupils' self-esteem and sense of identity, and therefore on their learning. In spite of the welcoming ethos of the school, many class teachers seemed unaware of the languages spoken by their pupils, unless they were recent arrivals and relatively new to English. Even during the first week of the school year, when the whole school focuses on diversity and what makes each of us unique, I noticed that language skills were rarely mentioned. I am always struck by the reticence of the multilingual pupils themselves to talk about the other languages they speak and how surprised they seem if anyone asks them about 'their language'. This is not the case, however, when I have the opportunity to work with pupils in a small-group situation. Then I find they are keen to read one of the dual-language books from the library, or to talk about their languages with other multilingual pupils, and they are usually very happy to help out by translating for a new arrival.

So as a first step in developing a more 'multilingual approach' to learning, I decided to set up an after-school Languages Club. I sent a letter of invitation to about 25 pupils from Years 4–6 (aged 9–11) who I knew to be multilingual. As I wanted groups of pupils from the same language background to work together if possible, I concentrated on speakers of eight of the most widely spoken languages in the school: Arabic, Spanish, Portuguese, Yoruba, Russian, Ukrainian, Mandarin and Albanian. The club was to take place for an hour on a Wednesday after school, in the second half of the summer term when the SATs exams were over and few other clubs were running. I was not surprised to find that the majority of the 14 who chose to attend were pupils who had previously worked with me in small groups and who therefore already knew that I was interested in finding out about the other languages they spoke.

Activities

As this was a voluntary after-school club, it was important that the pupils enjoyed themselves and wanted to attend. Some of my ideas came from the language awareness work that I had done many years ago when teaching Modern Languages in a secondary school, and some from my more recent reading about activities to promote learning for multilingual pupils. I had already decided that we would have a quiz every week, and I also invited some of my multilingual colleagues to come along to read a story in their first language. In the first session we brainstormed other ideas for activities as I wanted the pupils to feel some ownership of the club. There were many interesting suggestions, some more practical than others!

The quizzes proved to be the most popular of the activities and ranged from naming different flags to identifying the scripts from the languages spoken by the pupils. The favourite, however, was a quiz where the pupils looked at clips of different traditional songs, which I was able to put together from the internet, and then worked in groups to work out which language was which.

Storytelling was also a popular activity: our first invitations were to one of the class teachers who is a Spanish speaker and to one of the teaching assistants whose first language is Arabic. I was also able to arrange for one of my ex-students, a Chinese speaker, to come along to read a traditional story in Mandarin. In our first session I started the storytelling with a French children's story that I have often used in my teaching, chosen because it contains a large number of cognates with English.

The pupils were fascinated by the different scripts they saw in both the Chinese and the Arabic story. As the story chosen in Arabic by our teaching assistant was a version of *Goldilocks*, we initially discussed which words we would expect to be in the story and then each group was asked to identify one of the words and produce it in Arabic at the end of the reading. This activity also enabled the Muslim pupils in the group, who were themselves not Arabic speakers, to identify a number of other words which they recognised from attending classes at the local mosque.

Before listening to the traditional Chinese story, our visitor explained a little about the writing system and the pupils enjoyed learning the numbers from one to ten and practising how to write them. After we had heard the Mandarin version, the pupils focused on picking out and recognising numbers as they occurred in the written text. I was delighted when two of the Year 4 pupils, Paula, a Spanish speaker from Bolivia, and Djoumana, a girl of Algerian origin who speaks both Arabic and Kabyle, a Berber language, subsequently asked if they could present stories themselves. Paula chose to read a dual-language book from the school library, which I scanned so that the whole group were able to follow the text in both Spanish and English as she read it to them, and together we spotted cognates, identified vocabulary and discussed possible meanings. The other Spanish speakers were very keen to give their interpretations and particularly to point out how the word order differed from that of English. Djoumana played us a typical Kabyle poem set to music which she had found on the internet; she explained the meaning of the words as well as telling us the traditional story on which it was based. The other pupils were very interested and some were able to think of similar stories that they knew; they were also most impressed when our 'expert' showed us how to write some of the words in the distinctive Kabyle script.

The pupils seemed just as keen to find out about the other languages spoken by their peers as they were to talk about their own, so I included a number of language awareness activities. One of the more successful focused on the concept of language families and involved the pupils comparing counting systems in a range of different languages. I was struck by how quickly they spotted similarities between the numbers and by their interesting theories as to why this should be the case. The pupils wanted to have a party in our final session of the term, which also happened to be someone's birthday. As we shared the birthday cake, we talked about what you would say in the different languages and the pupils enjoyed talking about how birthdays were traditionally celebrated in their families. I also took the opportunity to get some feedback about the club and to give the pupils the chance to give suggestions for activities they would like to do on future occasions.

Impact

I was not expecting to see much impact on the pupils' school work after only seven sessions, but I was pleased with the enthusiasm of the pupils for the club – 12 of them attended every session. Whenever I saw the pupils around the school they were keen to assure me that they would be at the club that week and, in their final feedback, all said they would attend again if the club ran in the next school year. Other pupils came up to me in the playground to ask why they had not been chosen – being invited to the Languages Club was definitely seen as a privilege!

One of the Year 6 boys, Ahmed, a Yoruba speaker who was generally viewed as 'difficult' in class, surprised us all by coming back to school to attend the club after a day out at his new secondary school. The enthusiasm of Xiao Yu, a Year 4 girl with a Chinese background, was also unexpected; painfully shy in class, she rarely shared any of her home experiences with her close friends, let alone with

(Continued)

(Continued)

her teachers. Xiao Yu attended every session of the club and amazed the other pupils by not only being able to introduce herself in Mandarin, but also by seemingly effortlessly writing whole phrases in Chinese, in spite of previously maintaining that she only spoke English! Although she was not confident enough to chat to our Chinese visitor, she clearly understood the language of the traditional story and was heard to explain some of the words to her friends and to help them with the pronunciation.

Feedback from the parents was also very positive: two mothers told me that their younger children, who would be in Year 4 the following year, were really looking forward to attending the club in the future. Another parent spoke to me about how her daughter, who had previously not been interested in speaking anything but English at home, had been asking to have stories read to her in Russian. I felt it was important that all the languages spoken by the pupils were given equal emphasis during the sessions and I believe that this is one of the reasons why the club was so successful - the look of delight on each child's face as they recognised their own language in one of the activities made the sometimes difficult task of finding examples in Albanian or Yoruba worthwhile! In their feedback, the pupils also said that one of the reasons that they enjoyed the club was that they were able to make new friends and learn something about their languages, and I think this experience was enhanced by the fact that the sessions provided an opportunity - and a reason - for the pupils to talk about their own languages in the company of other multilinguals. For once, speaking another language was being presented as both normal and even an asset.

Future plans

The club ran again the following academic year. The pupils did presentations to the rest of the group on typical foods (with tasting sessions!), on traditional games and music, and on places to visit in the other countries they knew well. As they become more confident in speaking about their own languages, they took part in school assemblies in the International Week. Some of the older pupils were also keen to add a section to the school website with information about the different languages spoken by pupils in the school. After the success of the storytelling sessions, I worked with some groups of pupils to produce some dual-language books of their own to display and to add to the school library. Perhaps the pupils' obvious enthusiasm for such activities will even encourage the class teachers to find the time in an already overcrowded curriculum to develop a more multilingual approach in their own teaching.

2.4 DUAL LANGUAGE BOOKS

Dual language books are a powerful resource for learning in many ways. The University of East London website (UEL, 2014) is the best source of information and ideas, along with Raymonde Sneddon's book (2009) (see Further Reading at the end of the chapter). Dual language books are usually stories published in two languages, and there are also a few information texts. Both languages can be shown on one page or the two languages can face each other on alternate pages. Books published in the UK generally have English as one of the languages and many publishers produce series of dual language books where the same story is presented in different languages, all along with English. Sets of these can be very useful in promoting language diversity. Pupils who are not speakers or readers of the languages concerned but who can read English can read and compare the texts of the story in the different languages.

Cummins and Early's book *Identity Texts* (2011) discusses the importance of dual language books, reporting projects done round the world where they have proved to be 'an effective and inspirational way of engaging learners in multilingual schools'. The importance of helping pupils to develop a positive identity as learners was discussed in Chapter 2, and dual language books can be a very effective means to do this. The story of Mushtaq (Chapter 3, p. 57) illustrates this clearly. Dual language books made by the pupils themselves were a powerful way for him to use his knowledge of literacy in Bengali as a means to becoming a reader of English.

RESEARCH FOCUS

Dual language texts

For pupils who can read their home language, like Mushtaq, dual language texts can provide a means of learning English, as well as developing their literacy in their home language. They can also promote **metalinguistic awareness**, which is important for understanding and analysing academic language. Dual language books can be useful for pupils who can speak but not read their home language. Discussing the pictures can help them follow the story and develop their understanding of the structure, character, setting and so on. The University of East London (UEL) has done extensive research into dual language books – you can find information and lots of practical ideas on their website: https://www.uel.ac.uk/schools/cass/research/dual-language-books/personal-books-and-young-authors.

ACTIVITY 8.6

Dual language texts

Find out what you can about dual language texts – Mantra Lingua is one of the main publishers and they have an extensive website: http://uk.mantralingua.com. If you are able to, get hold of some dual language texts representing the languages of the pupils you are teaching and share them with a small group of pupils.

---

3 WORKING WITH MULTILINGUAL COLLEAGUES

There are many ways of using home languages and cultures to help open out pupils' conceptual understanding in subjects across the curriculum. In a school with a positive, welcoming ethos, knowledge of languages is seen as something to be celebrated and – more importantly perhaps – to be shared as a resource to use in strategies that promote pupils' learning. Multilingual colleagues have an important role to play in this. Their importance is not just in supporting the learning of their pupils, but also in raising all pupils' awareness of the importance of multilingualism in our society and as a role model of the positive benefits of multilingualism.

Sadly, multilingual teachers are still very much in the minority in mainstream schools in England. It is more common to have multilingual teaching assistants or support assistants who work alongside the teacher and support individual or small groups of pupils. Their presence can benefit the whole class. Varian-Roper (in Gravelle, 2000, pp. 73–4) has some excellent examples of the ways that multilingual assistants can link content teaching and language teaching in maths and also provide a bridge for parents. Zofia Donnelly's case study in Chapter 3 (p. 47) shows how a visiting teacher can both support and open out the learning and the teacher–pupil relationships in a multilingual setting. Here are some suggestions of ways of working with multilingual colleagues.

- Tell a story together in two languages.

- Jointly assess pupils in different areas of the curriculum in order to evaluate their conceptual understanding as well as their language.

- Jointly plan an activity where you identify the language demands and think of ways that the concepts could be introduced multilingually.

- Colleagues with a group of pupils whose language they share discuss the activities they are doing and prepare their answers (which will be in English for the rest of the class).

- Ask your multilingual assistant to prepare materials to be sent home which explain some of the things you have done in school and also how parents can support their pupils at home.

The following vignette illustrates good collaboration between multilingual colleagues. A primary trainee used his own basic knowledge of French to help a child new to English to engage actively in a science task. With the support of the school's Languages teacher, who was a French specialist, he was able to support the child in showing how much he understood about the concepts being developed in the lesson.

■■ VIGNETTE ■■■■■■■■■■■■■■■■■■■■■■■■■■■■■■■■■■■■■

Working with multilingual colleagues

Ben undertook his first block placement on his PGCE Primary course in a Year 3 class in a large school where most of the pupils were multilingual. There was one 'new to English' child in the class, of Pakistani heritage but recently arrived from France where members of his extended family lived. Ben discovered that the child was fluent in French as well as Urdu. The class were doing a science topic where they were exploring the qualities of different materials and Ben had prepared a recording sheet for the pupils to write down their findings about different objects in the classroom. With the help of the teacher responsible for Languages, Ben wrote a French translation of the questions and statements above the English version on the sheet for the new pupil. The child was then able to carry out the investigation himself and write the names of the objects and some descriptive words in French on the sheet. In this way, Ben could appreciate his pupil's understanding of the science concepts in the activity, at the same time as providing a link for him to learning the words in English. Figure 8.4 shows the sheet which the child produced. The teacher's writing appears above each question and the child's answers in the relevant spaces.

3.1 USING PERSONAL FUNDS OF KNOWLEDGE

The two case studies in this section show ways of using personal funds of knowledge in the classroom. First Charlotte Wood, a secondary science teacher, discusses how she used her knowledge of Spanish in order to help a newly arrived pupil feel included and begin to learn the subject content of the lessons.

Figure 8.4 Science worksheet in French and English

Then, Shila Begum, an Early Years teacher, describes how she learned place value in Bangla as a child, and what it showed her about the importance of valuing children's knowledge of counting in their home languages.

SPANISH IN SCIENCE – CASE STUDY BY CHARLOTTE WOOD

Throughout my first placement on my PGCE in Secondary Science, I had the privilege of working along-side a Spanish EAL student. She was the only Spanish speaker in a very diverse school and was finding it hard to be included in mainstream lessons. As a result, her English was progressing very slowly. She was in a low-ability GCSE biology group whom I taught twice a week. As a Spanish speaker, I could speak to the learner in her home language and prepare suitable bilingual resources to support her in her learning.

Creating a safe environment

My initial focus was to make the student feel welcome in the classroom, as learning can best take place if the learner is in a 'safe space'. I made sure I knew the correct pronunciation of her name, smiling as she entered the classroom and having a small conversation with her in Spanish: '¡Hola! ¿Como estás?' – 'Hello, how are you?' and asking about her day. I started to build a positive relation-ship with the student and broke down any initial communication barriers that she may have thought were there. I tried out a variety of techniques to see which was the most effective in supporting her learning. I found it useful to explain a task to her in her first language. This would allow her to under-stand the activity and what I wanted her to achieve. For example, as part of the lesson on decay I had asked the students to design a compost bin which met four criteria: it would attract decomposers, have insulation from the cold, be able to circulate air and allow some water to enter to provide mois-ture. I told the student in Spanish to imagine that she lived in the countryside near Barcelona and wanted to recycle waste food to be more environmentally friendly. I then went on to tell her that she

(Continued)

183

(Continued)

had to include all four criteria to produce the best compost bin. As a result of associating the task with her life back in Barcelona, she designed a compost bin with all the required criteria.

Use of key words and questioning

Having seen that the use of key words was valuable in the development of the student's English skills, I provided her at the beginning of each lesson with a key word sheet including Spanish translations. Instead of asking her to find the words in the dictionary, I asked her to learn these words for the next lesson, when I checked to see if she could remember them. This was a quick activity while other students were completing a different starter activity, recapping what we had learnt in the previous lesson. It also allowed me to prepare questions. Closed questions are generally thought to be unhelpful, but they can be very helpful in some instances. I found that by asking the student a closed question which required her to answer with a key word that she had learnt, she was able to answer quickly and correctly. I made sure I didn't ask her to describe or explain a concept without building up steps to get to the answer. This allowed the learner to build understanding gradually and so scaffolded her understanding of the science concepts. For example, during a lesson on the carbon cycle I would ask questions such as 'Which process produces carbon dioxide, respiration or photosynthesis?', 'What do plants do to get rid of carbon dioxide?'

As part of a revision exercise I gave the class a range of exam questions on a learning mat. The students had to move around the classroom to help each other complete the learning mats and answer all the questions. I differentiated this resource for my Spanish-speaking student by providing her with a learning mat that contained closed questions, usually only requiring recall of knowledge or one-word answers such as 'Name three food groups.' Although this wasn't initially stretching the student to answer the more complex questions, her level of English at the time of the activity didn't allow for her to answer questions such as 'Explain why these food groups are important.'

Matching activities – using first language

In science, many words have a Latin origin and so are similar in different languages. By using key words in a card sort activity, the student was able to build upon her own prior science learning from Spain to gain an understanding of the topic being covered. For example, in a lesson on photosynthesis I made it clear that the word in Spanish was 'fotosíntesis' and so very similar to the English version. She was instantly able to associate what we were learning with her prior experience, giving a foundation for new learning to develop. I also used visual cues. The students had to match pictures to key words and definitions. This helped the Spanish student by activating her prior knowledge of the key words, associating them to images and definitions, thus deepening her understanding and also improving her English skills.

Conclusion

As the weeks progressed, I discovered what styles of learning suited my student, so that I could focus further on resources linked to those styles. In particular, the use of visual aids was very important. The most productive resource for me, however, was my Spanish-speaking skills. As well as meaning I was able to converse with the student, I could also make resources containing written Spanish to allow the student to access the work that the other students were covering during the lessons. It was clear that my knowledge of Spanish was a useful resource and through using it with one student, I learned a lot of generic skills that will be valuable in the future for working with EAL learners.

LEARNING PLACE VALUE IN BANGLA – CASE STUDY BY SHILA BEGUM

As a small child growing up in a remote village in Bangladesh I would often hear family members counting out money when they bought something from the local market or from the traders that came directly into the village. I would hear people counting their cows, chickens and ducks and I was aware of a game called five pebbles. My first vague awareness of numbers was when I went with my uncle to pick up my older sister and cousins from school. I remember walking to the school, often barefoot, and from quite a distance hearing the rhythmic chanting of numbers. I couldn't help but tap my hands and feet to the rhythm and soon looked forward to hearing it each day. As a young child I didn't ask any questions about the rhyme or express the enjoyment I felt by listening to it.

In 1986, aged five and a half, I left Bangladesh and came to England. Soon my knowledge and under-standing of numbers in English flourished. I was taught how to count and write the numerals as well as perform different number operations. At around the age of seven, my parents sent me to Bangla classes at the local mosque. There I heard the same familiar rhythmic chanting of numbers as I had heard in Bangladesh. Once again I felt an irresistible urge to tap my hands and feet to the rhythm, just like I did all those years ago back in Bangladesh.

This time I was much more curious and very eager to discover what this incredible rhyme was so I hurried home to confront my older sister. My sister was surprised by my inquisitive questioning and informed me it was a special number rhyme in Bangla to help children to learn the numbers from 0 to 100. I asked my sister if she would teach me the rhyme and she did. Both my parents and sister were delighted about my sudden desire to learn the Bangla numbers and were equally surprised at how quickly I picked them up. They were also fascinated when I tapped my hands and feet along with the rhyme, though my sister explained that if I had behaved like that in a school in Bangladesh I would have been punished.

The place value rhyme is very simple and not only does it enable children to learn the numbers 0 to 100 but it also teaches about place value and the multiples of ten to a hundred. The example below demonstrates how the rhyme goes.

0	1	2	3	4	5	6	7	8	9
One		ten		zero		10			
One		ten		one		11			
One		ten		two		12			
One		ten		three		13			
One		ten		four		14			
One		ten		five		15			
One		ten		six		16			
One		ten		seven		17			
One		ten		eight		18			
One		ten		nine		19			
Two		tens		are		20			
Three		tens		are		30			
Four		tens		are		40			
Five		tens		are		50 ... and so on.			

(Continued)

(Continued)

I decided to try out this number rhyme at the Saturday class I work at with multilingual children aged five to eleven. I wanted to see how the children responded to the rhyme. They received it very well and soon beat to the rhythm as I had done when I was a child. Some children commented on how they thought it sounded like a rap and you could dance to it. Even though the rhyme was initially done in Bangla with a group who were mainly Punjabi speakers, the children became familiar with the pattern and were soon able to predict the next equivalent number in English, for example after the number 29 one child remarked '3 tens are 30 Miss, it is like the times tables.' The children were fascinated and amazed at how they could apply their knowledge and understanding of numbers to a rhyme in a different language. I encouraged the children to listen to the rhythm and demonstrated how they could tap on their hands and soon children began to tap along with the rhyme. Isa commented, 'It makes you want to dance Miss.' Later we came up with an English and Punjabi equivalent to the rhyme, which demonstrated to the children the universal nature of numbers. We accompanied the activity with visual number cards to reinforce understanding of place value and numbers further.

CHAPTER SUMMARY

The four learning outcomes for this chapter are all to do with linking the theories you read about in Chapters 2 and 3 to your thinking about the kinds of strategies and resources that will promote learning for your EAL and multilingual learners. You may be able to take some of the specific ideas described in the chapter into your own planning, but it is more likely that you will use your professional judgement to adapt them to your own classroom setting and the pupils you are teaching.

Self-assessment questions

1. As well as the examples discussed in this chapter, what other kinds of 'funds of knowledge' do you think could be used in your teaching across the curriculum?

2. (If you are not multilingual yourself) What issues do you think you might face in working with multilingual colleagues to promote pupils' learning? Think of some examples of ways in which you could work with a multilingual colleague, using your different expertise positively.

3. (If you are multilingual yourself) What issues do you think you might face in using your multilingual expertise to promote pupils' learning? Think of some examples of ways in which you could work with the pupils and with your colleagues using your multilingual skills to promote learning.

FURTHER READING

Conteh, J. (ed.) (2006) Promoting Learning for Multilingual Pupils 3–11: Opening Doors to Success. London: Paul Chapman.

This book contains chapters written by teachers about projects they planned and carried out to promote listening and speaking with their multilingual and EAL learners. The examples show how they build a multilingual approach as an integrated part of their ongoing planning and teaching, not as an add-on. In this way, they open out the learning and promote independence in their pupils.

Sneddon, R. (2009) Bilingual Books – Biliterate Pupils: Learning to Read Through Dual Language Books. Stoke-on-Trent: Trentham Books.

Developed from action research work by primary teachers, this book features case studies of multilingual pupils aged from six to ten, and the ways in which dual language books support their learning. It illustrates how young pupils can work simultaneously in two languages to read unfamiliar texts and to analyse the differences between their languages. It offers ideas for teaching pupils languages as well as developing their multilingualism.

STUDYING AT MASTER'S LEVEL

Critical reading:

Conteh, J. and Brock, A. (2010) '"Safe spaces"? Sites of bilingualism for young learners in home, school and community', *International Journal of Bilingual Education and Bilingualism*, 14 (3), pp. 347-60.

In this article, Avril Brock and I argue that multilingual learners need 'safe spaces' to reach their full potential in education. We define safe spaces theoretically as based on notions of culture, context and identity, and argue for the importance of an ecological model of learning to understand the experiences of both teachers and learners from diverse backgrounds and identify the best ways to help multilingual learners to succeed.

After reading the article, consider the following questions, ideally in discussion with colleagues:

1. On p. 349, we discuss Bronfenbrenner's ideas about 'an individual's ecology'. He talks about this as 'nested networks of interactions'. What do you think he means by this? Can you think of any practical examples?

2. Can you think of examples of 'ideologies and inequalities' that might be 'embedded in the ways that the wider society constructs and mediates its languages and their speakers'? How might such ideologies and inequalities influence multilingual pupils' opportunities for success? How are they reflected in the transcript of Arafa's interview on p. 9?

3. Do you agree that the learning experiences that Shila describes on p. 10 are 'powerful'? If so, what do you think makes them powerful?

4. In our conclusion, Avril and I argue that teachers and trainee teachers need safe spaces to develop their learning as well as children, so that they can model 'the ways in which they can construct learning with their own pupils'. Do you agree? What aspects of your own training have helped you to do this?

REFERENCES

Allwright, D. and Hanks, J. (2009) *The Developing Language Learner: An Introduction to Exploratory Practice*. London: Palgrave Macmillan.

Conteh, J. (2003) *Succeeding in Diversity: Culture, Language and Learning in Primary Classrooms*. Stoke-on-Trent: Trentham Books.

Conteh, J., Martin, P. and Robertson, L. (eds) (2007) *Multilingual Learning Stories in Schools and Communities in Britain*. Stoke-on-Trent: Trentham Books.

Cummins, J. and Early, M. (eds) (2011) *Identity Texts: The Collaborative Creation of Power in Multilingual Schools*. Stoke-on-Trent: Trentham Books.

Datta, M. and Pomphrey, C. (2004) *A World of Languages: Developing Children's Love of Languages*. London: National Centre for Languages.

Department of Education and Science (DES) (1985) *Education for All – The Report of the Committee of Inquiry into the Education of Children from Ethnic Minority Groups (Swann Report)*. London: HMSO.

Gravelle, M. (2000) *Planning for Multilingual Learners: An Inclusive Curriculum*. Stoke-on-Trent: Trentham Books.

Sneddon, R. (2009) *Multilingual Books – Biliterate Pupils: Learning to Read Through Dual Language Books*. Stoke-on-Trent: Trentham Books.

University of East London (UEL) (2014) *Multiliteracy in Action: Using and Researching Dual Language Books for Children*. Available at http://www.uel.ac.uk/duallanguagebooks/index.htm (accessed 5 December 2018).

Wolfe, S. and Alexander, R. J. (2008) *Argumentation and Dialogic Teaching: Alternative Pedagogies for a Changing World*. Available at http://www.robinalexander.org.uk/wp-content/uploads/2012/05/wolfe-alexander.pdf (accessed 5 December 2018).

SUGGESTED ANSWERS FOR ACTIVITIES 8.1 AND 8.2

These are just some ideas for each activity - there are no 'right' answers, and many other possibilities than those given here.

Activity 8.1

Q1: I think that most teachers would agree that Episode 2 gives a better example of independent learning, for some of the following reasons (there are others, which may emerge in your discussion):

- It affords more space for pupils to use their own ideas and knowledge gained from the previous lessons, mainly because the pupils are not organised in ability groups.

- The letter writing task is open-ended and pupils can respond freely, using the information they have gained; it can be described as 'differentiated by outcome' rather than within the task itself. On the other hand, the comprehension activity about the poem is closed with no real opportunity for negotiation.

- There is a range of reference materials available in the classroom to help pupils develop their answers, whereas in the first episode, the only reference material is the poem which the pupils have already been studying in detail.

Q2: There are different ways the activities in Episode 1 could be developed to promote independence. Here are a couple of ideas:

- Pupils could be given answers, to which they have to devise plausible questions.

- Pupils could be organised in mixed-ability groups and asked to devise their own questions to put to another group.

Activity 8.2

Here are some possible function words and learning objectives for the eight activities in Activity 8.2. There are many others, and your ideas may be better than these:

Activity	Function words	Learning objectives
1	narrate	to put simple information into words
	discuss	to compare simple ideas
2	analyse	to form a range of questions correctly
	justify	to justify question choices for an interview on a specific topic
3	explain	to recall simple information
	analyse	to discuss possible questions and answers in a game
4	narrate	to narrate personal information
	imagine	to explore locations of countries in the world
5	discuss	to analyse key information
	explore	to justify answers to questions
6	narrate	to recall prior knowledge
	explain	to explain a particular maths topic
7	evaluate	to compare different ways of checking information
	justify	to justify choices in information retrieval
8	speculate	to compare words in different languages
	evaluate	to identify similarities and differences in languages

9
CONCLUSIONS: SYNTHESISING LEARNING AND MOVING ON

Your initial training as a teacher can only give you an introduction to the professional attributes, knowledge and skills you need in order to understand multilingual and EAL learners' needs and make provision for their successful learning in your classroom. This is the same for any aspect of becoming a teacher. In this final chapter, at the start of your career as a teacher, you are invited to reflect on what you have learnt so far. Through considering the knowledge you have gained from reading this book, as well as other experiences you may have had in your course of training, you will synthesise your understanding of EAL as a central aspect of becoming a teacher. Following this, you are invited to think about how you might move on in the development of your professional expertise in this important and growing aspect of the teacher's role, in both primary and secondary contexts. At the end of the chapter, there are suggestions for further reading. Do not forget, also, about the further reading suggestions at the end of each chapter in the rest of the book as well as the invitations to Master's level study.

As you have no doubt become aware through your experience in school and through your reading, the whole field of EAL teaching and learning is a growing one. Over recent years, it is increasingly becoming recognised that there is a body of both theoretical and practical knowledge that all teachers need in order to develop language-based and culturally informed pedagogies that will benefit all pupils, not just EAL learners. One of the aims of this book is to provide you with the principles that underpin such pedagogies, which see language diversity as a resource rather than a problem in classrooms. Through the more theoretical chapters in Part 1 as well as the more practical chapters in Part 2 with their case studies from practising teachers in specific classrooms, we have tried to show how theory and practice need to work together in developing principled responses to meet the needs of multilingual and EAL learners. We have shown how you can play to your learners' strengths, recognising what they bring to their learning, rather than applying ready-made, commercially published 'packages' of teaching strategies and activities. The understanding that your learners are active, creative individuals is crucial in developing an EAL pedagogy, as is recognising the professional agency that you have as a teacher, along with those of other professionals you will be working with.

These are exciting times, with rich possibilities for newly qualified teachers who have the interest in and the commitment to the positive, inclusive values that promoting EAL in this way offers. A well-structured, theory-informed and thoughtful EAL pedagogy will not only promote success for multilingual and EAL learners, it will also contribute to more positive attitudes generally towards language and cultural diversity and thus to greater awareness and opportunities for learning for all pupils. Both researchers and practitioners are coming to recognise the importance of the 'multilingual turn' in languages education and its benefits for society generally, both inside and outside of language classrooms. Recognising multilingualism as a positive resource rather than a problem brings many benefits for social cohesion and justice in the wider community. Becoming specialist teachers and future leaders in the field of EAL offers many professional rewards, as well as fulfilling vital roles in our future education system.

1 MYTHS REVISITED

In Chapter 1, I introduced four 'myths' about language teaching and learning. I suggested that they needed to be challenged, as they represent commonsense, intuitive, but often unhelpful notions that are not supported by research about language and learning in relation to multilingual and EAL learners. In order to help you synthesise your knowledge and understanding about EAL, this section provides a brief reflection on each of the myths, showing how what you have learnt in this book reveals their shortcomings and suggests positive ways of moving forward.

1.1 LANGUAGES SHOULD BE KEPT SEPARATE IN THE CLASSROOM OR LEARNERS WILL BECOME CONFUSED (SOMETIMES CALLED 'LANGUAGE INTERFERENCE')

In the first part of the book, there are many ideas that call the 'language interference' myth into question. Language, identity and learning are intimately connected, as the theories introduced in Chapter 2 show. A child whose accent or dialect is ignored or treated as a form of 'bad' English in the classroom is just as likely to feel excluded as a bilingual or multilingual child who is made to feel that it is unacceptable to speak any other language than English. In Chapter 3, the examples of 'translanguaging', such as Sameena's counting in two languages (p. 45), as well as Cummins' theoretical idea of the CUP (p. 56) and the definition of bilingualism as 'living in two languages' (p. 16) all show in different ways how it is wrong to construct languages as separate systems that must be kept apart. Similarly, the principle about linking home and school learning is illustrated by many different practical examples in the second part of the book, especially in Chapter 8, which shows how the theoretical concept of 'funds of knowledge' plays out in practice. Dual language books, cross-curricular work with artefacts, a worksheet in science with additional French words that 'opened up' the science concepts for a newly arrived child – these are all examples of practical ways to bring funds of knowledge into classroom learning in order to promote your pupils' conceptual learning and language development multilingually.

1.2 PUPILS WILL 'PICK ENGLISH UP' NATURALLY IN THE CLASSROOM – THEY DO NOT NEED TO BE EXPLICITLY TAUGHT (SOMETIMES CALLED 'IMMERSION')

The vignettes of different 'EAL learners' presented in Chapter 1 show a range of ways in which pupils clearly do not simply 'pick up' English in the classroom and somehow become successful learners without any conscious understanding and planning on the part of the teacher. 'Immersion', if it is not properly understood and managed, can very quickly become 'submersion'. For social and cultural reasons through no fault of himself or his family, Joseph, in section 2.3 (p. 17), was struggling to do as well as he clearly had the capacity to do. If his teachers had been able to find out more about his home background and country of origin, this might have helped them to think about how to support him in more informed and appropriate ways. Safina, in section 2.1 (p. 15), was doing very well in speaking and listening, but had found the written demands of the Year 6 SATs difficult. The evidence is that she will find it harder and harder to cope with the academic language demands of the subjects she is learning as she progresses through secondary school. The contrasts between Stefan's and Jan's progress as new arrivals in section 2.2 (p. 16) clearly indicate that it was not simply a matter of 'picking up' English for them.

Many of the theoretical questions raised by these examples are addressed in Chapter 3 with Cummins' model of BICS and CALP, which explains some of the complexities of the development of academic language, essential for success in the ways demanded by the school. Then, the approach to planning for both language and conceptual progression provided in Chapter 4 offers principled and practical ways to ensure that pupils are provided with carefully structured activities to support both their language and conceptual development across the curriculum. Chapter 6 gives many suggestions for providing a language-rich classroom environment and linking language, literacy and content in your teaching. Chapter 7 provides advice on assessing conceptual learning for pupils whose English development is at an early stage, as well as a way of understanding multilingual pupils' development as distinctive from those who are not learning multilingually.

1.3 LANGUAGE DIVERSITY IS A 'PROBLEM' AND IT IS BETTER IF PUPILS SPEAK ENGLISH ALL THE TIME IN CLASSROOMS

In Chapter 1, it is established that language and cultural diversity have long been a feature of everyday life in Britain, and the clear signs are that they will always remain so. The children of Safina, Stefan, Jan, Joseph, Hamida and Radia, should they choose to remain in Britain, will be citizens of an increasingly multilingual and multicultural society. In Chapter 2, I argued that we all experience language diversity in our daily lives, even if we think of ourselves as being monolinguals whose only language is English. Following this, in Chapter 3, I present the idea of multilingualism as a continuum or spectrum. Some of us may place ourselves towards the 'monolingual' end of the continuum in our experiences and knowledge of language diversity, and others may see themselves positioned more towards the more expert, multilingual end, with high levels of competence in listening, speaking, reading and writing in different languages. Language diversity is a theme in all the chapters in Part 2 and it takes centre stage in Chapter 8. Here, there are many practical ideas for making language diversity a positive feature and resource in your classroom, no matter what languages are spoken by the pupils you teach or their ages. Even simple activities like doing the register in different languages can promote a positive ethos in a very accessible way and open doors to learning about different languages for your pupils, as well as reinforcing the links between identity and learning for those whose languages are represented.

1.4 IT IS IMPOSSIBLE, OR VERY DIFFICULT, TO LEARN A NEW LANGUAGE BEYOND A YOUNG AGE (SOMETIMES CALLED 'THE CRITICAL PERIOD')

The vignettes in Chapter 1 show multilingual learners of different ages mostly becoming competent and confident speakers, readers and writers of English. The important point to draw from this is that they do so in a variety of ways, and so need different kinds of teaching and support. The example of Stefan and Jan (p. 16), both from the same language background and in the same school in England for the same length of time, illustrates very clearly that there is no universal, standardised way to becoming a competent user of English. The learner's age is only one factor that must be taken into account, as are the languages they already know in both spoken and written modes. Mushtaq, whose story appears in Chapter 3, arrived in England at the age of nine. His experience of learning to read was a positive one. It should encourage us to have confidence in our pupils as independent learners. Mushtaq understood how to manage his own learning and quickly became a competent reader and writer of English, once his skills and capacity in his first language of Bengali were recognised.

All these examples illustrate how the idea of the 'critical period' in the sense of there being an age beyond which it is always very difficult to learn a new language is a myth. However, it is also clear that the distinctiveness of pupils' 'EAL development' at different ages must be understood. The *Language in Common* steps offer excellent starting-points for assessing individual pupils' progress as bilingual language users. They are also helpful in developing your own understanding of the distinctiveness of multilingual and EAL learners' development and progress.

2 MOVING FORWARD – SOME SUGGESTIONS FOR FURTHER READING AND PROFESSIONAL DEVELOPMENT

A major concern of this book has been to help you to understand the importance of theory for your classroom practice and for your professional understanding and development as a teacher, no matter what your subject area or age range. Of course, theory by itself is of no value in teaching, but neither are packages of strategies or lists of practical suggestions with no theoretical rigour behind them and no clear statement of the principles from which they have been developed. If you depend on these in your teaching, you will quickly run out of ideas and be at the mercy of ready-made plans with no real understanding of how and why they have been constructed in the way they have.

This book gives you a theoretical explanation for all the practical advice it provides, as well as the practical implications of the theories. This is intentional – the hope is that you will be able to go on to develop your own theory-informed and principled ways to plan, teach and assess the learning of the pupils you teach, especially those who are multilingual. As you move through your induction year as an NQT, you could suggest to your school mentor that you use some of the activities in this book to help develop your professional expertise in the field of EAL.

The further reading and Master's level study sections suggested at the end of each chapter give you some starting-points for your CPD. The list given below, mostly taken from the references for each chapter, will help you to move further in your understanding of how to integrate theory and practice in your teaching to promote the learning and achievement of multilingual and EAL learners. Books speak to readers in different ways – these are mostly titles which have inspired me in my teaching and to which I have returned many times, with some new ones added in. I hope some of them will speak to you and become your favourites, as well as offering you useful guidance for your teaching and forming the basis of further study. As time goes on, you may be offered the opportunity or feel the need to pursue higher qualifications, and the study of EAL has rich potential. Use the **NALDIC** website (www.naldic.org.uk) – and join the association – to keep up to date with developments in the field of EAL, including opportunities for further study and professional development.

3 SUGGESTIONS FOR FURTHER READING

Cummins, J. (2001) *Negotiating Identities: Education for Empowerment in a Diverse Society*, **2nd edn. Ontario, CA: California Association for Bilingual Education.**

This book gives a thorough explanation of Cummins' three key theories which run through this book – CUP, linguistic interdependence, BICS and CALP – showing how his ideas have developed over the years. Other important ideas are also discussed and the educational implications are fully explained.

Cummins, J. and Early, M. (eds) (2011) *Identity Texts: The Collaborative Creation of Power in Multilingual Schools.* **Stoke-on-Trent: Trentham Books.**

This book provides a collection of case studies and examples of 'identity texts', which are texts created by multilingual learners in a wide range of educational settings round the world. They illustrate how such work can contribute to a pedagogy that plays to the strengths of pupils from diverse language and cultural backgrounds.

Datta, M. (2007) *Bilinguality and Biliteracy: Principles and Practice*, **2nd edn. London: Continuum.**

This book shows how multilingual children can benefit academically from opportunities to develop their biliterate skills. With case studies and examples of children's work, it shows how children's bilinguality provides opportunities for the development of literacy throughout the curriculum.

García, O. (2009) *Bilingual Education in the 21st Century: A Global Perspective.* **Chichester: Wiley-Blackwell.**

This inspiring book provides an overview of bilingual education theories and practices throughout the world. It questions assumptions regarding bilingual education and proposes a new theoretical framework for the teaching and assessment of bilingual learners. It explains why bilingual education is good for all children and adults throughout the world and gives examples of successful bilingual programmes.

Gonzalez, N., Moll, L. and Amanti, C. (eds) (2005) *Funds of Knowledge: Theorizing Practices in Households, Communities and Classrooms.* **New York: Routledge.**

The concept of 'funds of knowledge' is based on the premise that all people have valuable knowledge formed from their life experiences. This book gives readers the basic methodology of funds of knowledge research and explores its applications for classroom practice. It argues that instruction must be linked to students' lives and that effective pedagogy should be linked to local histories and community contexts.

Gregory, E. (2008) *Learning to Read in a New Language: Making Sense of Words and Worlds.* **London: Sage.**

This book introduces an 'Inside-Out' (starting from experience) and 'Outside-In' (starting from literature) approach to teaching children to read. It draws on examples of children from different countries engaged in learning to read nursery rhymes and songs, storybooks, letters, the Bible and the Qur'an in languages they do not speak fluently. It argues that there is no universal method to teach children to read but rather a shared aim which they all aspire to: making sense of a new world through new words.

Kenner, C. and Ruby, M. (2012) *Interconnecting Worlds: Teaching Partnerships for Bilingual Learning.* **Stoke-on-Trent: Trentham.**

Working together with multilingual pupils and their teachers from both mainstream and complementary schools in London, Kenner and Ruby developed some powerful strategies, which played to the children's strengths and used all their language resources for learning. They write about them in inspiring ways in this book.

Nieto, S. (1999) *The Light in Their Eyes: Creating Multicultural Learning Communities.* **New York: Teachers College Press.**

Another inspiring book which focuses on the significant role of teachers in transforming students' lives. It considers recent theories, policies and practices about the variability in student learning and culturally responsive pedagogy and examines the importance of student and teacher voice in research and practice.

APPENDIX 1: SUGGESTED ANSWERS TO THE SELF-ASSESSMENT QUESTIONS

The learning outcome questions at the end of each chapter are, on the whole, very open and there are no fixed answers for many of them. They are intended to help you reflect on the issues raised in the chapters and develop your own professional understanding of them. The points given below help you to do this by suggesting possible factors you might consider.

CHAPTER 1 INTRODUCING MULTILINGUAL AND EAL LEARNERS

1. This question is designed to get you to think about your own identity and what matters to you as an individual, as this can sometimes become problematic when you are working with children from different language and cultural backgrounds. Traditionally, identity has been defined by broad, general factors such as gender, social background or ethnic group. But it may also be about features that are more personal to you, such as where in the UK you come from, your religion, your family circumstances, your political views, the music you like, the football team you support and so on. Think about times when you might have felt annoyed, upset or threatened because of something that was important personally to you. What do you think caused your negative feelings?

2. The aim of this question is to get you to think about specific out-of-school factors that may impinge on children's learning and influence their achievements and attainment. These may relate to issues connected with the family's home circumstances, or there could be things which, if you knew about them, would be important in helping to promote their learning and academic success, e.g. literacy skills in another language.

3. This question is designed to get you to reflect on the choices teachers can make in dealing with individual children. There are no fixed answers. In many circumstances, there are no 'right' ways to behave as a teacher, but you need to use professional judgement and experience. What you read in this book and other books like it may help you to consider some principled ways of understanding children's progress more widely than simply through what is happening in the classroom. For example, Joseph's teacher(s) might have tried to find out more about Sierra Leone than the fact that there had been a war when some awful things happened.

4. Again, no fixed answers here, but try writing your vignette based on the models given in the chapter. When you have done so, you could share it with colleagues or classmates to widen your awareness of bilingual and EAL learners.

5. Many Gypsy and Roma pupils coming from Eastern Europe have suffered racism over many years in their countries of origin, and can thus be very reluctant to send their children to school. Aspirations are low, and some parents fear 'losing' their children if they apply for university or

courses away from home. There have been negative reports in the media about Gypsy and Roma families arriving in some towns in England, and also programmes about marriage customs that, it can be argued, present stereotypical images of traditional cultural practices.

CHAPTER 2 ALL ABOUT LANGUAGE AND LEARNING

1. The main implications of sociocultural theories and the ZPD relate to the kinds of activities that will offer the greatest opportunities for learning. These clearly need to focus on speaking and listening, and involve children in using talk in a wide range of ways, with plenty of time devoted to small-group discussion-type activities. The progression in cognitive demand also needs to be considered, so medium-term planning is important in order to ensure that the learning objectives become increasingly demanding. At the same time, contextual support needs to be maintained.

2. The main differences are to do with what aspects of language the grammars encompass and what their purposes are. Most conventional grammars consider words and perhaps sentences. They deal with semantics (meanings), morphology (grammar within words – the morphemes with which words are made up) and syntax (the order of words in sentences). Functional grammars, on the other hand, consider whole texts, including features like layout, paragraph structure, and so on. They are concerned with the ways that language is used in the construction of texts, according to the purposes and audiences of the text and the content it is intended to communicate. Functional grammars are more about understanding languages in use as part of culture and society and conventional grammars are more about describing languages as systems without reference to their social and cultural contexts.

3. Sociocultural theories argue that interaction, through talk as well as other means, is at the centre of the learning process. They emphasise the importance of making talk a central aspect of all the learning that pupils are expected to do in their classrooms, no matter what the subject or conceptual learning involved.

4. For the reasons given above, i.e. that it is through engaging in activities that focus on talk that children will learn most effectively. This is a key conclusion of the *National Curriculum Review* (DfE, 2011), which contains many useful references to support the development of your understanding in this area.

5. This is an open question – you may be able to find out by observing and talking to your pupils.

CHAPTER 3 WHAT DOES IT MEAN TO BE MULTILINGUAL?

1. This question obviously needs to be answered through reflecting on your own views and opinions. It would be useful, perhaps, if you reflected on what you thought about bilingualism and multilingualism before reading the chapter and what you thought about it afterwards. The conventional view is that bilingualism is about having full competence in two or more languages, whereas the ideas expressed in the chapter are intended to help you to see it as a much more fluid, diffuse concept, including social and cultural aspects as well as language.

2. Again, the answer to this question depends very much on your own personal and educational experiences. Perhaps you could also make it the topic of a group discussion as part of developing your professional understanding about the role of language diversity and bilingualism in children's learning.

3. The answer to this question would include ideas such as using a wider range of ways of assessing learning than the usual writing-focused tasks, possibly using practical activities and perhaps visual means. There is also the possibility of assessing children's conceptual understanding of the particular subject content in their home languages.

CHAPTER 4 EAL IN THE EARLY YEARS: BEGINNING SCHOOLING IN A NEW LANGUAGE AND CULTURE

1. The answer to this question is likely to relate to the age of the children and to the fact that parents are much more likely to be involved in their children's schooling in the early years than at later stages.

2. The curricula are different, as are the approaches to learning and assessment. In general, working with early years children is likely to mean that you need to know much more about the children's home and family circumstances in the early years than at later stages.

3. 'Planning play' is more about planning structured activities that use play equipment and involve the children following guided instructions, whereas 'planning for play' is more about setting up an environment in which children can develop their own play activities, thus taking ownership of their own learning.

CHAPTER 5 EAL AND LITERACY: LEARNING TO READ INDEPENDENTLY IN A NEW LANGUAGE

1. This question is open in that issues will differ in relation to individual learners, but in gerenal issues could be about EAL learners needing to gain cultural knowledge so that they can understand inferences, connotations and so on in the texts they read. Pupils also need to learn to read critically so that they can understand and be aware of the possible ways that facts can be used to persuade and influence opinions, and the ways that biases can be developed. They also need to be able to read in order to infer meanings and the viewpoints of the writer.

2. The debate about phonics has been shown to have hindered the progress of EAL learners in that it is too common for them to be used with older pupils when other, more holistic approaches would be more beneficial. Time taken up with phonics means that pupils are not given oppirtunities to develop independence, which is the main theme of the chapter.

3. There are many ways, such as in topics in history, geography and RE, and in English literature – an example could be finding texts that relate to the countries of origin or histories of your pupils and their communities.

4. Reading for pleasure is crucial as without it, pupils will not sustain their efforts in reading and go on to become independent readers. It is vital for pupils at all stages of learning to read. There are lots of ways of communicating reading for pleasure in classrooms, but the most effective, perhaps, is actually finding ways to do it with your pupils.

CHAPTER 6 PLANNING FOR LEARNING ACROSS THE CURRICULUM FOR MULTILINGUAL AND EAL LEARNERS

The questions here are open, but these general points could be taken into account when considering your practice in relation to promoting speaking and listening and working with other colleagues:

1. Drawing out the language demands is important because it will help you in your planning to ensure that you develop clear progression in increasing the complexity of the language demands of the activities and also become aware of the kinds of academic language you are introducing to your pupils. It will also help you to understand better the ways in which you can introduce the concepts of the subject to your pupils.

2. Think about organising your classroom and your lessons to promote discussion and to allow pupils to work sometimes with peers who share the same home languages so they can use this in their conversations. As a teacher, you need to model ways of speaking and listening and give your pupils opportunities to practise as well as engage fully in speaking and listening activities.

3. The key here is to engage in collaborative planning as far as possible, and to plan in to your lessons ways of sharing the teaching according to your different strengths and expertise.

4. Language awareness activities are a positive resource in all schools, and particularly in schools with low numbers of multilingual pupils as they may not have the awareness and experience of language diversity that pupils living in more linguistically and culturally diverse areas may have – this can be a disadvantage as they grow up. In these settings, the first strategy would be to find out what language diversity is present in the local community and then perhaps arrange visits for the children to relevant places and/or for visitors to come into school. The same principle of building on personal and community resources applies.

CHAPTER 7 ASSESSING MULTILINGUAL AND EAL LEARNERS ACROSS THE CURRICULUM

1. The purposes of assessment *for* learning, sometimes known as formative assessment, are to find out what your learners can do and what they find difficult, in order to plan how to help them make further progress. Assessment *of* learning is the same as summative assessment, and its main purpose is to identify what point children have reached on an externally decided, standardised scale of attainment in order to assign levels or other external criteria. In assessing the achievements and attainment of EAL and bilingual learners, the distinctive nature of their language development and learning always has to be borne in mind.

2. The main reason is that if we do confuse *learning needs* and *language needs* for bilingual and EAL learners, we will not be able to make the appropriate provision to help them make progress and succeed in education.

3. AfL processes are very valuable for multilingual and EAL learners as they offer a range of ways to find out about their learning more holistically. Using custom-made tools such as the DfE Proficiency

Scale or the *Language in Common* steps will enable you to reach a deep understanding of a child's strengths and needs and what to do to help them make progress. The issues faced in sampling the work of a child who is relatively new to English are, of course, to do with communication. The child may not understand what is expected of her or him, there may be cultural issues in the task that you are not aware of and finally the child may understand the concept under consideration but not have enough English to express or explain it in a way that is comprehensible to you.

4. The main point here is to recognise that parents from different cultural backgrounds may express their concerns and interest in their children's progress in different ways. Sometimes, parents can appear passive as they do not question their child's teacher or engage in discussion. This may be because they see the teacher as the authority figure, and that their role is to support what the teacher says rather than agree or disagree with it.

CHAPTER 8 PROMOTING INDEPENDENCE: USING HOME LANGUAGES AND CULTURES IN LEARNING

These are open questions and the answers will largely depend on your own experiences and opinions. The suggestions given are indicative.

1. Besides knowledge of other languages and cultural backgrounds, the kinds of things that may occur to you here could be practical skills such as cooking, sewing, carpentry, etc., artistic and musical expertise, personal knowledge related to family and community, and so on.

2. Points here might include anxiety about trying to speak languages you do not feel very confident with, not understanding completely what is going on, losing control of the lesson and so on. You could discuss this with a multilingual colleague and perhaps come up with ideas about how you might work together.

3. Points here might include anxiety about being considered an 'expert' in a particular language, about performing in that language which you have never done before, about understanding how to assess what pupils say or write, and so on. You could discuss this with a colleague who is not multilingual, and perhaps come up with ideas about how you might work together.

APPENDIX 2: GLOSSARY

Academic language Academic language is the kind of language that is used in textbooks, in tests and in formal classroom discourse, and the kind of language we need in order to learn and make progress in school and beyond. Learners need to understand and be able to use it themselves in speaking and writing in order to carry out cognitively complex activities and to achieve success academically.

Accent Accent refers to the ways people pronounce the languages they speak. Accents can be specific to a country, a region, a town or city, a social group or an individual. Speakers of English have many different accents according to their social and cultural backgrounds and where they come from.

Achievement An assessment of achievement reveals the knowledge, skills, understandings and capabilities of a learner, as well as the progress they are making compared with learners of similar age and capability.

Additive bilingualism Additive bilingualism is where the acquisition of a new language does not replace the first or earlier languages; instead the earlier languages are enhanced by the learning of the new language. It is linked to high self-esteem and improved cognitive flexibility.

Attainment Attainment is a measure of how well a learner is performing in a particular subject at a particular point in time, linked to an external set of criteria such as the National Curriculum Attainment Targets assessed through the SATs (see below).

Authentic language In contrast with the language used in many school textbooks, curriculum programmes and teaching resources, authentic language is the kind of language that people use in their everyday lives to do the things they want to do.

BICS (basic interpersonal communication skills) Cummins made a distinction between two kinds of language knowledge and proficiency (see CALP below). BICS refers to the conversational fluency that most learners of a new language can develop relatively quickly in everyday, face-to-face social interactions.

Bilingual A word with many definitions, in this book it refers to anyone who has access to and uses more than one language in their everyday life, no matter what their level of proficiency.

CALP (cognitive academic language proficiency) CALP is the second type of language knowledge and skill that Cummins identified in his research (see BICS above). CALP is associated with academic learning and is the language of cognitive processes such as analysing, synthesising, arguing and persuading.

Codeswitching Codeswitching refers to a speaker's use of more than one language in one utterance or conversation. It is a natural and normal aspect of the speech of many bilingual and multilingual people.

Cognitive language Cognitive language is the kind of language required to engage in cognitively challenging activities, e.g. Latinate words, complex grammatical structures and long, tightly structured texts. It is linked to academic language (see above).

Complementary/supplementary schools These are schools outside of the mainstream system, usually funded and run by different linguistic and cultural communities outside of school hours, sometimes in the premises of mainstream schools but often in other community premises. Their purpose is most often to maintain and develop knowledge of heritage languages and cultures. Many pupils who study their home languages in such schools go on to do GCSEs and 'A' levels in those languages.

Context of use Part of the functional grammar approach, the context of use of a text is the set of social and cultural factors which surround it and contribute to its construction, i.e. why, when, how and where it was produced (the purposes), who it was produced for (the audience) and what it is about (the content).

CUP (common underlying proficiency) CUP relates to Cummins' theories of bilingualism and is a term to describe the ways in which our processing of language is supported by all the languages we know. Rather than possibly 'interfering' with each other, it is clear from many different kinds of research that knowledge of different languages feeds into a common 'reservoir' of knowledge, understanding and capacity to express meaning.

DARTS (directed activities related to texts) DARTs are activities that encourage the learner to analyse how a text is constructed and how its meanings are expressed at word, sentence and text level. There are two types: 'disruption' activities where the learner is expected to alter the text in some way, e.g. changing the tenses or other linguistic features, and 're-construction' activities where the text needs to be re-assembled or completed in some way, such as a cloze activity.

Dialect Dialects are the varieties of a language in terms of grammar and vocabulary. English has many different dialects, both regional within Britain and international across the globe.

Dialogic talk and teaching This term was introduced by Robin Alexander, who has written extensively about it. He is referring not just to a teaching strategy or technique, but to a whole approach to teaching which values the knowledge and viewpoints of the learner as well as the teacher and so seeks to develop ways in which they can be voiced and integrated into the construction of knowledge in the classroom.

EAL (English as an additional language) EAL is a term whose 'official' definition has changed many times. It is used to refer to those children in the education system who speak, and possibly read and write, other languages besides English. The term EAL is now increasingly used to identify a distinctive 'field' of language teaching and learning.

EFL (English as a foreign language) EFL refers to the branch of English language teaching and learning concerned with teaching people from other countries who plan to live, work or travel in England or other English-speaking country (see TEFL below).

ELT (English language teaching) A broad term used to cover the range of fields of English language teaching and learning.

Emergent literacy A term used in Early Years education, referring to the ways in which young children develop as readers and writers through their everyday interactions with the world around them without formal teaching.

Formative assessment The kind of assessment that seeks to understand how much learners know about a particular topic or concept, and what problems they may have, in order to plan future teaching to meet their needs. It is sometimes also called Assessment for Learning.

Functional approach (to language, including grammar and literacy) The functional approach to language is one which considers whole texts (either spoken or written, see below) in their contexts of use (see above) and the choices the speaker or writer has made in constructing them. The main implications of the approach are the need to teach grammar and literacy in context, rather than in discrete exercises.

Funds of knowledge 'Funds of knowledge' refers to the learning, often social and cultural and sometimes academic, which a child engages in within their home and community contexts and which forms the prior experience they bring to school.

Genre Genres are different text types, defined by the purposes and audiences for which they are intended and the kinds of language and structural elements with which they have been constructed.

Grammar Grammars are systematic ways of describing languages. There are many different kinds of grammars, which each pay attention to different aspects and elements of language.

Graphic organisers These are visual ways of organising knowledge, concepts, information and ideas, showing the links between them, in order to aid understanding. Examples of graphic organisers are charts, tables, Venn diagrams, webs and so on.

Halal Anything which is halal is acceptable within Islamic rules and standards. Something which does not meet these standards is defined as *haram*.

Heritage languages In England, the term 'heritage languages' normally refers to the languages of the individual's country of origin, spoken by people who have migrated to England or whose ancestors did so.

Home languages This is the term used in the book for languages that children know which are not represented in the school system or officially in wider British society. Other terms frequently used are first languages (L1) and community languages.

Hot seating Hot seating is a technique used in drama and role play where a participant is asked to sit on a chair in the role of a character, e.g. from a story or from a historical period, and answer questions put to them by the audience in that role. It is a valuable teaching strategy in different subjects across the curriculum.

Identity The word 'identity' is used in many different ways to describe an individual's sense of who they are, where they belong and how they would define themselves.

Identity text A term invented by Jim Cummins and Margaret Early to describe creative work by students which leads to the construction of written and visual texts that present and affirm their identities in positive ways.

Jigsawing Jigsawing is a technique used in discussion-based activities where participants each have partial information about the topic under consideration and have to collaborate in different ways in order to disclose the full information.

Language awareness This is defined as explicit knowledge about language, and conscious perception of its importance in language learning, language teaching and language use.

Language diversity This term refers to the range of languages, besides English, that are used by people in Britain on a daily basis.

Linguistic interdependence Another of Cummins' theories, linguistic independence refers to the idea that knowledge and understanding of one language links to and supports the development of knowledge and understanding in another.

Metalanguage This is the language that we need in order to be able to talk about, investigate and analyse language.

Metalinguistic awareness Metalinguistic awareness is the deeper understanding of how languages work as systems and the capacity to explain them, gained from studying and analysing languages and comparing different languages.

Monolingualising Monolingualising is a term introduced by some researchers to describe the way that the curriculum can impose a message that English is the only language that matters and that other languages are much less important.

Multilingual/multilingualism With the recognition that societies are becoming increasingly multilingual, the term is being used more and more to capture the sense that we need to understand more about how people live in settings where different languages are increasingly used alongside each other and the implications for education.

Multiliterate The capacity to read and/or write more than one language, at any level.

Multi-modal Texts which are multi-modal are constructed with a mix of forms, usually including aural and visual elements and also conventional text forms.

NALDIC (National Association for Language Development in the Curriculum) NALDIC is the national subject association for English as an additional language (EAL). It was founded in 1992 and is recognised today as the foremost organisation promoting effective teaching and learning for bilingual and EAL children in schools in the UK.

Pedagogy The processes of teaching which are informed by professional knowledge, skills and understanding, mediated by the judgements made by the individual teacher.

Received pronunciation (RP) RP is the prestigious form of pronunciation of English that is associated with high status and educational success. Traditionally, it is the way of speaking that had to be adopted by members of society who wished to be received in court.

Repertoire Repertoire refers to the whole range of knowledge about languages an individual possesses in terms of listening, speaking, reading and writing. It can change many times over an individual's life course, according to a wide range of social, cultural, academic and personal factors.

SATs (Standard Attainment Tests) SATs are the tasks in English and maths, commissioned by the government, to identify and record the attainment of children at the age of 7 (Key Stage 1) and 11 (Key Stage 2), and in English, maths and science at 14 (Key Stage 3).

Scaffolding Scaffolding is an idea (sometimes called a 'theory of instruction') that goes along with the notion of the ZPD (see below). It refers to an approach to planning activities in order to offer learners opportunities to acquire new knowledge securely while at the same time developing as independent learners.

Semantics Semantics is the part of language knowledge and study to do with meaning in words, sentences and whole texts.

SLA (second language acquisition) SLA is the process of developing the skills and knowledge to communicate in an additional language, as distinct from the knowledge that might be learnt through direct teaching.

Standard English Standard English is the high-status form of English grammar and vocabulary associated with educational and economic success, spoken by people in England. For many people, it is one of several kinds of English they have in their repertoires. People speak standard English with a wide range of regional and social accents.

Summative assessment This is formal, normative assessment which seeks to identify an individual's attainment judged according to fixed measures or standards.

Superdiverse Superdiverse is a term from sociology to describe contemporary societies where different migrations over many years have led to complex communities whose members possess an increasingly wide range of language, cultural, social and economic backgrounds.

TEFL (teaching English as a foreign language) TEFL is a pedagogy for teaching English to people who wish to live in, work in or visit Britain and other English-speaking countries. It is often carried out before the learners travel and can also take place in short courses in the English-speaking host country.

Texts Texts can be either spoken or written. They are complete, communicative events transacted through language that has been selected to take account of the speaker(s)' or writer(s)' purposes, meanings and audiences.

Transitional bilingualism Transitional bilingualism is a contrasting term to additive bilingualism (see above). It describes the situation where an individual, in acquiring a new language, loses their capacity to use existing languages in their repertoires. It is associated with low levels of academic attainment and success and poor self-image.

Translanguaging Translanguaging is a recently developed term used to describe the ways that multilinguals make choices from their language repertoires to express their meanings and perform their identities in the ways most appropriate to them. Unlike the term 'codeswitching' (see above), it helps us to consider languages as fluid and seamless, rather than as separate and isolated systems.

Word class All words belong to lexical categories called word classes (which are sometimes called parts of speech) according to the part they play in a sentence. Words can belong to different classes according to the jobs they are doing in the text.

ZPD (zone of proximal development) The idea of the ZPD comes from Vygotsky's theories about learning as a sociocultural process, in which the interactions between learners and their teachers are an important element. The ZPD is Vygotsky's term to describe the 'gap' between what the learner knows and what they do not yet know, which can be bridged with the support of a more knowledgeable other.

APPENDIX 3: PRINCIPLES FOR PLANNING FOR MULTILINGUAL LEARNERS

These six key principles for planning lessons and activities for multilingual learners have been developed from the ideas discussed in Chapters 1 to 3. In Chapters 4 to 7, I use these principles to present practical examples of activities and strategies to promote multilingual children's learning in speaking and listening, reading and writing across the curriculum.

1. Developing a positive ethos that reflects language and cultural diversity at whole-school level, supports home–school links and encourages families and schools to work in partnership.

2. In the classroom, providing opportunities for multilingual pupils to use their first languages in everyday activities opens out the potential for learning and affirms their identities.

3. Pupils need every possible opportunity to explore ideas and concepts orally in all subjects across the curriculum.

4. Before beginning extended writing activities, pupils need plenty of chances for collaborative discussion and practical experience.

5. Promoting awareness of language systems and structures by allowing multilingual pupils to analyse and compare the different ways of saying things in the languages they know helps develop their CALP and also promotes language awareness among their monolingual classmates.

6. Providing extensive opportunities for hands-on experience enhances language learning and learning more generally.

INDEX

Page numbers followed by 'g' indicate a term in the glossary